• TROPHIES •

Intervention
TEACHER'S GUIDE
Grade 4

Harcourt

Orlando   Boston   Dallas   Chicago   San Diego

Visit *The Learning Site!*
www.harcourtschool.com

Printed in the United States of America

ISBN 0-15-325346-0

6 7 8 9 10 048 10 09 08 07 06 05 04

Table of Contents

What are Intervention Strategies?

Intervention strategies are designed to facilitate learning for those students who may experience some difficulty no matter how well we have planned our curriculum. These strategies offer support and guidance to the student who is struggling. The strategies themselves are no mystery. They are based on the same time-honored techniques that effective teachers have used for years—teaching students on their instructional reading level; modeling previewing and predicting; directed and giving direct instruction in strategic-reading, vocabulary, phonics, fluency, and writing.

Intervention works best in conjunction with a strong core program. For an intervention program to be effective, instruction should focus on specific needs of students, as determined by systematic monitoring of progress.

Components of the Intervention Program

The goal of the *Trophies* Intervention Program is to provide the scaffolding, extra support, and extra reading practice that below-level readers need to succeed in the mainstream reading program. The program includes the following components:

- *Skill Cards* to preteach and reteach the Focus Skill for each lesson
- *Intervention Practice Book* with the following practice pages for each lesson:

    Fluency Page with word lists and phrase-cued sentences that parallel the reading level of the *Intervention Reader* selection

    Phonics Practice Page that reinforces prerequisite phonics/decoding skills and can be used as a teacher-directed or independent activity

    Comprehension Practice Page that gives students an opportunity to respond to the *Intervention Reader* selection and show that they have understood it

    Focus Skill Review Page that provides an additional opportunity to practice and apply the focus skill for that lesson

- *Intervention Reader* to provide reading material at students' instructional reading level
- *Vocabulary Game Boards* and related materials to provide additional practice and application of vocabulary skills
- *Intervention Assessment Book* opportunities to monitor progress and ensure success

Using the *Intervention Teacher's Guides* with *Trophies*

The *Intervention Teacher's Guide* gives support for below-level readers in key instructional strands of *Trophies*, plus prerequisite phonics skills and oral-reading fluency. Each *Intervention Teacher's Guide* lesson includes the following resources:

■ The **Phonics/Decoding Lesson** reviews prerequisite phonics and word analysis skills. Each skill is systematically applied in the corresponding *Intervention Reader* selection.

■ **Preteach/Reteach Vocabulary** activities to teach key vocabulary that appears in both the *Intervention Reader* selection and the corresponding *Trophies Pupil Edition* selection.

■ **Fluency Builders** reinforce important vocabulary while providing reading practice to promote oral reading fluency. You may also wish to use the *Oral Reading Fluency Assessment* periodically to measure student progress.

■ **Preteach/Reteach Focus Skill** activities reinforce the objective of *Trophies* Focus Skills, ensuring that below-level readers get the in-depth instruction they need to reach grade skill-level standards.

■ **Preview and Summarize** provide support for comprehension of each main selection in *Trophies Pupil Editions*.

■ **Directed Reading Lesson** for the *Intervention Reader* selection that reinforces basic comprehension skills, using questions and teacher modeling.

■ **Writing Support** for writing lessons in *Trophies* provides interactive writing experiences for the key aspects of the corresponding writing forms and skills.

■ **Weekly Review** provides additional support as students review phonics, vocabulary, and focus skills and prepare for testing.

■ **Self-Selected Reading** suggests titles that students can read independently with success and also offers specific suggestions for encouraging student expression and participation through conferencing.

The *Intervention Teacher's Guide* lessons clearly identify the most appropriate times during the *Trophies* lesson plan to provide supplemental instruction. Look for the BEFORE or AFTER tag that appears next to each of the key instructional strands, along with page numbers from the core program. For example:

BEFORE
Skills/Strategies
pages 305I–305J

This tag alerts you that *before* you teach the Skill and Strategy lessons that appear in *Trophies* on pages 305I–305J, intervention strategies may be useful. Appropriate preteach activities are provided. Reteaching activities are indicated by the AFTER tag.

Depending on your individual classroom and school schedules, you can tailor the "before" and "after" instruction to suit your needs. The following pages show two options for pacing the instruction in this guide.

Suggested Lesson Planners

Option 1:

DAY 1	DAY 2
BEFORE **Building Background and Vocabulary** **Review Phonics** ■ Identify the sound ■ Associate letters to sound ■ Word blending ■ Apply the skill **Introduce Vocabulary** ■ Preteach lesson vocabulary	**BEFORE** **Reading the *Trophies* Selection** **Focus Skill** ■ Preteach the skill ■ Use Skill Card Side A **Prepare to Read the *Trophies* selection** ■ Preview the selection ■ Set purpose
AFTER **Building Background and Vocabulary** **Apply Vocabulary Strategies** ■ Use decoding strategies ■ Reteach lesson vocabulary **Fluency Builder** ■ Use *Intervention Practice Book*	**AFTER** **Reading the *Trophies* Selection** **Reread and Summarize** **Fluency Builder** ■ Use *Intervention Practice Book*

Option 2:

DAY 1	DAY 2
AFTER **Weekly Assessments** **Self-Selected Reading** ■ Choosing books ■ Conduct student-teacher conferences **Fluency Performance** ■ Use passage from *Intervention Reader* selection	**AFTER** **Building Background and Vocabulary** **Apply Vocabulary Strategies** ■ Use decoding strategies ■ Reteach lesson vocabulary **Fluency Builder** ■ Use *Intervention Practice Book*
BEFORE **Building Background and Vocabulary** **Review Phonics** ■ Identify the sound ■ Associate letters to sound ■ Word blending ■ Apply the skill **Introduce Vocabulary** ■ Preteach lesson vocabulary	**BEFORE** **Reading the *Trophies* Selection** **Focus Skill** ■ Preteach the skill ■ Use Skill Card Side A **Prepare to Read the *Trophies* selection** ■ Preview the selection ■ Set purpose

DAY 3

BEFORE Making Connections

Directed Reading of *Intervention Reader* selection
- Read the selection
- Summarize the selection
- Answer *Think About It* Questions

AFTER Skill Review

Focus Skill
- Reteach the skill
- Use Skill Card Side B

Fluency Builder
- Use *Intervention Practice Book*

DAY 4

BEFORE Writing Lesson

Writing Support
- Build on prior knowledge
- Construct the text
- Revisit the text
- On Your Own

AFTER Spelling Lesson

Connect Spelling and Phonics
- Reteach phonics
- Build and read longer words

Fluency Builder
- Use passage from *Intervention Reader* selection

DAY 5

BEFORE Weekly Assessments

Review Vocabulary
- Vocabulary activity

Review Focus Skill
- Use *Intervention Practice Book*

Review Test Prep
- Use the core *Pupil Edition*

AFTER Weekly Assessments

Self-Selected Reading
- Choosing books
- Conduct student-teacher conferences

Fluency Performance
- Use passage from *Intervention Reader* selection

DAY 3

AFTER Reading the *Trophies* Selection

Reread and Summarize

Fluency Builder
- Use *Intervention Practice Book*

BEFORE Making Connections

Directed Reading of *Intervention Reader* selection
- Read the selection
- Summarize the selection
- Answer *Think About It* Questions

DAY 4

AFTER Skill Review

Focus Skill
- Reteach the skill
- Use Skill Card Side B

Fluency Builder
- Use *Intervention Practice Book*

BEFORE Writing Lesson

Writing Support
- Build on prior knowledge
- Construct the text
- Revisit the text
- On Your Own

DAY 5

AFTER Spelling Lesson

Connect Spelling and Phonics
- Reteach phonics
- Build and read longer words

Fluency Builder
- Use passage from *Intervention Reader* selection

BEFORE Weekly Assessments

Review Vocabulary
- Vocabulary activity

Review Focus Skill
- Use *Intervention Practice Book*

Review Test Prep
- Use the core *Pupil Edition*

Fluency

"So that students will understand why rereading is done, we have involved them in a discussion of how athletes develop skill at their sports. This discussion brings out the fact that athletes spend considerable time practicing basic skills until they develop speed and smoothness at their activity. Repeated readings uses this same type of practice."

S. Jay Samuels
The Reading Teacher, February 1997
(originally published January 1979)

In the years since S. Jay Samuels pioneered the technique of repeated reading to improve fluency, continuing research has confirmed and expanded upon his observations. Ideally, oral reading mirrors the pacing, smoothness, and rhythms of normal speech. Fluency in reading can be defined as a combination of these key elements.

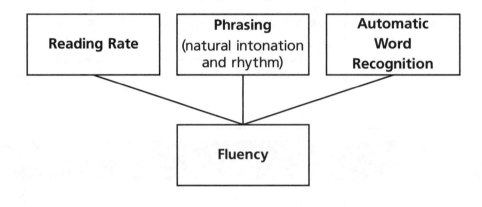

How Do Students Become More Fluent Readers?

Research and the experiences of classroom teachers make it clear that certain practices can and do lead to significant improvements in reading fluency. Techniques that have been shown to be successful include

- Teacher modeling

- Repeated reading of short passages

- Daily monitoring of progress

A program that incorporates these three elements will help struggling readers gain fluency and improve their comprehension.

Using Fluency Builders in the *Intervention Teacher's Guide*

The plan for each lesson in the *Intervention Teacher's Guide* includes daily fluency practice that incorporates the elements of teacher modeling, repeated reading, and self-monitoring.

The fluency portion of the lesson is designed to be completed in five or ten minutes, although you may adjust the time according to students' needs and as your schedule allows.

About the *Intervention Practice Book* Fluency Page

The *Intervention Practice Book* Fluency Page is designed to correlate with the phonics elements taught in the *Intervention Teacher's Guide*, as well as with key vocabulary from the *Trophies* and *Intervention Reader* selections. A total of twenty words that fall into these three categories are listed at the top of the Fluency Page for each lesson.

On the bottom half of the page, you will find a set of numbered sentences that incorporate the words from the lists. Slashes are used to divide each sentence into phrases. To help students improve natural phrasing, model reading each phrase smoothly, as a unit, and encourage students to follow the same procedure in their repeated-reading practice.

This chart gives an overview of the fluency portion of the Intervention Program.

Day	Materials	Explanation
1	*Intervention Practice Book* Fluency Page	Teacher models reading aloud word lists. Students then practice reading aloud the word lists with partners.
2	*Intervention Practice Book* Fluency Page	Teacher models reading aloud the phrased fluency sentences. Students then practice repeated rereadings of the sentences with partners.
3	*Intervention Practice Book* Fluency Page	Students read the fluency sentences on tape, assess their own progress, and then reread the sentences on tape to improve pacing and tone.
4	*Intervention Reader* selection	Students read aloud a selected short passage from the *Intervention Reader* selection three times, monitoring their progress after each reading.
5	*Intervention Reader* selection	Students read the same passage aloud to the teacher. Both teacher and student assess the student's progress.

Phonemic Awareness

Rhyming Activities

Rhyme-a-Day

Start each day by teaching students a short rhyme. Periodically throughout the day, repeat the rhyme with them. Say the rhyme together, have them say it alone, pause and leave out words for them to insert, or ask volunteers to say each line. Students will develop a repertoire of favorite rhymes that can serve as a storehouse for creating their own rhymes.

Rhyme Sort

Place on a tabletop pictures of items that rhyme. Have students sort the pictures into groups, according to names that rhyme. You may also want to try an "open sort" by having students create categories of their own to sort the picture cards.

Rhyme Pairs

To assess students' ability to recognize pairs of words that rhyme, say a list of twenty or more pairs of words. Half of the word pairs should rhyme. Students tell which word pairs rhyme and which do not. Have students indicate *yes* with a card marked *Y* or another symbol.

If working with **one child** (or small group), have students use one of the Game Boards. For each correct response, the player can move a marker ahead one space. Provide word pairs until the player has completed the game.

What Word Rhymes?

Use theme-related words from across the curriculum to focus on words that rhyme. For example, if you are studying animals, ask: *What rhymes with snake? bear? fox? deer? ant? frog? goat? hen? fish? whale?* If a special holiday is approaching, ask: *What rhymes with flag, year, or heart?* Use these word groups for sound-matching, sound-blending, or sound-segmenting activities.

Sound-Matching Activities

Odd Word Out

Form a group of four students. Say a different word for each group member to repeat. The student with the word that does not begin (or end) like the other words must step out of the group. For example, say *basket, bundle, cost, bargain*. The student whose word is *cost* steps from the group. The odd-word-out player then chooses three students to form a new group and the procedure continues.

Head or Toes, Finger or Nose?

Teach students the following rhyme. Be sure to say the sound, not the letter, at the beginning of each line. Recite the rhyme together several times while touching the body parts.

> /h/ is for *head.*
> /t/ is for *toes.*
> /f/ is for *finger.*
> /n/ is for *nose.*

Phonemic Awareness Activities • Intervention Teacher's Guide

Explain that you will say a list of words. Students are to touch the head when you say a word that begins with /h/, the toes for the words that begin with /t/, a finger for words that begin with /f/, and the nose for words that begin with /n/. Say words such as *fan*, *ten*, *horn*, *hat*, *feet*, *nut*, *ham*, *nest*, *toy*, *fish*, *note*, *tub*, *nail*, *time*, *fox*, and *house*.

Souvenir Sound-Off

Have students imagine that a friend has traveled to a special place and has brought them a gift. Recite the following verse, and ask a volunteer to complete it. The names of the traveler, the place, and the gift must begin with the same letter and sound.

- My friend [person]
  My friend Hannah

- who went to [place]
  who went to Hawaii

- brought me back a [gift].
  brought me back a hula skirt.

After repeating this activity a few times, ask **partners** to recite the missing words. As an alternative, you can focus on words with initial blends and digraphs. Students can focus on social studies and phonics skills by using a world map or globe to find names of places.

Match My Word

Have students match beginning or ending sounds in words. Seat students in pairs, sitting back-to-back. One student in each pair will say a word. His or her partner will repeat the word and say another word that begins with the same sound. Repeat the activity, reversing the roles of partners and focusing on ending sounds.

Sound Isolation Activities

What's Your Name N-N-N-Name?

Invite students to say their names by repeating the initial phoneme in the name, such as *M-M-M-M-Michael* or by drawing out and exaggerating the initial sound, such as *Sssss-erena*. Have students say the names of others, such as friends or family members.

Singling Out the Sounds

Form groups of three students. Students can decide who will name the beginning, the middle, and the ending sounds in one-syllable picture names. Given a set of pictures, the group identifies a picture name, and then each group member isolates and says the sound he or she is responsible for. Group members can check one another.

Chain Reaction

Have students form a circle. The student who begins will say a word such as *bus*. The next child must isolate the ending sound in the word, /s/, and say a word that begins with that sound, such as *sun*. If the word is correct, the two students link arms, and the procedure continues with the next child isolating the final sound in *sun* and giving a word that begins with /n/. You will want all students to be able to link arms and complete the chain, so provide help when needed.

Sound-Addition, Deletion, or Substitution Activities

Add-a-Sound

Explain that the beginning sound is missing in each of the words you will say. Students must add the missing sound and say the new word. Some examples follow.

Add:

/b/ to *at* (bat)	/f/ to *ox* (fox)	/k/ to *art* (cart)
/f/ to *ace* (face)	/p/ to *age* (page)	/h/ to *air* (hair)
/w/ to *all* (wall)	/j/ to *am* (jam)	/r/ to *an* (ran)
/b/ to *and* (band)	/d/ to *ark* (dark)	/f/ to *arm* (farm)
/d/ to *ash* (dash)	/s/ to *it* (sit)	/s/ to *oak* (soak)
/h/ to *eel* (heel)	/b/ to *end* (bend)	/m/ to *ice* (mice)
/n/ to *ear* (near)	/f/ to *east* (feast)	/b/ to *each* (beach)
/f/-/l/ to *at* (flat)	/sk/ to *ate* (skate)	/t/-/r/ to *eat* (treat)
/g/-/r/ to *ill* (grill)	/sh/ to *out* (shout)	/p/-/l/ to *ant* (plant)

Remove-a-Sound

Reinforce rhyme while focusing on the deletion of initial sounds in words to form new words. Ask students to say:

- *hat* without the /h/ (at)
- *fin* without the /f/ (in)
- *tall* without the /t/ (all)
- *box* without the /b/ (ox)
- *will* without /w/ (ill)
- *peach* without the /p/ (each)
- *nice* without the /n/ (ice)
- *meat* without the /m/ (eat)
- *band* without the /b/ (and)

Continue with other words in the same manner.

Mixed-Up Tongue Twisters

Think of a simple tongue twister such as *ten tired toads*. Say the tongue twister for students, but replace the initial letter in each word with another letter, such a *p*, to create nonsense words: *pen pired poads*. Explain to students that you need their help to make sense of the tongue twister by having them replace /p/ with /t/ and say the new tongue twister. Use the same procedure for other tongue twisters.

- copper coffee cups
- nine new nails
- two ton tomatoes
- long lean legs

Then ask partners to do this activity together.

The Name Game

Occasionally when a new sound is introduced, students might enjoy substituting the first sound of their names for the name of a classmate. Students will have to stop and think when they call one another by name, including the teacher. For example, Paul would call Ms. Vega, Ms. Pega; Carmen becomes Parmen; Jason becomes Pason; and Kiyo becomes Piyo. Just make certain beforehand that all names will be agreeable.

Take Away

New words can be formed by deleting an initial phoneme from a word. Have students say the new word that is formed.

flake without the /f/ (lake)

bring without the /b/ (ring)

swing without the /s/ (wing)

swell without the /s/ (well)

shrink without the /sh/ (rink)

shred without the /sh/ (red)

spread without the /s/-/p/ (read)

gloom without the /g/ (loom)

fright without the /f/ (right)

snout without the /s/-/n/ (out)

score without the /s/ (core)

slip without the /s/ (lip)

bride without the /b/ (ride)

block without the /b/ (lock)

spoke without the /s/ (poke)

snail without the /s/ (nail)

Sound-Blending Activities

I'm Thinking of a Word

Play a guessing game with students. Tell students that you will give them clues to a word. Have them listen closely to blend the sounds to say the word.

- I'm thinking of something that has words— /b/-/o͞o/-/k/. (book)
- I'm thinking of something that comes in bunches— /g/-/r/-/ā/-/p/-/s/. (grapes)
- I'm thinking of something that shines in the night sky— /s/-/t/-/är/-/z/. (stars)
- I'm thinking of something that moves very slowly— /s/-/n/-/ā/-/l/. (snail)

What's in the Box?

Place various objects in a box or bag. Play a game with students by saying **In this box is a /k/-/r/-/ā/-/o/-/n/. What do you think is in the box?** (crayon) Continue with the other objects in the box, segmenting the phonemes for students to blend and say the word.

Sound-Segmenting Activities

Sound Game

Have **partners** play a word-guessing game, using a variety of pictures that represent different beginning sounds. One student says the name on the card, separating the beginning sound, as in **p-late**. The partner blends the sounds and guesses the word. After students are proficient with beginning sounds, you could have them segment all the sounds in a word when they give their clues, as in **d-o-g**.

Count the Sounds

Tell students that you are going to say a word. Have them listen and count the number of sounds they hear in that word. For example, say the word *task*. Have children repeat the word and tell how many sounds they hear. Students should reply *four*.

tone (3)	four (3)
great (4)	peak (3)
pinch (4)	sunny (4)
stick (4)	clouds (5)
flake (4)	feel (3)
rain (3)	paint (4)

Vocabulary Games

Vocabulary Game Boards

To give students additional vocabulary practice, use the Vocabulary Game Boards and copying masters provided in the Intervention Kit. Two different games can be played on each game board. Directions for each game are printed on the back of the board on which the game is played. There are a total of five game boards, which students can use to play ten different games. For best results, use the games to review vocabulary at the end of each theme, so that there are more words to play with.

Copying Masters

The copying masters that accompany the game boards provide some other materials that students will need to play the games. These include: spinners, game pieces, game cards, number cards.

Illustrated directions on the copying masters show students how to create the game materials. They may need scissors, crayons or colored markers, and glue. Pencils and paper clips are used to construct spinners. When game markers are called for, provide students with buttons, counters or some other small item.

Additional Materials

When the directions for a game call for **word cards**, use the vocabulary word cards from *Trophies*. In addition, some games require the use of a vocabulary list, definition cards that students can create, a dictionary, and commonly available items such as a coin or pebble, or a paper bag.

Use the following charts to plan for and organize the vocabulary games.

Game Board I: Hopscotch

Games	Skills Practiced	Players	Additional Materials
Definition Hop	definitions	2	*Trophies* word cards coin or pebble paper and pencil
What's That Word?	definitions	4	*Trophies* word cards list of vocabulary words paper bag coin or pebble paper and pencil

Game Board 2: Mountain Challenge

Games	Skills Practiced	Players	Additional Materials
Zany Tales	creating a continuing story	2–4	Zany Tales Copying Master *Trophies* word cards paper bag dictionary
Syllable Climb	number of syllables	2–4	Syllable Climb Copying Masters *Trophies* word cards dictionary

Game Board 3: Wagon Train

Games	Skills Practiced	Players	Additional Materials
Pioneer Spin	syllables, definitions, and sentences	2–4	Pioneer Spin Copying Masters *Trophies* word cards dictionary
Let's Go West, Partner!	definitions	4	Let's Go West, Partner Copying Masters *Trophies* word cards list of vocabulary words dictionary two paper bags pencil

Game Board 4: Five-in-a-Row

Games	Skills Practiced	Players	Additional Materials
Syllable-O	number of syllables	2	Syllable-O Copying Master *Trophies* word cards small items for game markers dictionary
May I Mark It?	syllables, definitions, and sentences	3	2 sets of small items for game markers 2 sets of *Trophies* word cards dictionary small items for game markers

Game Board 5: Remember It

Games	Skills Practiced	Players	Additional Materials
Meaning Match	definitions	2	2 sets of *Trophies* word cards 2 sets of definition cards that match each word
Matching for Points	number of syllables	2	Matching for Points Copying Masters 2 sets of *Trophies* word cards dictionary paper and pencil

The six activities on the following pages provide additional opportunities for vocabulary practice and application. Two activities are offered for individual students, two for pairs of students working together, and two for small groups of three or four students. All require a minimum of preparation and call for materials that are readily available in the classroom.

Personal Glossary

INDIVIDUAL ACTIVITY

MATERIALS
- paper
- markers
- stapler or simple binding materials

As students progress through a theme, encourage them to identify new vocabulary words that they find particularly interesting or that they think will be especially useful to them. Have individual students create a page for each of the special words they choose. Encourage them to check the spelling of the word and to include the definition and other information they might find helpful, such as the part of speech, how the word is divided into syllables, how it is pronounced, whether it has a prefix or a suffix, synonyms and antonyms, and how the word may be related to other words they know. Students can also include example sentences or draw pictures with captions and labels where appropriate.

Upon completion of the theme, have students arrange their pages in alphabetical order and make a cover for their personal glossary. Staple the pages together or help students use simple materials to bind them. Encourage students to share their personal glossaries with classmates and to use them as a resource for their writing.

Draw the Cat

PARTNER ACTIVITY

MATERIALS
- list of vocabulary words from a complete theme
- either two sheets of paper and markers or chalk and chalkboard
- dictionary

Pairs of students can play this game on paper or on the board. Players should be designated Player 1 and Player 2. Player 1 begins by choosing a vocabulary word from the list for Player 2 to define. If Player 2 defines the word correctly, he or she gets to draw one part of a cat. If Player 2 cannot define the word correctly, he or she cannot draw on that turn. Players take turns choosing words for each other to define and adding parts to their cats each time they define a word correctly. Encourage students to use a dictionary to check definitions as necessary.

The first player to draw a complete cat wins the game. A completed cat drawing has ten parts, to be drawn in this order: (1) head, (2) body, (3) tail, (4) one ear, (5) the other ear, (6) one eye, (7) the other eye, (8) nose, (9) mouth, (10) whiskers.

1. cat's head
2. cat's body
3. cat's tail
4. one ear
5. other ear
6. one eye
7. other eye
8. cat's nose
9. cat's mouth
10. whiskers

Who Wants to Win 100?

SMALL GROUP ACTIVITY

MATERIALS
- list of vocabulary words from a theme
- scoreboard
- chalk
- dictionary

Students play the roles of quizmaster, contestant, "lifeline," and judge. The quizmaster chooses vocabulary words from the list for the contestant to define. The contestant earns 25 points for each word he or she defines correctly. If the contestant is not sure about a word, he or she can ask the lifeline for help and still earn 25 points for a correct answer. The judge looks up each word in the dictionary and rules on whether or not

Kelly	Luis	Sarah	Tony
25	25	25	
25	25	25	
25	25	25	
25	25		
100	100		

the answer is correct, and the quizmaster adds up the points on the scoreboard. When the contestant has earned a total of 100 points, students exchange roles and play another game.

Tally-Ho!

INDIVIDUAL ACTIVITY

MATERIALS
- list of vocabulary words from a theme
- pencil and paper
- dictionary

Make a list of eight to ten vocabulary words that may have given students some difficulty. Have students copy the words from the list and write a definition for each word from memory. Then have them use a dictionary to check their definitions. Tell them to make tally marks to show the number of words they defined correctly.

Then have students copy the words from the list in reverse order, beginning at the bottom. Have them again write a definition for each word from memory, check the definitions in a dictionary, and tally up the number they defined correctly. Tell students to compare this score to their first score to see how much they improved.

Show Time

SMALL GROUP ACTIVITY

MATERIALS
- list of vocabulary words from a theme
- paper
- pencil

Have groups of students work cooperatively to write and dramatize brief scenes for TV shows that include vocabulary words from the theme. Explain that the scenes may be from comedy, drama, documentary, news, or other types of shows. Challenge students to use as many words as possible from the vocabulary list in their scenes. They can keep track of the words they use by checking them off on the list. Give students an opportunity to present their dramatizations for classmates.

Yes or No

PARTNER ACTIVITY

MATERIALS
- list of vocabulary words from a theme
- scrap paper
- pencils

Display the list of vocabulary words where both players can see it. Students take turns choosing a word from the list for each other to guess. The student who is guessing may ask questions about the part of speech, meaning of the word, the number of syllables, whether it has a prefix or a suffix, or any other information they think may help them. However, every question can only be answered with *yes* or *no*.

Encourage students to jot down information that they find out about the word that can help narrow down the list. You may want to give examples of questions that players might ask and explain how they can use the information they obtain.

QUESTION: Is the word an adjective?
INFORMATION: If the answer is yes, you can rule out all the other words on the list and focus on the adjectives. If the answer is no, you can rule out the adjectives and ask questions that will help you narrow the list further.

QUESTION: Does the word have an -*ed* ending?
INFORMATION: If the answer is *no*, you can rule out all words with -*ed* endings. If the answer is *yes*, focus on the words with -*ed* endings. Ask more questions to figure out which of those words is the correct one.

Use with

"The Gardener"

Review Phonics: Short Vowel /a/a; Long Vowel /ā/a-e

Identify the sounds. Have students repeat this sentence aloud twice: *Sam plants yams with Tran.* Ask them which words have the /a/ sound. (*Sam, plants, yams, Tran*) Then have them repeat this sentence twice: *Jake ate some cake.* Ask which words have the /ā/ sound. (*Jake, ate, cake*)

Associate letters to sounds. Write on the board the above sentences. Underline words with the /a/ sound in the first sentence, and point out the consonant-vowel-consonant (CVC) pattern in each. Explain that words with this pattern usually have a short vowel sound. Then underline the words in the second sentence with the /ā/ sound and point out the *a-e* pattern in each. Explain that when *e* is added to many words with a short *a* sound, the new word usually has the /ā/ sound.

Word blending. Model how to blend and read the word *cake*. Touch the *e* and say that it is silent. Slide your hand under the word as you elongate the sounds /kkāāk/. Then say the word naturally—*cake*. Repeat with *Jake*, *ate*, *plants*, and *yams*.

Apply the skill. *Vowel Substitution* Write these words on the board, and have students read each aloud. Make the changes necessary to form the words in parentheses. Have students read aloud the new words.

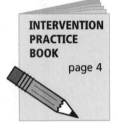

INTERVENTION
PRACTICE
BOOK
page 4

fad (fade)   **glad** (glade)   **pan** (pane)   **plan** (plane)   **scrap** (scrape)

Introduce Vocabulary

PRETEACH **lesson vocabulary.** Tell students that they are going to learn six new words that they will see again when they read a story called "The Gardener." Teach each Vocabulary Word using the process shown below.

Use the following suggestions or similar ideas to give the meaning or context.

> Write the word.
> Say the word.
> Track the word and have students repeat it.
> Give the meaning or context.

anxious	Role-play being very nervous; look around and fidget.
retire	This is a multiple-meaning word. Explain that *to retire* means "to rest." People retire from work at a certain age.
vacant	Point to a vacant chair. Explain that the chair is vacant because it is currently not being used.
sprucing	Clean your desk. Explain that you are sprucing it up.

| adore | Show a picture of a pet. Hold it close to your heart and say you adore this pet. Explain that *adore* means "to love." |
| recognizing | Point out the *-ing* ending. Explain that *recognize* means "to know." |

For vocabulary activities, see Vocabulary Games on pages 2–7.

For vocabulary activities, see Vocabulary Games on pages 2–7.

Vocabulary Words

anxious nervous; excited

retire to stop working after reaching a certain age

vacant empty; unused

sprucing decorating or making neat

adore to love very much

recognizing knowing who someone is or what something is

AFTER
Building Background and Vocabulary

Apply Vocabulary Strategies

Use sentence and word context. Write this sentence on the board: *When my grandfather retires from his job, he'll go fishing more often.* Tell students that sometimes they can figure out the meaning of a word by reading the sentence. Model using the strategy.

> **MODEL** When I read this sentence, I am not sure what *retires* means. Since the second part of the sentence says Grandfather will be able to fish more often, I think *retires* must have something to do with leaving his job. I know people leave their jobs when they are older. *Retire* must mean "to stop working when you get older."

Guide students in using a similar procedure to figure out the meaning of other Vocabulary Words.

RETEACH lesson vocabulary. Have students listen to each of the following sentences. Tell them to nod their heads if the sentence you say is true. If the sentence is false, students should clasp their hands together.

1. A **vacant** lot has a building on it. (*false*)
2. A dog lover **adores** dogs. (*true*)
3. Planting flowers is a good way of **sprucing** up your yard. (*true*)
4. **Recognizing** a stranger is hard to do. (*true*)
5. Many people get **anxious** before a big test. (*true*)
6. When I **retire**, I will go to my job every day. (*false*)

FLUENCY BUILDER Have students look at *Intervention Practice Book* page 3. Read the words in the first column aloud. Invite students to track each word and repeat the words after you. Then have students work in pairs to read the words in the first column aloud to each other. Follow the same procedure with each of the remaining columns. After partners have practiced reading aloud the words in each of the columns, have them practice all of the words.

INTERVENTION PRACTICE BOOK
page 3

★ (Focus Skill) Narrative Elements

PRETEACH the skill. Tell students that the most important elements in a story, or narrative, are setting, characters, and plot. These elements help readers understand why characters act the way they do.

Have students look at **side A of Skill Card 1: Narrative Elements**. Read the definitions of setting, characters, and plot. Then read the story aloud while students read along.

Now call attention to the chart. Point to the setting box, the characters box, or the plot box as appropriate. Ask:

- **What are the main characters doing?** (*Possible response: They are playing soccer.*)

- **How does the setting affect the characters and the plot?** (*Possible response: The outside setting means the girls have to go inside because of the storm.*)

Explain that identifying and understanding the characters, setting, and plot can help students understand a character's motivations and actions.

Prepare to Read: "The Gardener"

Preview. Tell students that they are going to read a selection called "The Gardener." Explain that this story is realistic fiction and that it has a setting, characters, and plot. Tell them that "The Gardener" is a story about a girl who loves to plant. Then preview the selection.

LEAD THE WAY pages 22–43

- **Pages 22–23:** I see the title, "The Gardener," and the names of the author and the illustrator on page 23. The picture shows a girl and her grandmother in a big garden.

- **Pages 24–27:** On these pages, I see the grandmother helping the girl pack a suitcase. The next illustration shows the girl sitting in a train. She must be going on a trip.

- **Pages 28–35:** The illustrations let me know that the girl went to a city. It looks like the girl is doing some baking in another illustration. The decorations on pages 30–31 suggest that it is holiday time.

- **Pages 38–43:** The illustrations have lots of plants and flowers. The girl is hanging up signs that say "Please go up" and "You've arrived." I can guess that she finds a way to garden in the city.

Set purpose. Model setting a purpose for reading "The Gardener."

MODEL From my preview I can see that a girl who loves gardening goes on a trip to the city and continues to enjoy gardening. I will read to find out what happens to the girl and why the story's title is "The Gardener."

Reread and Summarize

Have students reread and summarize "The Gardener" in sections, as described in the chart below.

Pages 26–27
Let's reread pages 26–27 to recall what we learned about Lydia Grace.

Summary: Lydia Grace is shy. She knows a lot about gardening but nothing about baking. She feels pretty wearing the dress her mother made for her, and the train ride is making her sleepy.

Pages 28–29
Now let's read page 29 to remember how Lydia Grace felt when she first arrived in the city.

Summary: Lydia Grace was excited. She saw window boxes and couldn't wait to grow something.

Pages 34–35
As we reread the letters on pages 34–35, let's find out who knows about Lydia Grace's secret place.

Summary: No one else knows about the secret place but Otis, the cat. Uncle Jim sees Lydia Grace working, but he never sees her working in her secret place.

Pages 42–43
Now let's reread the letter on page 43 to find out what Uncle Jim did when he closed the store at lunch.

Summary: He told Lydia Grace, Ed, and Emma to go upstairs and wait. He brought up a beautiful cake and told Lydia Grace the news that she was going home.

FLUENCY BUILDER Redirect students to *Intervention Practice Book* page 3. Lead students to look at the bottom half of the page. The slashes break the sentences into natural phrases. Tell students that their goal is to read each phrase with expression and at a good pace. Model reading aloud these sentences. Have students repeat after you, imitating your expression, phrasing, and pace. Encourage partners to practice reading the sentences to each other.

INTERVENTION
PRACTICE
BOOK
page 3

Directed Reading: "Gram's Plant Parade," pp. 6–12

**MOVING
AHEAD**
pp. 6–12

Pages 6–7

Read aloud the title of the story. Ask students what they think a plant parade might be. Then have students read to find out who is telling the story and who the story is about. (*Blake is telling the story. It is about his grandmother, who loves plants.*) Ask: **Why do you think Gram plants things in such unusual places?** (*Possible response: She loves plants so much she plants them anywhere she can.*) **SPECULATE**

Ask: **What do you think Gram's idea is when she sees the empty lot? Why do you think so?** (*Possible response: Gram wants to plant something in the lot by the station. She says, "Vacant land to plant!"*) **MAKE PREDICTIONS**

Ask: **Why do you think Gram might want to plant things in the vacant lot?** (*Possible response: to make it beautiful*) **INTERPRET CHARACTERS' MOTIVATIONS**

Ask: **What is the setting for this story?** (*Possible response: at the corner station*) (★Focus Skill) **NARRATIVE ELEMENTS**

Pages 8–9

If necessary, point out the bulbs in the illustration and tell students that some flowering plants, including tulips and daffodils, sprout from bulbs. Then have students read pages 8–9 to find out if their predictions about Gram's plans are correct. Ask: **What was Gram's plan?** (*to plant a lot of bulbs by the station*) **CONFIRM PREDICTIONS**

Read aloud the paragraph on page 8 with the word *spade*. Model using the strategy of using context to confirm meaning:

> **MODEL** When I read page 8, I was not sure what a *spade* was. Blake said, "I take the spade." Then Gram said, "Hand me my spade and stand back. I have to plant." I think that a spade must be like a shovel and you might use a spade to plant. The illustration and the sentences confirm my prediction that a spade is like a shovel and you use it to plant. (★Focus Strategy) **USE CONTEXT TO CONFIRM MEANING**

Discuss whether students agree with your definition of *spade* and if your definition makes sense in the sentence.

Pages 10–11

Ask students to read to find out whether there really is a "plant parade" in the future, as Gram has promised. Ask: **What happened to the bulbs Gram planted?** (*They sprouted, and dozens of beautiful flowers grew.*) **SEQUENCE**

Ask: **How do you think Blake feels now that the bulbs have sprouted and the flowers have spruced up the station?** (*Possible response: He probably feels proud.*) **DETERMINE CHARACTERS' EMOTIONS**

Ask students to find out if Blake's feelings about plants have changed.

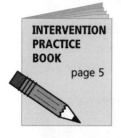
Ask: **Have Blake's feelings changed? How can you tell?** (Possible response: *Yes. Now Blake wants to fill empty land with flowers, too. He says he wants to share Gram's plant craze and that there is another plant parade in their future.*) **DRAW CONCLUSIONS**

Summarize the selection. Have students share their opinions of Gram and her efforts to make the neighborhood beautiful. Then help them summarize the story.

Answers to *Think About It* Questions

1. Gram plants in all the vacant spaces she can find. **SUMMARY**
2. Blake thinks it might not be all right to plant there. He thinks everyone is looking at him and Gram. **INTERPRETATION**
3. Accept reasonable responses. Students should use standard letter format with a salutation and closing. **WRITE A LETTER**

AFTER

Skill Review
pages 48–49

USE SKILL CARD 1B

(Focus Skill) Narrative Elements

RETEACH **the skill.** Have students look at **side B of Skill Card 1: Narrative Elements**. Read the skill reminder aloud, and invite students to read along.

Then have students read the paragraph aloud with you. Direct them to create a chart similar to the one shown that will help them identify the narrative elements in this story.

After students have identified the narrative elements in this story, have them share their chart with the group. Discuss any differences among students' charts.

FLUENCY BUILDER Be sure students have copies of *Intervention Practice Book* page 3. Tell students that today they will practice reading the sentences on the bottom half of the page by echoing the sentences after you. Encourage students to copy your tone, inflection and pace. Read aloud each sentence, phrase by phrase. Have students repeat (echo) the sentences, phrase by phrase.

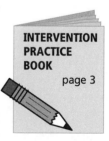

INTERVENTION
PRACTICE
BOOK

page 3

Descriptive Writing: Descriptive Paragraph

Build on prior knowledge. Tell students that you are going to write a paragraph together describing the experience of being in a park and watching a fireworks show set to music. Display the following information:

see	hear	smell	touch
the <u>twinkling</u> lights	a <u>thunderous</u> crash	a <u>fragrance</u> of flowers	the <u>soft fuzziness</u> of a blanket
a <u>glaring</u> flash	a <u>soothing</u> melody	the <u>stench</u> of smoke	the <u>coarse roughness</u> of burlap

Read the descriptive phrases aloud. Remind students that vivid words and phrases help the reader picture the event in his or her mind. Ask students to explain how the underlined words in each description affect how they feel about the topic. For example, *twinkling* makes the lights sound pleasant; *glaring* makes the flash seem annoying. Invite students to add other sensory details using words that help create vivid descriptions.

Construct the text. "Share the pen" with students in a collaborative group writing effort. As students dictate words and phrases, write them on the board or on chart paper, guiding the process by asking questions and offering suggestions as needed. Guide students in writing descriptive sentences about the fireworks show using words and phrases from the chart. Follow these steps:

- Choose a phrase from the chart. Ask students to identify the descriptive words and explain how the description makes them feel.

- Ask a student to say the phrase in a sentence that fits the description. Have a volunteer write that sentence on the chart.

- Continue until everyone in the group has had an opportunity to record a sentence.

Revisit the text. Have students reread their sentences to be sure they are complete. Ask: **Can I add other words to make my description more vivid?** Remind them that each sentence should begin with a capital letter and end with correct punctuation. Read aloud the sentences, emphasizing the sensory words.

On Your Own

Have students write descriptive sentences about a family celebration or event. Tell them to include sensory words and phrases that describe the event and help the reader understand how they felt.

Connect Spelling and Phonics

RETEACH **Short vowel /a/ *a*; Long vowel /ā/ *a-e*.** Write the words *land* and *stale* on the board. Explain that you will say more words with the short *a* and long *a* sounds. Then dictate the following words, and have students write them. After students write each word, display the correct spelling so they can proofread their work. Have them draw a line through a misspelled word and write the correct spelling beside it.

I. land*	2. glad*	3. stale	4. spade*
5. plant*	6. frame*	7. skate*	8. landscape

*Word appears in "Gram's Plant Parade."

Dictate the following sentence for students to write: *Stan skates to the lake.*

Build and Read Longer Words

Introduce compound words. Write *clambake* on the board. Tell students that when they see a word such as this, they can look to see if it is made up of two smaller words. Cover the word *bake,* and have students read the word *clam.* Cover *clam,* and have students read the word *bake.* Have students blend the word parts to form the longer word *clambake.* Repeat with *landscape, classmate,* and *namesake.*

Display these words in a pocket chart or on the board: *hand* and *land.* Invite students to work in small groups to write as many compound words as they can think of that contain these words. For example, students might list *handbag, handball, handbook,* and *handcuff.* Allow five minutes per word. Compile a class list, taking suggestions from the small groups.

INTERVENTION ASSESSMENT BOOK ✔

FLUENCY BUILDER Have students select a page from "Gram's Plant Parade" to read aloud to a partner. You may have students choose pages that they found particularly interesting, or have them choose one of the following options:

- Read the last two paragraphs on page 9 and continue reading through the end of the story. (Total: 98 words)

- Read pages 8–9. (Total: 102 words)

Students should read their selected passages aloud to their partners three times. Have the student rate his or her own reading on a scale from I to 4.

SCALE
I Not good
2 Pretty good
3 Good
4 Great!

Review Vocabulary

Review the Vocabulary Words before the weekly assessment. Invite students to fold a piece of paper in half the long way and then into thirds so the paper will have a total of six boxes. Have students write the six Vocabulary Words in the boxes in any order. Read aloud the definitions of the words and have students place a marker on the word that is being defined. Markers can be beans, buttons, or slips of colored paper. Tell students to say "Bingo" once they have a completed row or three markers in a row.

You may want to display the Vocabulary Words and definitions on page 9 and have students copy them to use when they study for the vocabulary test.

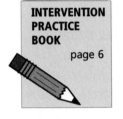

INTERVENTION
PRACTICE
BOOK
page 6

⭐ (Focus Skill) Review Narrative Elements

To review narrative elements before the weekly assessment, distribute *Intervention Practice Book* page 6. Select a volunteer to read the paragraph aloud. Tell students to listen and identify the setting, characters, and plot. Guide students to complete the chart with these narrative elements.

Review Test Prep

Invite students to turn to page 49 of the *Pupil Edition*. Read aloud and review the two tips for answering the test questions. Remind students that knowing the elements in the story— the setting, the characters, and the plot—can help them answer not only the test questions about the story on this page but also other test questions like these. Tell students that understanding and identifying the narrative elements will help them understand a character's actions and motives.

LEAD
THE WAY
page 49

INTERVENTION
ASSESSMENT
BOOK

Have students follow along as you read aloud each test question and the tip that goes with it. Discuss why knowing where Sam is from would help you know how he feels about life in the country.

Self-Selected Reading

Have students select their own books to read independently. They might choose books from the classroom library, or you may wish to offer a group of appropriate books from which students can choose. Titles might include:

- *Kenny's Tomatoes.* (See page 49M of the *Teacher's Edition* for a lesson plan.)

- *Wanda's Roses*, by Pat Brisson. Boyds Mills, 1994

- *Cabbages and Kings*, by Elizabeth Seabrook. Viking Penguin, 1997

You may also wish to choose additional books that are the same genre or by the same author.

After students have chosen their books, give each student a copy of My Reading Log, which can be found on page R38 in the back of the *Teacher's Edition*. Have students fill in the information at the top of the form. Then have them use the log to keep track of their reading and to record their responses to the literature.

Conduct student-teacher conferences. Allow time to confer with each student about his or her self-selected reading choices. Encourage students to share their Reading Log with you and to select a favorite passage to read aloud to you. Ask questions about the content of the book and why the student selected it. Discuss the narrative elements of the book. Ask questions about the characters, their actions and emotions, as well as the setting and the plot.

FLUENCY PERFORMANCE Invite students to read aloud to you the passage they practiced from "Gram's Plant Parade." Keep track of the number of the words each student reads correctly and incorrectly. Ask the student to rate his or her own reading on the 1–4 scale. Give students the opportunity to continue practicing and then to read the passage to you again.

See *Oral Reading Fluency Assessment* for monitoring progress.

LESSON 2

BEFORE

Building Background and Vocabulary

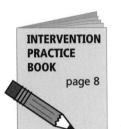

INTERVENTION PRACTICE BOOK

page 8

Use with

"Donavan's Word Jar"

Review Phonics: Short Vowel /i/*i*; Long Vowel /ī/*i-e*

Identify the sound. Have students repeat *Rick is sick of jam* three times. Ask students which words have the /i/ sound they hear in *wig*. (*Rick, is, sick*) Then have students repeat three times: *Mike likes the kite.* Ask them to identify the words with the /ī/ sound they hear in *spike*. (*Mike, likes, kite*)

Associate letters to sounds. Write on the board the words *fig* and *brim*. Underline the *i* in *fig* and point out that *i* stands for the /i/ sound in *brim*. Explain that when a word has a vowel between two or more consonants, it usually has a short vowel sound. Write *fin, spin,* and *flip* on the board. Ask students to identify the CVC pattern and read the words aloud. Write the word *kite*. Point out the *i-e* pattern in *kite*. Explain that words with this pattern usually have a long vowel sound.

Word blending. Model how to blend and read the word *kite*. Touch *k* and say /k/. Touch *i* and *e* and say /ī/. Touch *t* and say /t/. Then slide your hand under all the letters, elongating the sounds /kīīt/. Then say the word naturally—*kite*. Repeat with *Rick, sick, Mike,* and *likes*.

Apply the skill. *Vowel Substitution* Write these words on the board, and have students read each aloud. Make the changes necessary to form the words in parentheses. Have volunteers read aloud the new words.

fin (fine)   **strip** (stripe)   **slid** (slide)   **grip** (gripe)   **hid** (hide)

Introduce Vocabulary

PRETEACH lesson vocabulary. Tell students that they are going to learn six new words that they will see again when they read a story called "Donavan's Word Jar." Teach each Vocabulary Word using this process.

Use the following suggestions or similar ideas to give the meaning or context.

> Write the word.
> Say the word.
> Track the word and have students repeat it.
> Give the meaning or context.

leisure Sit back and pretend to read a book. Explain that you enjoy doing this in your leisure time.

disappointment Open an empty wrapped box. Show disappointment.

perseverance Work to solve a math equation. Explain that *perseverance* means "to continue to try."

uneasy Point out the root word *easy* and the prefix *un-*, meaning "not." Explain that to be *uneasy* is to be uncomfortable.

compromise	Ask two students to pretend to argue over a book and then reach an agreement for sharing it. Explain that they have compromised.
chortle	Laugh out loud. Tell students that *chortle* is another word for *laugh*.

For vocabulary activities, see Vocabulary Games on pages 2–7.

Building Background and Vocabulary

Apply Vocabulary Strategies

Use prefixes and suffixes. Write the word *disappointment* on the board. Remind students that often they can figure out a word's meaning by using prefixes and suffixes. Model using the strategy.

> **MODEL** As I look at the word, I see the prefix *dis-*. I have seen this in the word *disobey*, which I know the meaning of. I think *dis-* means "not." Then I see the suffix *-ment*, which means "condition." When I blend these parts together with the root word *appoint*, I get *disappointment*. I know I've heard this word before. I think it is a feeling or condition that someone has when something that was expected does not happen.

Guide students to figure out meanings of other words in a similar way.

RETEACH lesson vocabulary. Have volunteers pantomime the Vocabulary Words for classmates to guess. If a student has trouble creating a pantomime, offer suggestions:

1. **leisure** Play basketball, draw, play on the computer.
2. **disappointment** Hold up a *D* grade and look disappointed.
3. **perseverance** Practice shooting a basket repeatedly.
4. **uneasy** Pretend to walk on a tightrope, act cautious, and look down a lot.
5. **compromise** Argue over the computer with another student; point to the clock and work out a 10-minute compromise.
6. **chortle** Pretend to laugh, holding your belly.

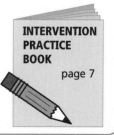

Vocabulary Words

leisure time free from work

disappointment the feeling that comes when one's hopes are not met

perseverance the habit of continuing in spite of troubles

uneasy worried

compromise to reach an agreement after each side gives up part of its demands

chortle to laugh or chuckle loudly

FLUENCY BUILDER Using *Intervention Practice Book* page 7, read each word in the first column and have students repeat it. Follow the same procedure with each of the remaining columns. After students have repeatedly read each of the words in the columns, invite them to read these lists of words to a partner.

INTERVENTION PRACTICE BOOK
page 7

BEFORE

Reading
"Donavan's
Word Jar"
pages 52–70

USE SKILL CARD 2A

(Focus Skill) Prefixes, Suffixes, and Roots

PRETEACH the skill. Tell students that many words are made up of smaller word parts. Use *uncomfortable* as an example: *un comfort able.*

Invite students to look at **side A of Skill Card 2: Prefixes, Suffixes, and Roots**. Read the definitions aloud. Then read the words in the word box. Point out the chart and explain that each word has a prefix, a suffix, or both. Ask:

- **What is the prefix in the word** *unhook*? (*un-*)
- **What is the root word in** *reconstruct*? (*construct*)
- **What is the suffix in the word** *blissful*? (*-ful*)

Explain that adding a prefix or a suffix to a word changes the word's meaning. Ask students how adding *un-* to these words would change their meaning: *tie, dress, likely, plug.*

Prepare to Read: "Donavan's Word Jar"

Preview. Tell students that they are going to read a realistic fiction story called "Donavan's Word Jar." Explain that the boy in this story has an unusual hobby, or collection. Then preview the selection.

LEAD THE WAY
pages 52–70

- **Pages 52–55:** I see the title, "Donavan's Word Jar," on page 53 and the names of the author and illustrator. I think that Donavan has words written on the pieces of paper in that jar. On page 55, it looks as if he is taking his word jar somewhere.

- **Pages 56–61:** On pages 57–60, there are photos of people, and on page 58, there is an illustration of a woman. I can tell that this woman is someone Donavan is close to because she is putting her arms around him on page 61.

- **Pages 63–65:** The people on page 63 look very sad and lonely. It looks like a miserable rainy day outside. On page 65, the people are smiling and holding up a slip of paper. I think it is a slip of paper from Donavan's word jar.

- **Pages 66–69:** On page 67, Donavan looks surprised that the people are taking his words. His jar is empty on page 69 and the woman is talking to him. I guess she is talking to him about his word jar and what happened to his words.

Set purpose. Model setting a purpose for reading "Donavan's Word Jar."

MODEL From what I have seen in my preview, it looks as if people take words from Donavan's word jar and enjoy reading the words. One purpose for reading is to find out about characters or events. I will read to find out what happens to Donavan's words.

Reread and Summarize

Have students reread and summarize "Donavan's Word Jar" in sections. The chart below offers suggestions on how to reread the story.

Pages 53–57

Let's reread pages 53–57 to find out why Donavan is taking his word jar to his grandma's house.

Summary: Donavan is hoping Grandma can help him solve his problem. Grandma has lots of collections. He wants to keep collecting words, but his word jar is too full.

Pages 58–61

Now let's reread pages 58–61 to see if Grandma has any suggestions for Donavan.

Summary: Grandma and Donavan enjoy reading the words and remembering stories that went with the words. Grandma thinks other people would enjoy the words too, but Donavan does not want to give his words away.

Pages 62–64

As we reread pages 62–64, let's find out what Grandma's neighbors are doing.

Summary: Mr. Perkins was looking out the window. Miss Millie was staring into space. Mr. Crawford, the mailman, was rubbing his feet. Miz Marylou and Mr. Gut were shouting at one another.

Pages 65–70

Let's reread pages 65–70 to recall what happens as the people read Donavan's words.

Summary: After Grandma's neighbors read the words, they are walking about, laughing, and talking. The words inspire them.

FLUENCY BUILDER Invite students to look at the bottom half of *Intervention Practice Book* page 7. These sentences have been broken into phrases. The slashes break the sentences into natural phrases. Tell students to repeat these phrases after you, imitating your tone, inflection, and speed. After students have repeated each sentence, invite them to practice reading the sentences to a partner.

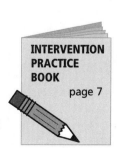

INTERVENTION PRACTICE BOOK

page 7

Directed Reading: "Click!" pp. 14–21

Pages 14–15

Invite students who have collections (stamps, coins, caps, and so on) to describe them. Then have students read aloud the title of the story and view the illustration on pages 14–15. After reading the pages, ask: **What kind of person does the teacher in this picture seem to be? What do you think she collects?** (*She is fun and makes the kids in her class smile.*) **DETERMINE CHARACTERS' TRAITS**

MOVING
AHEAD
pp. 14–21

Ask: **What does Miss Wise say about collecting pins?** (*Possible response: that she does it in her leisure time; that she gets disappointed when she doesn't find the pin she wants*) **NOTE DETAILS**

Ask: **How does the suffix -or help you figure out the meaning of collector?** (*Possible response: The suffix -or means "doer" or "action" so a collector must be "someone who does" the action of collecting.*)
⭐(Focus Skill) **PREFIXES, SUFFIXES, AND ROOTS**

Pages 16–17

Ask: **Do you think Tim sees his group of hats as a collection at first? Why or why not?** (*Possible response: No, because he asks Mike whether his hats are a collection.*) **DRAW CONCLUSIONS**

Have students read page 17 to find out what Jill collects. (*stamps*) Ask: **What does Mike do everywhere he goes?** (*He takes pictures.*) **SUMMARIZE**

Does this give you a clue about what his collection might be? (*Possible response: Maybe he collects photographs.*) **MAKE PREDICTIONS**

Pages 18–19

Have students read pages 18–19 to find out what else Miss Wise's students collect. Ask: **What does Linda collect?** (*pigs*) **NOTE DETAILS**

Why does Mike suggest that Linda collect cats instead of pigs? (*Possible response: He thinks she collects real pigs. He is worried that real pigs might bother the neighbors.*) **DRAW CONCLUSIONS**

Does Mike continue to take pictures? (*yes*)

Ask a volunteer to read the last paragraph on page 18. Notice the pronunciation of the word *chortles*. Model using the use decoding-phonics strategy:

> **MODEL** When I come to a word like this, that I don't know, I break the word down into smaller parts. I know that when the letters *c* and *h* are together, they make the sound /ch/. The next two letters in this word are a word I already know: *or*. I know the letters at the end of this word and the sounds these letters make. I can blend them all together: *t* is /t/, *le* is /əl/, and the letter *s* makes the sound /s/. I can put all these sounds together. *ch-or-təls*. ⭐(Focus Strategy) **USE DECODING/PHONICS**

Page 20

INTERVENTION PRACTICE BOOK page 9

Have students recall their predictions about Mike's collection. After they read, ask: **What does Mike collect?** (*smiles that he captures in photographs*) **CONFIRM PREDICTIONS**

Why might this be a good collection? (*Responses will vary.*) **PERSONAL OPINION**

Summarize the selection. Ask students which collections they liked the best: the pins, hats, stamps, pigs, or photos. Then have them complete *Intervention Practice Book* page 9 to help them summarize the story.

Page 21

Answers to *Think About It* Questions

1. Mike collects smiles. He collects them by taking pictures of all the kids in his class. **SUMMARY**

2. Possible response: She wants kids to find out about the fun of collecting. **INTERPRETATION**

3. News stories should be brief, factual descriptions of the collections mentioned in the story and may include descriptions of other collections as well. **WRITE A NEWS STORY**

AFTER

Skill Review *pages 76–77*

USE SKILL CARD 2B

(Focus Skill) Prefixes, Suffixes, and Roots

RETEACH the skill. Have students look at **side B of Skill Card 2: Prefixes, Suffixes, and Roots**. Read the skill reminder with students and have a volunteer read aloud the words in the word box.

Ask another volunteer to read aloud the directions. Explain that students should create this chart on their own. Encourage students to make at least four rows, but tell them they can have more if they wish. The directions ask students to break apart four words, but twelve words are provided.

After students have completed their chart, have them share and compare definitions. Create a class chart of all twelve words.

FLUENCY BUILDER Tell students that today they will reread the sentences on the bottom of *Intervention Practice Book* page 7. Have students locate and point to the first sentence. Tell students that everyone is going to read the sentence together. This choral reading will provide students with an opportunity to hear others and listen to the natural phrasing of the sentences. Choral read each of the sentences several times.

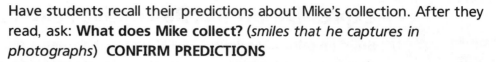

INTERVENTION PRACTICE BOOK page 7

Expressive Writing: Descriptive Sentences

Build on prior knowledge. Tell students that they are going to write descriptive sentences for a character from a book they have recently read. Display the following chart:

Physical Traits	Feelings or Actions
How does the character look?	What does the character do?
	How does the character feel?

Construct the text. "Share the pen" with students in a collaborative group writing effort. As students dictate words and phrases for their descriptive sentences about a character, write them on the board or on chart paper, guiding the process by asking questions and offering suggestions as needed.

- Is the character tall, short, large, or small? Does he or she have any special physical traits?

- Does the character behave in a certain way? Does he or she express specific feelings? Why do you think the character acts the way he or she does?

Revisit the text. Go back and read the suggestions together. Ask: **Have we described this character clearly and used vivid descriptions? What could we do to make the sentences more interesting?** (add details or examples)

- Guide students in adding details or examples to their sentences. Encourage them to use adjectives to describe the character.

- Have students read their completed descriptive sentences aloud.

On Your Own

Have students write descriptive sentences about a member of their family. Tell them to include words and phrases that describe not only how the person looks but also how that person makes them feel.

Connect Spelling and Phonics

Write the word *five* on the board. Explain that you will say some words that have a long *i* sound. Explain that the words will have a silent *e* on the end that causes the *i* to have the long *i* sound. Tell students you will also read three words that have a short *i* sound. Remind them to listen carefully. Then read the following words, and have students write them. After they write each one, display the correct spelling so that students can proofread their work. Have them draw a line through a misspelled word and write the correct spelling beside it.

I. grins*	2. kick*	3. smile*	4. nine*
5. click*	6. hides	7. time*	8. glide

*Word appears in "Click!"

Dictate the following sentence for students to write: *Jim likes to fix pipes*.

Build and Read Longer Words

Explain that a syllable is a word part that can be said by itself and that every syllable has one vowel sound. Clap your hands once as you say *spin*. Explain that this word has one syllable. Then clap your hands twice as you say *spinning*. Explain that this word has two syllables. Say these words: *swim*, *swimming*, *plan*, *planning*, *grin*, *grinning*. Have students clap once after each one-syllable word and twice after each two-syllable word. Explain that when the ending *-ing* is added to a word with the CVC pattern, the final consonant is usually doubled. When such a word is divided into syllables, it is usually broken between the double consonants. Write these words on the board: *clap*, *win*, *hop*, and *cut*. Select volunteers to come to the board and make these words two-syllable words by adding *-ing* to them. Remind them to double the consonant at the end of the word before adding *-ing*. (*clapping*, *winning*, *hopping*, *cutting*)

**INTERVENTION
ASSESSMENT
BOOK**

FLUENCY BUILDER Pair students and have them read passages from "Click!" aloud to each other. Students may select a passage that they enjoyed, or have them choose one of the following options:

- Read page 14 and the first paragraph on page 15. (Total: 99 words)

- Read pages 18–20. (Total: 108 words)

Encourage students to read the selected passage aloud to their partners three times. Have the student rate his or her reading on a scale from 1 to 4.

SCALE
I Not good
2 Pretty good
3 Good
4 Great!

Review Vocabulary

To revisit the six Vocabulary Words prior to the weekly assessment, use these synonyms. Read aloud these words, and have students identify the Vocabulary Word that is similar in meaning.

laugh (chortle)

agreement (compromise)

continued effort (perseverance)

setback (disappointment)

free time (leisure)

worried (uneasy)

Then encourage students to think of words that are antonyms, or opposites, for each Vocabulary Word. You may want to display the Vocabulary Words and definitions on page 19 and have students copy them to use when they study for the vocabulary test.

**INTERVENTION
PRACTICE
BOOK**
page 10

(Focus Skill) Review Prefixes, Suffixes, and Roots

Have students complete *Intervention Practice Book* page 10 to review prefixes, suffixes, and roots. Choose a volunteer to read the directions aloud. Select a second volunteer to read the words in the word box. Guide students to complete the page.

Review Test Prep

Ask students to turn to page 77 of the *Pupil Edition*. Direct students' attention to the tips. Tell students that these tips will help them answer the questions on this page and other test questions as well. Remind them that knowing different prefixes and their meanings will help them understand and define many new words.

**LEAD
THE WAY**
page 77

**INTERVENTION
ASSESSMENT
BOOK**

Ask students to follow along as you read aloud the test questions and the tips. Discuss how knowing the meanings of *micro* and *scope* will provide students with the meaning of *microscope*. Then ask students what *un-* means and how it changes the meaning of *tidy*.

Self-Selected Reading

Have students select their own books to read independently. They might choose books from the classroom library shelf, or you may wish to offer a group of appropriate books from which students can choose.

- *Family Pictures* by Carmen Lomas Garza. Children's Press, 1990

- *Jacob's Collection* by Brian Mundt. Steck-Vaughn, 1997

Groups of books could be by the same author or about the same subject.

After students have chosen their books, give each student a copy of My Reading Log, which can be found on page R38 in the back of the *Teacher's Edition*. Have students fill in information at the top of the form. Then have them use the log to keep track of their reading and to record their responses to the literature.

Conduct student-teacher conferences. Arrange time for each student to confer with you individually about his or her self-selected reading. During this conference, invite students to share their opinions about the books they selected. Encourage students to read a passage from the book to you or share their Reading Log with you. If students have difficulty sharing during this time, ask leading questions about the book that help initiate the discussion. Invite them to show you a favorite illustration and ask why it is their favorite.

FLUENCY PERFORMANCE Listen to students read the passages from "Click!" that they selected and practiced earlier. Note the number of words the student reads correctly and incorrectly. Have students rate their own oral reading on a scale of 1 to 4. Allow them the opportunity to read the passage again if they were not satisfied with their fluency.

See *Oral Reading Fluency Assessment* for monitoring progress.

Use with

"My Name Is María Isabel"

Review Phonics: Short Vowel /o/*o*; Long Vowel /ō/*o-e*

Identify the sounds. Have students repeat this sentence three times: *Tom did not find the note at home.* Ask them to identify the words that have the /o/ sound. (*Tom, not*) Then have them repeat the sentence twice and identify the words that have the /ō/ sound. (*note, home*)

Associate letters to sounds. Write the sentence *Tom did not find the note at home.* on the board. Underline the words *not* and *note*. Point out the addition of *e* in *note* and ask students how the vowel sound changed when the *e* was added. Explain that words that have the CVC letter pattern usually have a short vowel sound; words that have the letter pattern in *note* (CVCe) usually have a long vowel sound. Repeat with *Tom* and *home*.

Word blending. Model blending the letters to read *note*. Touch *n* and say /n/. Touch *o* and *e* and say /ō/. Touch *t* and say /t/. Slide your hand under the whole word as you elongate the sounds /nnōōtt/. Then read the word naturally—*note*. Follow a similar procedure with *Tom, not,* and *home*.

Apply the skill. *Vowel Substitution* Write the following words on the board, and have students read each aloud. Make the changes necessary to form the words in parentheses. Have students read each new word aloud.

rod (rode)	**glob** (globe)	**mop** (mope)	**tot** (tote)
rob (robe)	**slop** (slope)	**hop** (hope)	**lop** (lope)

Introduce Vocabulary

PRETEACH **lesson vocabulary.** Tell students that they are going to learn six new words that they will see again when they read a story called "My Name Is María Isabel." Teach each Vocabulary Word using this process.

Use the following suggestions or similar ideas to give the meaning of each word.

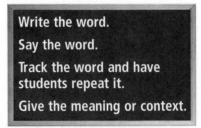

Write the word.

Say the word.

Track the word and have students repeat it.

Give the meaning or context.

pageant Relate to a beauty pageant or a fashion show. Explain that a pageant is a show on a stage.

restless Point out the suffix *-less* and explain that it means "lack of." *Restless* means "lack of rest," or "unable to be still."

tropical Show pictures of a tropical island. Name tropical birds. Explain that a *tropical* location is hot and humid.

rehearsals	Ask students who play instruments what they do to prepare for concerts. They practice, or rehearse.
attentively	Point out the *-ly* ending and the root word *attentive*. Demonstrate listening attentively.
troublesome	Explain that *troublesome* is an adjective. Adjectives are words that describe things, so *troublesome* describes something that causes trouble.

For vocabulary activities, see Vocabulary Games on pages 2–7.

For vocabulary activities, see Vocabulary Games on pages 2–7.

Vocabulary Words

pageant a show based on stories or events from previous times

restless unable to be still

tropical found in the warm, wet regions of the Earth, near the equator

rehearsals practices for a play or other performance

attentively in a way that shows complete concentration; with concern

troublesome trouble-causing; disturbing

AFTER

Building Background and Vocabulary

Apply Vocabulary Strategies

Use sentence and word context. Write this sentence on the board: *Brad was listening attentively to the teacher giving the directions.* Tell students that sometimes they can figure out the meaning of a word by reading the rest of the sentence. Model using the strategy.

> **MODEL** When I read this sentence, I am unsure what the word *attentively* means. If I continue reading, I can figure out that it must mean "carefully" or "closely." I'll reread it, substituting these words to see if the meaning makes sense.

RETEACH **lesson vocabulary.** Have students listen to each sentence. Ask them to say *Yea!* if the sentence is true and *Nay!* if the sentence is false.

1. You can build a snow fort on a tropical island. (*Nay!*)
2. You should listen attentively to directions. (*Yea!*)
3. A restless person can't sit in a chair for very long. (*Yea!*)
4. People don't need many rehearsals to put on a great show! (*Nay!*)
5. Some people find long division troublesome. (*Yea!*)
6. An auditorium is a good place to hold a pageant. (*Yea!*)

FLUENCY BUILDER Have students look at the top of *Intervention Practice Book* page 11. Read the words in the first column aloud and have students repeat the words after you. Have partners read the words in the first column aloud to each other. Follow a similar procedure with the words in the other two columns.

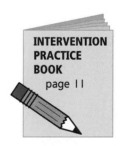

INTERVENTION PRACTICE BOOK
page 11

BEFORE

Reading
"My Name Is
María Isabel"
pages 80–95

USE SKILL CARD 3A

(Focus Skill) **Narrative Elements**

PRETEACH **the skill.** Remind students that narrative elements consist of the setting, characters, and plot. Explain that most stories have a problem, or conflict, and the resolution, or answer, to the problem.

Have students look at **side A of Skill Card 3: Narrative Elements.** Read the first sentence. Then ask a volunteer to read aloud the paragraph. Encourage students to listen for the problem. Direct students' attention to the chart, and have volunteers take turns reading each box aloud. Ask:

- **What could the boys have done to avoid the problem?** (Possible response: Flown the kite in a place with no trees)

- **Suppose the wind had not blown the kite out of the tree. What do you think the boys would have done?** (Help students understand that there are other solutions to their problem.)

Explain that identifying the problem in a story can help students understand the steps characters take to resolve that problem.

Prepare to Read: "My Name Is María Isabel"

Preview. Tell students that they are going to read a story called "My Name Is María Isabel." Explain that it is realistic fiction. It has characters and events that are like real-life people and events, but the story is made up. Explain that this story is about a girl named María Isabel and a problem she has. Then preview the selection.

**LEAD
THE WAY**
pages
80–95

- **Pages 80–85:** I see the title, "My Name Is María Isabel," and the author's and illustrator's names. I think the girl must be María Isabel. Then I see a snowman, a candle, some stars, and a bell. These things make me think that it could be holiday time.

- **Pages 86–89:** In the illustration on page 87, María Isabel looks disappointed, tired, or even sad. On pages 88–89, there is a pig. I'm not sure what the pig has to do with this story. I'll have to read to find out.

- **Pages 90–95:** On page 90, there is a paper with the title "My Greatest Wish." It could be a story that María Isabel wrote. I see the guitar and musical notes, so the story must be about music. On page 94 there is a butterfly and the title "Candles of Hanukkah." This is probably a song.

Set purpose. Model setting a purpose for reading "My Name Is María Isabel."

MODEL From what I have seen in my preview, I can tell that it is winter time and that María Isabel sings and writes a story. I will read to find out what her problem is and how she solves it.

Reread and Summarize

Have students reread and summarize "My Name Is María Isabel" in sections, as described below.

Pages 81–83

Let's reread pages 81–83 to recall María Isabel's problem and what the Winter Pageant is all about.

Summary: María Isabel wants a part in the Winter Pageant but she doesn't respond when the teacher calls her Mary Lopez. The Winter Pageant is a show about holidays around the world.

Pages 84–87

Now let's reread pages 84–87 to find out what María Isabel daydreams about and how she felt about the book *Charlotte's Web*.

Summary: María Isabel daydreams about being a famous singer. She feels as if she is caught in a spider web similar to Charlotte's.

Pages 88–91

As we reread pages 88–91, let's recall what María Isabel's greatest wish is.

Summary: María's greatest wish is to be called María Isabel Salazar Lopez. These family names remind her of special people and her heritage.

Pages 92–94

Let's reread pages 92–94 to remember what happens to make María Isabel feel special.

Summary: The teacher calls her by her name and then asks her to sing for the class. María Isabel's father buys her some butterfly barrettes for her hair. María performs in the Winter Pageant after all.

FLUENCY BUILDER Be sure students have copies of *Intervention Practice Book* page 11. Have students look at the sentences on the bottom half of the page. Remind students that the slashes break the sentences into phrases. Read aloud each sentence and model the appropriate phrasing and expression. Have students repeat each sentence after you, imitating your phrasing and expression.

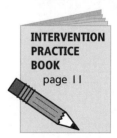

INTERVENTION
PRACTICE
BOOK
page 11

Directed Reading: "A Troublesome Nose," pp. 22–28

Pages 22–23

Read the title of the story aloud. Point out the stage, children, teacher, and props. Then have students read to find out what the class is doing. (*planning a holiday pageant*) Ask: **What do you think the troublesome nose is?** (Possible response: *the fox's nose one boy is holding up*) **SPECULATE**

MOVING
AHEAD
pp. 22–28

Why do you think Ron wants a role in the pageant? (*Possible response: The students will be acting out Ron's favorite book.*) **INTERPRET CHARACTERS' EMOTIONS**

Pages 24–25

Have students read page 24. Then ask: **What is the problem in this story?** (*Ron's fox nose is too big; it flops over his eyes or flops down over his lips.*) (Focus Skill) **NARRATIVE ELEMENTS**

Ask: **How does the big nose affect Ron's performance?** (*When it flips up, Ron cannot see. When it flops down, the others can't hear his lines.*) **CAUSE-EFFECT**

Ask a volunteer to read aloud the first two paragraphs on page 25. Model the make and confirm predictions strategy:

> **MODEL** When I read this part, I wondered what Ron would do about his troublesome nose. I asked myself what I would do. I think I would try and fix the nose so it wouldn't move around. I predict Ron will find a way to fix the nose so it doesn't flip up or flop down. Let's read on to see if I am right. After reading the rest of page 25, I see that Ron's dad suggests using tape. That's a great idea. I think Ron will make the nose tighter. (Focus Strategy) **MAKE AND CONFIRM PREDICTIONS**

Pages 26–27

Have students look at the illustration on pages 26–27. Ask students if the pageant appears to be a success. Then have them read pages 26–27 to confirm. (*Yes, it is a success.*) Ask: **Does Ron's fox nose slip?** (*yes*) **NOTE DETAILS**

How does this affect Ron's performance? (Possible response: *It makes his funny role even funnier.*) **DRAW CONCLUSIONS**

INTERVENTION
PRACTICE
BOOK
page 13

Ask: **Did you expect this outcome? Why or why not?** (Possible responses: *No, I thought he would fix the nose using the tape; no, I thought the nose would ruin his performance.*) **CONFIRM PREDICTIONS**

Summarize the selection. Have students think about Ron's problem and how he solved it. Then have them complete *Intervention Practice Book* page 13 and summarize the story in one sentence.

Answers to *Think About It* Questions

1. Ron is the fox in the pageant. He likes the role because all his lines are jokes. **SUMMARY**
2. Possible response: The big nose does not work well, but it makes the kids laugh and clap for Ron. **INTERPRETATION**
3. Postcards should tell about the jokes and the nose from Ron's point of view. **WRITE A POSTCARD**

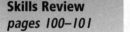

AFTER

Skills Review
pages 100–101

USE SKILL CARD 3B

(Focus Skill) Narrative Elements

RETEACH the skill. Have students look at **side B of Skill Card 3: Narrative Elements.** Read the skill reminder with them, and select a volunteer to read the paragraph aloud. Discuss the problem, the steps to resolving the problem, and the solution in this story.

Read aloud the next set of directions. Explain that students should now create their own flow chart to fill in the information about the plot of this story. Remind them to write one event in each box.

After students have completed their flow chart, have them share their chart with a partner. Suggest they compare the charts and discuss any differences.

FLUENCY BUILDER Invite students to look at *Intervention Practice Book* page 11. Tell students that they will practice reading the sentences on the bottom of this page. Have partners take turns reading the sentences aloud to each other and then reading them on tape. Encourage them to listen to the tape together and suggest ways they can improve their oral reading. Now have them reread the sentences on tape again, keeping in mind their partner's suggestions.

INTERVENTION PRACTICE BOOK
page 11

Expressive Writing: Personal Narrative

Build on Prior Knowledge. Tell students that they are going to write sentences about experiences they have had at recess. Display the sentences shown below. Point out the different sentence types.

Construct the Text. "Share the pen" with students in a collaborative group writing effort. Guide them in creating a variety of sentences.

> Have you ever played tetherball?
>
> We play tetherball at recess all the time.
>
> Wow, it is a blast!
>
> Why is tetherball your favorite activity to play at recess?
>
> Tetherball is a great activity to play with a friend, and it builds strength in your arms.

- Reread the sentences. Ask: **What activity will we focus on?** Guide students to write a declarative sentence stating the topic.

- Encourage students to write a sentence that expresses an emotion about their activity.

- Work with them to write a compound sentence about their activity.

Revisit the Text. Go back and read the sentences together. Ask: **Have we used a variety of sentences? What other types of sentences could we include?**

- Guide students in rewriting sentences for variety. For example, the first sentence could pose a question about the topic. The closing sentence could express a feeling using an exclamation.

- Have students read their completed sentences aloud.

On Your Own

Invite students to write four sentences about an after-school activity. Remind them to use different types and lengths of sentences.

Connect Spelling and Phonics

RETEACH **short vowel /o/o; long vowel /ō/o-e.** Write the words *hop* and *hope* on the board. Tell students that you will say four words that have the short *o* sound as in *hop* and that you will say four words that have the long *o* sound as in *hope*. Have students write the numbers 1–8 on a sheet of paper, and then dictate the following words. After students write each one, display the correct spelling so they can proofread their work. They should draw a line through a misspelled word and write the correct spelling beside it.

1. flops*	2. role*	3. nose*	4. prop
5. joke*	6. fox*	7. globe	8. problem*

***Word appears in "A Troublesome Nose."**

Dictate the following sentence for students to write: *The pot broke on the stones.*

Build and Read Longer Words

Remind students that when the ending *-ing* is added to a word with a short vowel sound, the final consonant is usually doubled.

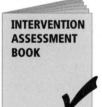

INTERVENTION ASSESSMENT BOOK

Write *mop* on the board and point out that the vowel between the two consonants has a short vowel sound. Then write *mopping* on the board and remind students that adding *-ing* also doubles the last consonant, *p*. Then write *mope* on the board. Remind students that words with this pattern have the long vowel sound. Write *moping* on the board. Tell students that when the ending *-ing* is added to a word with this pattern, the final *e* is dropped. Repeat the procedure with *joke/joking* and *slope/sloping*. Then write *hop* and *hope* on the board and ask volunteers to make the changes necessary to add *-ing* to each word. Have children create more words by asking them to add *-ing* to these words: *bob, pose, pop, rot, rob, sob, top*.

FLUENCY BUILDER Have students select a passage from "A Troublesome Nose" to read aloud to a partner. Students can choose one of the following options, or invite them to select a passage that they found particularly interesting.

- Read page 25 and the first paragraph on page 26. (Total: 84 words)

- Read the last two paragraphs on page 26 and all of page 27. (Total: 119 words)

Encourage students to read the selected passage aloud to their partners three times. Have each student rate his or her own reading on a scale from 1 to 4.

SCALE
1 Not good
2 Pretty good
3 Good
4 Great!

Review Vocabulary

Have students write the six Vocabulary Words on index cards, one word per card. Have two students stand next to each other. Read aloud the definition of a word. Have the two students identify the word being defined and hold up that Vocabulary Word. The first student to hold up the correct word trades places with the next student. Continue until all have had a turn. Students waiting to be quizzed should be seated and looking through their own cards. After hearing the definitions several times, students should be able to quickly identify the word being defined.

INTERVENTION
PRACTICE
BOOK
page 14

⭐ (Focus Skill) Review Narrative Elements

Distribute *Intervention Practice Book* page 14 to review narrative elements before the weekly assessment. Ask students to track the print and follow along as you read the paragraph aloud. Have students reread the paragraph and identify the problem, the steps to resolving the problem, and the solution.

Review Test Prep

Ask students to turn to page 101 of the *Pupil Edition*. Have students look at the tips for answering questions. Tell students that paying attention to these tips can help them answer not only the test questions on this page but also other test questions like these.

LEAD
THE WAY
p. 101

INTERVENTION
ASSESSMENT
BOOK

✔

Have students follow along as you read aloud each test question and the tip that goes with it. Explain that once they can identify the main character, they should search for details about the character's appearance, actions, and feelings. These details can help them answer questions about the main character and why he or she does specific actions.

Self-Selected Reading

Have students select their own books to read independently. They might choose books from the classroom library shelf, or you may wish to offer a group of appropriate books from which students can choose. Titles might include:

- *The Gold Coin*, by Alma Flor Ada. Atheneum, 1991

- *The Malachite Palace*, by Alma Flor Ada. Atheneum, 1998

The author of "My Name Is María Isabel" is also the author of these two books.

After students have chosen their books, give each student a copy of My Reading Log, which can be found on page R38 in the back of the *Teacher's Edition*. Have students fill in the information at the top of the form. Then have them use the log to keep track of their reading and to record their responses to the literature.

Conduct student-teacher conferences. Set aside time for each student to conference with you about his or her self-selected reading. Students may choose to share their Reading Log or to read a passage from their book aloud to you. If students are having difficulty talking about the book, prompt a discussion by asking questions about the book. Ask about the illustrations, what they learned, or their favorite part.

FLUENCY PERFORMANCE Listen to students read aloud the passage from "A Troublesome Nose" that they selected and practiced earlier. Tally the number of words each student reads correctly. Invite the student to rate his or her own performance on a scale of 1 to 4. Allow students to continue to practice and reread their passage until they are happy with their performance.

See *Oral Reading Fluency Assessment* for monitoring progress.

LESSON 4

BEFORE

Building
Background
and Vocabulary

Use with

"Lou Gehrig: The Luckiest Man"

Review Phonics: Short Vowel /e/e; Long Vowel /ē/ee, ea, ey

Identify the sounds. Have students say aloud three times: *Ben has the best donkey on our street.* Ask which words have the /e/ sound they hear in *bed.* (*Ben, best*) Then have students repeat the sentence and identify the words with the /ē/ sound they hear in *sneak.* (*donkey, street*)

Associate letters to sounds. Write the above sentence on the board. Underline the *e* in *Ben* and *best.* Point out the CVC pattern; remind students that in words with this pattern, the *e* usually stands for the short *e* vowel sound. Underline the *ee* in *street.* Point out the CVVC pattern. Explain that words with this pattern often have a long vowel sound. Underline the *ey* in *donkey,* and point out that these letters also stand for the long *e* vowel sound. Explain that in this word the *y* acts as a vowel.

Word blending. Model how to blend and read the word *beet.* Slide your hand under the letters, elongating the sounds /bbēētt/. Then say the word naturally—*beet.* Follow a similar procedure for *bet, team,* and *key.*

Apply the skill. *Letter Substitution* Write the following words on the board, and have students read each aloud. Make the changes necessary to form the words in parentheses. Have students read each new word.

ten (teen)   **Ken** (key)   **stem** (steam)   **red** (reed)

step (steep)   **fed** (feed)   **Ben** (bean)   **best** (beast)

INTERVENTION
PRACTICE
BOOK

page 16

Introduce Vocabulary

PRETEACH **lesson vocabulary.** Tell students that they are going to learn eight new words that they will see again when they read "Lou Gehrig: The Luckiest Man." Teach each Vocabulary Word using the process below.

Use the following suggestions or similar ideas to give the meaning or context.

courageous	Point out the suffix *-ous,* which means "full of." His *courageous* actions saved people's lives.
immigrants	Discuss people students know who may have lived in another country before they moved here.
appreciation	Point out the *-ion* suffix, meaning "state of being." Relate to being thankful.

> Write the word.
> Say the word.
> Track the word and have students repeat it.
> Give the meaning or context.

tremendous	Point to a large stack of papers and say, "This is a *tremendous* amount."
modest	Tell someone he or she did a great job on a test. Explain that a *modest* person may react by appearing shy.
sportsmanship	Have two students give each other high-fives or hand-shakes. Teams often do this after a game to show good *sportsmanship*.
valuable	Relate to expensive jewelry.
salary	Relate to people who receive a weekly paycheck.

For vocabulary activities, see Vocabulary Games on pages 2–7.

For vocabulary activities, see Vocabulary Games on pages 2–7.

Vocabulary Words

courageous brave

immigrants people who go to a country to live in it

appreciation showing that one recognizes the value of a person or thing

tremendous very large or great

modest humble; not boastful

sportsmanship playing fair and showing respect for opponents

valuable important; worth much

salary money paid at regular times to a worker

AFTER
Building Background and Vocabulary

Apply Vocabulary Strategies

Use prefixes and suffixes. Write the word *courageous* on the board. Explain that using root words, prefixes, or suffixes can sometimes help students figure out the meaning of a word. Model using the strategy.

> **MODEL** When I read the word *courageous*, the root word *courage* is familiar to me. I notice the suffix *-ous*, which means "full of." So *courageous* must mean "full of courage."

Guide students in using a similar procedure to decode *appreciation*.

RETEACH lesson vocabulary. Provide a set of word cards for each student or pair of students. Read aloud or write on the board the meaning of one of the Vocabulary Words and the first letter in that word. Students match the correct word card to the definition. Continue until students have matched all the words.

FLUENCY BUILDER Use *Intervention Practice Book* page 15. Invite students to point to the first word in the first column. Tell students that you are going to read all of the words in the first column and that you want them to read each word with you. Explain that this is called choral reading. Choral-read the next two columns of words. Have students practice reading the lists with a partner.

INTERVENTION PRACTICE BOOK

page 15

USE SKILL CARD 4A

 **Prefixes, Suffixes, and Roots**

PRETEACH **the skill.** Explain to students that some long words are made up of several parts. Give the example *unbelievable*. Separate the word into three parts: the prefix *un-*, the root word *believe*, and the suffix *-able*.

Have students look at **side A of Skill Card 4: Prefixes, Suffixes, and Roots.** Read the definitions. Next, have students look at the charts.

Have volunteers take turns reading the words in each chart. Ask:

- **In each word, how does the prefix or suffix change the meaning of the word *use*?** (*re-* makes it mean "use again" and *-ful* makes it mean "full of use")

- **How can knowing the meaning of prefixes and suffixes help you understand unfamiliar words?** (Help students see that the combination of these word parts with a root or a root word provides the word's meaning.)

Remind students that when they read long or unfamiliar words, they should look for familiar prefixes, suffixes, and roots. These word parts may help them figure out the meanings of some words.

Prepare to Read: "Lou Gehrig: The Luckiest Man"

Preview. Tell students that they are going to read a selection called "Lou Gehrig: The Luckiest Man." Explain that this is a biography, a story about a person's life written by another person. Then preview the selection.

LEAD THE WAY
pages 104–115

- **Pages 104–105:** I see the title, "Lou Gehrig: The Luckiest Man," and the names of the author and illustrator. I think that the man in this illustration must be Lou Gehrig.

- **Pages 106–109:** The illustrations on these pages lead me to believe that this story takes place in a big city. I can also guess that Lou Gehrig must be a baseball player.

- **Pages 110–111:** The newspaper headline in the illustration on page 110 says, "Gehrig Slumps." This makes me think that Gehrig was a good player but now has a streak of bad luck.

- **Pages 112–115:** On pages 112–113, it looks as though Lou Gehrig is talking to the crowd through a big microphone. He looks sad in this illustration. The illustration on page 114 shows his uniform, and his cap.

Set purpose. Model setting a purpose for reading "Lou Gehrig: The Luckiest Man."

MODEL From what I have seen in my preview, I can tell that this selection is about the life and baseball career of Lou Gehrig. I will read to find out why the author thinks Lou Gehrig is the luckiest man.

Reread and Summarize

Have students reread and summarize "Lou Gehrig: The Luckiest Man" in sections, as described in the chart below.

Pages 106–107

Let's reread pages 106–107 to recall where Lou Gehrig's parents immigrated from and how his mother felt about sports.

Summary: Lou Gehrig's parents came to the United States from Germany. Lou's mother thought games and sports were a waste of time.

Pages 108–111

Now let's reread pages 108–111 to find out how and why Lou earned the nickname Iron Horse.

Summary: Gehrig never missed a game and set a record when he played in 2,130 consecutive Yankees games. He played despite injuries and illness.

Pages 112–113

Let's reread page 113 to recall why Lou Gehrig considered himself the luckiest man.

Summary: Gehrig considered himself lucky because of his many blessings. He considered himself lucky to have the opportunity to play baseball and lucky to have such loyal fans and family.

Pages 114–115

Reread pages 114–115 to find out what the Yankees team did to honor Lou Gehrig that no other team had done before.

Summary: The Yankees retired Lou Gehrig's uniform and number.

FLUENCY BUILDER Be sure that students have copies of *Intervention Practice Book* page 15. Ask them to look at the sentences on the bottom of the page. Remind students that the slashes break the sentences into phrases. Tell them that their goal is to read each phrase fluently so that eventually the entire sentence will be read smoothly. Model appropriate pace, expression, and phrasing as you read each sentence aloud. Have students read each sentence after you. Then invite students to practice by reading the sentences aloud several more times with a partner.

INTERVENTION PRACTICE BOOK

page 15

Pages 30–31

Directed Reading: "Joe DiMaggio, One of Baseball's Greatest," pp. 30–37

MOVING
AHEAD
pp. 30–37

Read the title of the story aloud. Help students identify Joe DiMaggio. Have them read to find out why the Yankees fans were upset about Joe DiMaggio. (*He had a bad leg, and they wondered if he could hit and run around the bases.*) Ask: **Do you think DiMaggio was able to hit and run? How do you know?** (*Possible response: Yes, because the title says he was one of baseball's greatest.*) **MAKE PREDICTIONS**

Ask: **Why did DiMaggio's salary go up?** (*The manager noted that he hit the ball very well and that he was valuable to the team.*) **CAUSE-EFFECT**

Tell students to find a word on page 31 with the suffix *-able.* (*valuable*) Ask: **What is the root of this word?** (*value*) Ask: **How does knowing the root word and that *-able* means "likely to be" help you know the meaning of *valuable*?** (When I put the meanings together, I know *valuable* means "likely to be important.") (Focus Skill) **PREFIXES, SUFFIXES, AND ROOTS**

Pages 32–33

After students read pages 32–33, point out the illustration. Ask: **How do you think people got to see DiMaggio's sportsmanship?** (*Possible response: Even though the Yankees slid out of the top spot and his batting fell off a little, DiMaggio still met with the fans.*) **DRAW CONCLUSIONS**

How do you think the Yankees and DiMaggio did in 1941? (*Responses will vary.*) **MAKE PREDICTIONS**

Ask a volunteer to summarize the main events thus far. Model using the strategy of summarizing:

> **MODEL** When I read these pages, I make note of the dates that tell when the main events occurred. To summarize the events, I will make a time line to show the highlights for each year.
>
>   1937: 167 runs, 46 of them home runs
>   1938–1939: hot bat, home runs went down, batting up
>   1940: batting fell a little (Focus Strategy) **SUMMARIZE**

Pages 34–35

Have students read to confirm the predictions they made about the Yankees and DiMaggio. Ask: **How do you think the Yankees' manager was feeling during the 1941 season? Why?** (*Possible response: He was feeling happy because the Yankees won back the top spot.*) **DETERMINE CHARACTERS' EMOTIONS**

Ask: **What amazing feat did Joe DiMaggio begin on May 15, 1941?** (*a long hitting streak*) **NOTE DETAILS**

Have students read page 35 to find out what the fans expected of him. Ask: **What does the author mean when he says that DiMaggio "had a lot of heat on him in 1941"?** (*Possible response: People expected him to help the team win a lot of games.*) **UNDERSTAND FIGURATIVE LANGUAGE**

Ask: **What did DiMaggio do that still stands as a record today?** (*He did not miss getting a hit in 56 games.*) **IMPORTANT DETAILS**

Page 36

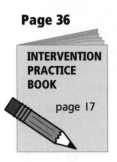

INTERVENTION PRACTICE BOOK

page 17

Have students read page 36 to find out how DiMaggio's baseball career ended. Ask: **Why do you think the Yankees and the fans were sad to see DiMaggio retire?** (*Possible responses: He helped the Yankees be a winning team; he was a great sportsman who cared a lot about the game.*) **THEME**

Summarize the selection. Have students consider what they learned about Joe DiMaggio's baseball career and what kind of a person he was.

Page 37

Answers to *Think About It* Questions

1. Possible response: He was voted in because he was such a good baseball player. He had a 56-game hitting streak. **SUMMARY**

2. Possible response: They liked him because he was modest and he was a very good hitter. **INTERPRETATION**

3. Diary entries should express excitement at seeing DiMaggio get another hit. **WRITE A DIARY ENTRY**

AFTER

Skill Review
pages 122–123

USE SKILL CARD 4B

(Focus Skill) Prefixes, Suffixes, and Roots

RETEACH the skill. Invite students to look at **side B of Skill Card 4: Prefixes, Suffixes, and Roots.** Read the skill reminder with them. Point out that the chart contains prefixes, root words, and suffixes.

Invite students to read the directions aloud. Demonstrate how to move across the chart, choosing prefixes, roots, and suffixes to form new words. After students have completed their chart, have them share their words. Ask them how knowing the different word parts helped them figure out the meanings of their words.

FLUENCY BUILDER Use *Intervention Practice Book* page 15. Explain that students will practice reading the sentences on the bottom half of the page by reading them aloud to a partner. One partner will read a sentence aloud three times and self-evaluate. (*How well did I read?*) The other partner will comment on how the reader improves each time. Students should then switch roles.

INTERVENTION PRACTICE BOOK

page 15

Expressive Writing: Expressive Sentences

Build on prior knowledge. Tell students that they are going to describe the weather. Then invite students to close their eyes. Say this sentence: *It was a beautiful day.* Wait a few seconds. Then say, *The fragrant red roses were blooming in the warm, bright sun.* Ask: **Which of these sentences did you prefer? Could you picture in your mind the place I was describing?** Remind students that expressive sentences often refer to a person's senses.

Construct the text. "Share the pen" with students in a collaborative group effort. As students dictate words and phrases, write them on the board or on chart paper, guiding the process by asking questions and offering suggestions. Guide students to write about today's weather. Think aloud the process of writing expressive sentences with the following steps:

- What do we see? Write one sentence that describes how the day looks.

- How can we tell our audience how the day feels? Write a sentence that compares the day to another object, using the words *is like*.

- How does the day sound? Write a sentence to describe the sounds of the day.

- How does the day smell? Write a sentence that describes the scents of the day.

Revisit the text. Invite students to reread the sentences written by the group. Encourage them to make sure the sentences include descriptive language and make sense. Ask them to check for correct punctuation, spelling, and grammar. Have students read the completed sentences aloud.

On Your Own

Have students write four expressive sentences about an athletic event. Tell them to describe people they may have seen or events that happened. Remind them to be sure to consider their choice of words carefully.

Connect Spelling and Phonics

RETEACH **short vowel /e/e; long vowel /ē/ee, ea, ey.** Write the word *sent* on the board, and tell students that in the next two words you will say, the /e/ sound is spelled with the CVC pattern as in *sent*. Have them write the words. Dictate the remaining words in sets of two, telling students which spelling of the /ē/ sound will be used in each pair. Use *fleet* for items 3–4, *leak* for items 5–6, and *honey* for items 7–8. After each word is written, display the correct spelling so students can proofread their work. They should draw a line through a misspelled word and write the correct spelling beside it.

1. went*	2. getting*	3. agreed*	4. speed*
5. streak*	6. heat*	7. money	8. trolley

Word appears in "Joe DiMaggio, One of Baseball's Greatest."

Dictate the following sentence and have students write it: *Jen gets green beans for a monkey.*

Build and Read Longer Words

Write the word *stepping* on the board. Remind students that when *-ing* is added to a word that has a short vowel sound, the final consonant is usually doubled. Then write these words on the board: *set*, *dig*, *get*, *stop*, *win*. Select volunteers to come to the board and add *-ing* to these words. Remind them to double the final consonant before they add the *-ing*.

Also remind students that two-syllable words are usually divided between the doubled consonants. Draw a line between the two *p*'s in *stepping*, and read each syllable as you point to it. Then read the word naturally— *stepping*. Follow a similar procedure with the words *setting*, *getting*, and *happen*.

INTERVENTION
ASSESSMENT
BOOK

FLUENCY BUILDER Ask students to select a passage from "Joe DiMaggio, One of Baseball's Greatest" to read aloud to a partner. Students may choose a passage they enjoyed, or have them choose one of the following options:

- Read page 32 and the first paragraph of page 33.
  (Total: 84 words)

- Read all of page 35 and the first paragraph on page 36.
  (Total: 100 words)

Have students read the selected passage aloud to their partners three times. Have the student rate his or her own reading on a scale from 1–4.

Review Vocabulary

To revisit the Vocabulary Words prior to the weekly assessment, play Dictionary Race. Distribute a dictionary to each student. Say a Vocabulary Word. Encourage students to quickly locate and point to the word in the dictionary. The first student to correctly locate the word can receive a small token such as a sticker. Select a volunteer to read the dictionary definition aloud. Continue racing to find the Vocabulary Words until all eight words have been found and defined. You may want to display the Vocabulary Words and definitions on page 39 and have students copy them to use when they study for the vocabulary test.

⭐(Focus Skill) Review Prefixes, Suffixes, and Roots

**INTERVENTION
PRACTICE
BOOK**

page 18

Distribute *Intervention Practice Book* page 18 to review prefixes, suffixes, and roots before the weekly assessment. Call attention to the box at the top of the page. Review these common prefixes and suffixes. Lead students to look at the words in the column on the left. Remind them to break each word apart into prefixes, suffixes, and root. Use the clues in the box to help them determine a definition. Direct students to draw lines from the word to its definition.

Review Test Prep

Invite students to review the test tips on page 123 of the *Pupil Edition*. Read the tips aloud and remind students to use these tips not only when they are answering the two questions on this page but whenever they are taking a test.

**LEAD
THE WAY**

page 123

**INTERVENTION
ASSESSMENT
BOOK**

✔

Discuss the prefixes, suffixes, and roots of the underlined words in each question. Ask students how understanding the prefixes, suffixes, and roots can help them figure out the correct answer to the questions. (*The word parts help me define the word.*)

Self-Selected Reading

Encourage students to select their own books to read independently. They may choose from the classroom library shelf, or you may wish to offer a group of appropriate books about baseball or other biographies from which students can choose. Titles might include the following:

- *The Kid from Brighton Beach.* (See page 123K of the *Teacher's Edition* for a lesson plan.)

- *The Baseball Birthday Party* by Annabelle Prager. Random House, 1995.

- *The Babe and I* by David A. Adler. Harcourt, 1999.

After students have chosen their books, give each student a copy of My Reading Log, which can be found on page R38 in the back of the *Teacher's Edition*. Have students fill in the information at the top of the form. Then have them use the log to keep track of their reading and to record their responses to the literature.

Conduct student-teacher conferences. Arrange time for each student to confer with you individually about his or her self-selected reading. Have students bring their Reading Logs to share with you at the conference. Students may wish to read a passage aloud to you. Ask questions about the book in order to generate discussion. For example, you might ask what information the student learned about a person's character or how a person faced challenges.

FLUENCY PERFORMANCE Ask students to read aloud the passage they practiced from "Joe DiMaggio, One of Baseball's Greatest." Keep track of the number of words the student reads correctly. Have the student rate his or her own performance on a scale of 1 to 4. Encourage the student to reread the passage until he or she is satisfied with his or her own reading.

See *Oral Reading Fluency Assessment* for monitoring progress.

LESSON 5

BEFORE
Building
Background
and Vocabulary

Use with

"Amelia and Eleanor Go for a Ride"

Review Phonics: Short Vowel /u/*u*; Long Vowel /o͞o/*u-e*

Identify the sounds. Have students say this sentence three times: *Luke runs up to the top of the dune.* Ask them to identify words that have the /u/ sound heard in *luck*. (*runs, up*) Repeat the sentence twice, and have them identify words that have the /o͞o/ sound heard in *tube*. (*Luke, dune*)

Associate letters to sounds. Write the above sentence on the board. Circle *runs*; point out the CVC pattern. Explain that words with this pattern usually have a short vowel sound. Underline the *u-e* in *dune*. Explain that words with the CVCe pattern usually have a long vowel sound.

Word blending. Model how to blend and read the word *dune*. Slide your hand under the whole word as you elongate the sounds /do͞o͞onn/. Then read the word naturally—*dune*. Write the words *scrub*, *tube*, and *fluff* on the board, and repeat the process.

INTERVENTION
PRACTICE
BOOK

page 20

Apply the skill. *Letter Substitution.* Write the following words on the board, and have students read each aloud. Make the changes necessary to form the words in parentheses. Have students read each new word aloud.

tubs (tubes)	**lug** (lube)	**plum** (plume)
duck (duke)	**tin** (tune)	**luck** (lute)	**run** (rude)

Introduce Vocabulary

PRETEACH **lesson vocabulary.** Tell students that they are going to learn eight new words that they will see again when they read "Amelia and Eleanor Go for a Ride." Teach each Vocabulary Word using the following process.

Use the following suggestions or similar ideas to give the meaning or context.

> Write the word.
> Say the word.
> Track the word and have students repeat it.
> Give the meaning or context.

outspoken   Explain that if a person is outspoken, it means he or she is frank and candid, saying whatever is on his or her mind.

practical   Relate to wearing comfortable shoes when taking a walk or a hike. Wearing high heels or sandals would not be practical.

brisk   This is a multiple-meaning word. Relate to very cool weather.

elegant   Show photographs of people in fancy clothing. These people might be called *elegant*.

 48   Lesson 5 • Intervention Teacher's Guide

elevations	Locate and point to several mountains on a map and read the elevation levels.
marveled	Point out the *-ed* ending. Relate to something wonderful. They *marveled* at the Grand Canyon.
miniatures	Display something miniature such as a tea set or a car.
starstruck	Underline the two words within this word. Discuss the meaning of each individual word and then what the words together mean.

For vocabulary activities, see Vocabulary Games on pages 2–7.

Vocabulary Words

outspoken bold or honest in speech

practical useful or sensible

brisk cool and stimulating, as weather can be

elegant tasteful, stylish, and beautiful

elevations heights above the ground or sea level

marveled became filled with awe or wonder

miniatures small-scale models of larger things

starstruck full of stars

AFTER

Building
Background
and Vocabulary

Apply Vocabulary Strategies

Use sentence and word context. Write this sentence on the board: *When the night air is brisk, I put on another blanket and open my window a crack.* Tell students that sometimes they can figure out the meaning of a word by reading the entire sentence. Model using the strategy.

> **MODEL** I know the word *brisk* is an adjective. I always need another blanket when it gets cool and if the window is open too, then the night air must be cold. I think *brisk* describes the cool night air.

Guide students in using a similar procedure to figure out the meaning of other vocabulary words.

RETEACH lesson vocabulary. Have students work in pairs. Give each pair sixteen index cards. Invite students to write a vocabulary word on one card and its definition on another card. Have students place all sixteen cards print side down on a desk or table. Tell students to take turns turning over two cards at a time to try matching a vocabulary word with its definition, continuing until all matches have been found.

FLUENCY BUILDER Distribute *Intervention Practice Book* page 19. Invite students to look at the first column. Tell students that you are going to read all of the words in the first column and that they should repeat each word after you. Repeat this echoing of words with the next two columns. Then have students practice reading the lists to a partner.

INTERVENTION PRACTICE BOOK

page 19

BEFORE

Reading "Amelia
and Eleanor Go for
a Ride"
pages 126–141

USE SKILL CARD 5A

(Focus Skill) Locate Information

PRETEACH **the skill.** Point out the different parts of a textbook: table of contents, index, and glossary. Guide students to describe where each part is located. Tell students that good readers use the parts of a book to locate information.

Have students look at **side A of Skill Card 5: Locate Information.** Read the information about book parts. Direct students' attention to the chart. Read aloud the information in the chart. Ask:

- **If you wanted to know where to find information on a specific topic, which book part would you use?** (*index*)

- **Why is the table of contents useful?** (*Possible response: It lists chapter names and page numbers so the reader can see what will be covered in the book and where to find it.*)

Explain to students that being able to locate information using different book parts will help them become better readers.

Prepare to Read: "Amelia and Eleanor Go for a Ride"

Preview. Tell students that they are going to read a selection called "Amelia and Eleanor Go for a Ride." Explain that it is historical fiction, which means it is based on events that really happened, but may not have happened exactly as written. Preview the selection.

LEAD THE WAY
pages 126–141

- **Pages 126–129:** I see the story title and that this selection is based on a true story. I can guess that the women in these pictures must be Amelia and Eleanor.

- **Pages 130–133:** The women are wearing gloves on pages 130–131. They are dressing up as if to go somewhere. I can see they are together now on pages 132–133. They look as if they are having a good time, and I can tell they like each other.

- **Pages 134–137:** It looks as if one woman is telling a story. The people appear to be fascinated with what she is saying. Then it looks as if the women are flying in an airplane at night.

- **Pages 138–139:** The women are standing in what looks like the doorway of a plane. It looks as though photographers are taking pictures, and reporters are writing about them.

Set purpose. Model setting a purpose for reading the story.

MODEL From what I have seen in my preview, I can see that these two women are good friends who like doing things together. One purpose for reading is to locate information. I will read to find historical details about the relationship between the two women.

Reread and Summarize

Have students reread and summarize "Amelia and Eleanor Go for a Ride" in sections, as described in the chart below.

Pages 128–129

Let's reread pages 128–129 to recall what we learned about Amelia and Eleanor.

Summary: Eleanor is the First Lady, married to President Franklin Roosevelt. Amelia is daring and likes to try things other women wouldn't even consider. Amelia is the first female pilot to fly alone across the Atlantic Ocean.

Pages 130–133

Now let's reread pages 130–131 to recall what Amelia and Eleanor do that makes them feel independent.

Summary: Eleanor has a new car. She likes to drive even though people think it is bold and dangerous. Amelia likes to fly planes, even though people think she is risking her life.

Pages 134–135

Let's reread page 134 to recall how Amelia describes flying at night.

Summary: The stars glitter all about and seem close enough to touch. The cities have twinkling lights and the clouds are white with dark islands in between.

Pages 136–139

As we reread pages 136–139, let's find out how Eleanor described flying at night.

Summary: Eleanor said it was like being on top of the world. She felt safe with Amelia. She could see the pinpoints of lights from the cities below.

FLUENCY BUILDER Use *Intervention Practice Book* page 19. Ask students to look at the sentences on the bottom of the page. Remind students that these slashes break the sentences into phrases. They should try to read each phrase fluently. Model appropriate pace, expression, and phrasing as you read each sentence. Have students repeat each sentence, imitating your expression. Have students practice reading these sentences to a partner.

INTERVENTION PRACTICE BOOK

page 19

Directed Reading: "Amelia's Flying Lesson," pp. 38–45

Pages 38–39

Read the title of the story aloud. Have students read to find out why Amelia is outside at night. (*Amelia is out looking at the stars.*) **Do you think June is interested in looking at the stars? How do you know?** (Possible response: *No, she tells Amelia she doesn't want to come out, but then she changes her mind.*) **DRAW CONCLUSIONS**

> MOVING AHEAD
> pp. 38–45

Ask students to locate the title of the story and the names of the author and illustrator. Ask: **What is this page called?** (*title page*) (Focus Skill) **LOCATE INFORMATION**

Ask: **How are Amelia and June different? How are they the same?** (*Amelia is outspoken; June is quiet. June likes to wear dresses; Amelia likes to wear pants. Amelia and June both enjoy being with each other.*) **COMPARE/CONTRAST**

Pages 40–41

Ask a volunteer to read aloud page 40. Then discuss how reading ahead would help students find out what Amelia wants to do with the wood planks. Model using the read ahead strategy.

> **MODEL** When I read the sentence "She pulled wood planks to the backyard" I was curious. What was she going to do with wood planks? I look ahead for the word *plank*. I can see in the picture on page 43 that the plank is going to be used as a ramp. (Focus Strategy) **READ AHEAD**

After students read page 41, point out the illustration. Ask: **Why do you think Amelia wants to know the elevation of the shed?** (Possible response: *She's planning to fly off the top of the shed.*) **DRAW CONCLUSIONS**

Pages 42–43

After students have read page 42 ask: **How do you think June is feeling? Explain why.** (*Possible response: June is hesitant about this whole thing. She tells Amelia she will only watch.*) **DETERMINE CHARACTERS' EMOTIONS**

Ask: **What did the author mean when she wrote, "Rumble, creak, rattle, clunk!"?** (*Possible response: That's the way the cart sounded going down the slide.*) **UNDERSTANDING FIGURATIVE LANGUAGE**

Ask: **What happened to Amelia at the bottom of the slide?** (*The wheels got stuck in the mud.*) **IMPORTANT DETAILS**

Page 44

> INTERVENTION PRACTICE BOOK
>
> page 21

Ask: **Why do you think the girls were so excited?** (*Possible responses: They did it! They made a cart and a slide, and they went so fast that they felt like they were flying.*) **INTERPRET THEME**

Summarize the selection. Have students think about what Amelia and June did in the selection. Have them complete *Intervention Practice Book* page 21 and summarize the selection in one sentence.

Answers to *Think About It* Questions

1. Amelia and June made a go-cart and a slide. **SUMMARY**

2. Possible response: This felt like flying to Amelia, and Amelia wanted to know what it felt like to fly. **INTERPRETATION**

3. Accept reasonable responses. Ask students to explain why they made their prediction. **MAKE PREDICTIONS**

AFTER

Skill Review
pages 146–147

USE SKILL CARD 5B

(Focus Skill) Locate Information

RETEACH the skill. Invite students to look at **side B of Skill Card 5: Locate Information**. Read the skill reminder aloud. Select a volunteer to read the book parts included in the word bank box.

Read aloud the directions. Ask students to first determine what book part they would use. Then have students create a chart similar to the one shown on the card. Tell them to list the book parts that answer the questions in the first column. Then invite them to write a brief description of the book part in the second column and the location of the book part in the third column.

After students have completed their charts, encourage them to share them with a partner to discuss their responses. Point out that many nonfiction books contain some or all of these book parts.

FLUENCY BUILDER Make sure students have copies of *Intervention Practice Book* page 19. Students will practice reading the sentences at the bottom of the page. Ask students to locate and point to several slashes. Remind students that these slashes divide the sentences into phrases. Students should practice reading these sentences aloud to a partner until they are comfortable with their pace and fluency.

INTERVENTION PRACTICE BOOK

page 19

Expressive Writing: Personal Narrative

Build on prior knowledge. Tell students that they are going to write a personal narrative paragraph about a recent class event. Explain that sometimes during a test, they may be given a specific length of time to complete their writing. Explain the importance of using their time wisely. Then write these words on the board: *First, Next, Finally*. Read this story.

> Last week my class went on a field trip to a very exciting place—the science center. *First*, we visited the hands-on exhibits where we operated machines and made electricity. *Next*, we saw a movie about the solar system. *Finally*, we saw fossils and models of dinosaurs. What a great day it was!

Discuss the time-order words in this story and how they helped students follow the events.

Construct the Text. "Share the pen" with students in a collaborative group writing effort. Guide them to write a five sentence personal narrative about a recent class event. Use these steps:

- What is the event? Guide students to write a catchy introductory sentence.

- Now work together to write three sentences that tell about three things they did. Use the words *First*, *Next*, and *Finally* to make the order of events clear.

- Guide students to conclude their sentences with a summarizing sentence that expresses how they felt about the event.

Revisit the Text. Go back and read the sentences together. Ask: **How do the time-order words help the reader follow the events?** (*They make it clear what was done and in what order.*)

- Guide students to check that their introduction will catch the reader's attention and that their closing sentence summarizes their experience.

- Have students read their completed sentences aloud.

On Your Own

Have students write a personal narrative about a recent trip their family took. This trip could be a vacation, a day trip to the park, or simply a trip to the grocery store. Tell them to use time-order words to connect the events of the story.

Connect Spelling and Phonics

RETEACH short vowel /u/*u*; long vowel /oo/*u-e*. Write the words *flute* and *cup* on the board. Underline the letter *u* in each of these words. Explain that you will say more words with the short *u* and long *u* vowel sounds. Then dictate the following words, and have students write them. After they write each one, display the correct spelling so students can proofread their work. They should draw a line through a misspelled word and write the correct spelling beside it.

I. just*	2. fumes	3. fun*	4. stuff*
5. tugged*	6. tune	7. plunk*	8. June*

*Word appears in "Amelia's Flying Lesson."

Dictate the following sentence, and have students write it: *Chuck plucks a tune on the lute.*

Build and Read Longer Words

Write the word *stunning* on the board, and underline *stun*. Remind students that two-syllable words that have double consonants are usually divided into syllables between the doubled consonants. Draw a line between the two *n*'s, and have students read the word aloud as you point to each syllable. Follow a similar procedure with these words: *plugging*, *strutting*, *humming*.

Invite students to add the *-ing* ending to these words to create three new words: *cut*, *tug*, *sun*. Remind them to double the consonants.

**INTERVENTION
ASSESSMENT
BOOK**

FLUENCY BUILDER Ask students to select a passage from "Amelia's Flying Lesson" to read aloud to a partner. Students may choose one of the following options or a passage they enjoyed:

- Read pages 39–40. (Total: 108 words)

- Read page 42. (Total: 101 words)

Encourage students to read the selected passage aloud to their partners three times. Have the student rate his or her own reading on a scale from I to 4.

Review Vocabulary

Review the Vocabulary Words. Write the words on miniature stars and the definitions on slightly larger stars. Tack the Vocabulary Words to the top of a bulletin board and the definitions along the bottom of the board. Staple a piece of yarn to the bottom of each Vocabulary Word. Have pairs of students connect the Vocabulary Word to its definition by moving the piece of yarn and tacking it to the definition. Check students' work after they have completed the activity.

(Focus Skill) Locate Information

INTERVENTION
PRACTICE
BOOK

page 22

Distribute *Intervention Practice Book* page 22 to review locating information in a nonfiction book. Select a volunteer to read aloud the directions and the words in the word bank. Tell students to read each row in the chart. Each row gives a description of a book part and where it is located within the book. Tell students to determine which book part is being described and write it in the first column. Guide them to use the book parts from the word bank.

Review Test Prep

INTERVENTION
ASSESSMENT
BOOK

Invite students to review the two test tips on page 147 of the *Pupil Edition*. Remind students that there are several places within a book that can help them find information. These tips will not only help them answer these two questions, but will help them locate information in the future.

LEAD
THE WAY

page 147

Have students follow along as you read aloud each question and the tip that goes with it. Discuss each of the possible answers.

Self-Selected Reading

Encourage students to select books to read independently. They may choose from the classroom library shelf, or you may wish to offer a group of appropriate books from which students can choose.

- *Laura Ingalls Wilder* by Alexandra Wallner. Holiday House, 1997

- *A Picture Book of Amelia Earhart* by David Adler. Holiday House, 1998

- *Zora Hurston and the Chinaberry Tree* by William Miller. Lee & Low, 1996

You may also wish to recommend other historical fiction selections or books about First Ladies or flying.

After students have chosen their books, give each student a copy of My Reading Log, which can be found on page R38 in the back of the *Teacher's Edition*. Have students fill in this information at the top of the form. Then have them use the log to keep track of their reading and to record their responses to the literature.

Conduct student-teacher conferences. Schedule time for each student to confer individually with you about his or her self-selected reading. Students may choose to read aloud from the book or share their Reading Log. If students have difficulty remembering the book, encourage them to flip through the book and comment on the illustrations. Ask questions about the illustrations to guide the discussion. For example, you might ask what was so important about the person in a biography and why the student thinks the author wrote the book.

FLUENCY PERFORMANCE Ask students to read aloud the passage they practiced from "Amelia's Flying Lesson." Keep track of the number of words the student reads correctly. Have the student rate his or her own performance on a scale from 1 to 4. Encourage students to reread the passage until they are satisfied with their reading.

See *Oral Reading Fluency Assessment* for monitoring progress.

BEFORE

Building
Background
and Vocabulary

INTERVENTION
PRACTICE
BOOK

page 24

Use with

"The Baker's Neighbor"

Review Phonics: Vowel Variant /ôl/*al, all*

Identify the sound. Have students repeat the following sentence aloud three times: *Pam calls Walt into the hall.* Have students identify the words that have the /ôl/ sound they hear in *ball.* (*calls, Walt, hall*)

Associate letters to sound. On the board write the above sentence. Circle the words *calls, Walt,* and *hall,* and ask students how these words are alike. (the /ôl/ sound; the letters *al* and *all*) Point out that in these words, the letters *al* and *all* stand for the /ôl/ sound. Then write *walk* and *talk* on the board. Explain that words with *alk* also have the /ô/ sound, but the *l* is silent. Read *walk* and *talk,* and have students repeat them.

Word blending. Model how to blend and read *tall.* Slide your hand under the letters as you elongate the sounds /tôôll/. Then say the word naturally—*tall.* Follow a similar procedure with *bald, stall,* and *halt.*

Apply the skill. *Consonant Substitution.*
Write *call, salt,* and *palm* on the board, and have students read each aloud. Make the changes necessary to form the following words indicated by the letters in parentheses. Ask students to read the new words aloud.

call	salt	palm
(b)all	(h)alt	(c)alm
(f)all	(m)alt	(b)alm
(sm)all		
(st)all		

Introduce Vocabulary

PRETEACH **lesson vocabulary.** Tell students that they are going to learn eight new words that they will see again when they read a story called "The Baker's Neighbor." Teach each Vocabulary Word using the following process.

Use the following suggestions or similar ideas to give the meaning or context.

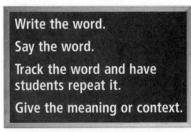

Write the word.

Say the word.

Track the word and have students repeat it.

Give the meaning or context.

privilege	Relate to something special students are allowed to do because of their age.
luxury	Discuss basic needs as being the opposite of luxuries.
elated	Role-play being excited. Relate to joy over success.
assent	Relate by giving approval for students to do something.
ad lib	Have a volunteer make up a poem or song on the spot.
shiftless	Point out the suffix *-less.* Relate to someone who is not able to keep a job because he or she is lazy.
indignantly	Role-play having your ball unfairly taken away at recess. Relate

to being offended because what happened was unjust.

shamefacedly Relate to how you would react if you were caught doing something wrong.

For vocabulary activities, see Vocabulary Games on pages 2–7.

Apply Vocabulary Strategies

Use familiar word parts. Write the word *shamefacedly* on the board. Tell students that sometimes they can figure out the meaning of a word by breaking it into familiar words and word parts. Model using the strategy.

> **MODEL** When I read this word, I try to break it into familiar words. I read the word *shame*, which means "a feeling caused by guilt." Then I read the familiar word *face*. When I add the ending *-ly*, I can figure out that *shamefacedly* must mean "in a way, or having a face, that shows guilt."

Guide students in doing the same to find the meaning of other words.

RETEACH lesson vocabulary. Have students listen to each of the following sentences. Tell them to raise one finger if the sentence is true and raise two fingers if the sentence is false.

1. We practiced all the lines to **ad lib** the scene. *(false)*
2. The lazy boy was **shiftless**. *(true)*
3. The child was **elated** when his favorite toy broke. *(false)*
4. My new video game machine is a **luxury**. *(true)*

5. He spoke **indignantly** after being unfairly accused. *(true)*
6. It will be my **privilege** to carry the flag. *(true)*
7. She **shamefacedly** returned the book she had torn. *(true)*
8. He showed his **assent** for the proposal by voting *no*. *(false)*

Vocabulary Words

privilege a special benefit, favor, or right enjoyed only under special conditions

luxury anything of value that gives comfort or pleasure but is not necessary for life or health

elated filled with joy or pride, as over success or good fortune

assent to agree or approve

ad lib to make up lines or music on the spot

shiftless not motivated; lazy

indignantly being angry about something that does not seem right or fair

shamefacedly in a way that shows shame for having done something bad

FLUENCY BUILDER Provide students with a copy of *Intervention Practice Book* page 23. Read the words in the first column aloud. Invite students to track each word as you say it. Then organize students into small groups. Have them read the first word aloud as a group. Then invite each student to say each word individually. Repeat this procedure for the words in all three columns.

INTERVENTION PRACTICE BOOK

page 23

USE SKILL CARD 6A

⭐ (Focus Skill) Cause and Effect

PRETEACH the skill. Point out that every cause has an effect. Explain that the effect may be easy to see, but you may need to look closer to find the cause. For example, you notice your ball won't bounce. (*the effect*) By looking more closely, you find the cause is a hole in the ball.

Have students look at **side A of Skill Card 6: Cause and Effect.** Read the definitions. Next, have students look at the pictures and describe them. Now call attention to the cause-and-effect chart. Ask:

- **Why does the chart show an arrow leading from the *Cause* box to the *Effect* box?** (*to show that a cause leads to an effect*)
- **Would it make sense if the boxes were reversed? Explain.** (*No, it wouldn't start to rain because the girl took out her umbrella.*)

Explain that identifying cause-and-effect relationships in a story will help them understand characters and the way they act.

Prepare to Read: "The Baker's Neighbor"

Preview. Tell students that they are going to read "The Baker's Neighbor." Explain that this is a play, a story told through dialogue. Explain that it is about a baker who learns an important lesson. Preview the selection.

LEAD THE WAY
pages 152–169

- **Pages 152–153:** I see the title and the names of the author and the illustrator. It also says *adapted by* so I know that the play was rewritten from a story. The picture shows a baker and the smell of his pastries filling the air.
- **Pages 154–155:** I see a man smelling the air and the baker looking as if he is taking away the pie that the man is smelling.
- **Pages 156–157:** The baker is counting his money. I also see the man who was smelling the pastries with children who have a coin. Maybe they plan to buy something.
- **Pages 158–161:** The man and the children are enjoying the smells. Then the children take the baker's hat. He looks mad.
- **Pages 162–163:** I see the baker and the man with another man. He may be a judge because he is holding a gavel.
- **Pages 164–165:** The man is smelling the air. The baker looks mad. Maybe he is angry that the man is smelling his pastries.
- **Pages 166–168:** The baker is counting money. Did the man have to pay for the smells? The baker is carrying a tray of food. The people look happy. He must be sharing with them.

Set purpose. Model setting a purpose for reading "The Baker's Neighbor."

MODEL From what I have seen in my preview, I know this is an entertaining play. I will read to find out what happens between the baker and the man.

Reread and Summarize

Have students reread and summarize "The Baker's Neighbor" in sections, as described below.

Pages 154–155

Let's reread pages 154–155 to recall what the problem is in this play.

Summary: Pablo comes to smell the baker's pastries every morning. The baker is angered by this because Pablo never buys anything.

Pages 156–157

Now let's reread pages 156–157 to find out what other people think about the baker.

Summary: People think that he is a miser. They believe that he cares more about money than about people.

Pages 158–161

As we reread pages 158–161, let's find out what game the children enjoy playing.

Summary: They like to pretend they are smells, sounds, or colors. They ask Pablo and the baker to tell them what sound they would like to be.

Pages 162–164

Now let's reread pages 162–164 to find out why the baker goes to get the judge.

Summary: The baker wants the judge to make Pablo pay for smelling the good smells around the store.

Pages 165–168

Let's reread pages 165–168 to recall what the judge decides and what lesson the baker learns.

Summary: The judge makes Pablo pay with his gold pieces. The judge lets the baker count the coins and tells him his payment is feeling the coins. The baker learns that friendship is better than money.

FLUENCY BUILDER Be sure that students have a copy of the *Intervention Practice Book* page 23. Call attention to the sentences on the bottom half of the page. Model reading aloud each sentence, pausing at each slash for the appropriate pacing, expression, and phrasing. Have students read aloud each sentence after you. Then have students practice reading the sentences aloud three times to a partner.

INTERVENTION
PRACTICE
BOOK

page 23

Directed Reading: "Can-Do Kid" pp. 46–52

Pages 46–47

Ask volunteers to read aloud the title of the story and describe the illustration. Be sure that students understand what is happening in the picture on page 46. Ask: **What do you think the kids are doing?** (Possible response: *They are at some kind of market. They are looking at CDs that a man is selling.*) **SPECULATE**

MOVING
AHEAD
pages 46–52

Note that the title is "Can-Do Kid." Ask: **What do you think the kid can do?** (Possible response: *Maybe he can buy things at the market.*) **MAKE PREDICTIONS**

Then have students read pages 46–47.

Pages 48–49

Have students read page 48. Ask: **What problem does Walt face?** (*He doesn't have enough money to buy the CD.*) **NOTE DETAILS**

Then ask: **How do you think he feels about this? Explain your answer.** (*Possible response: He feels bad about not having enough money. The direction for the actor playing Walt says that he says his line shamefacedly.*) **DETERMINE CHARACTERS' EMOTIONS**

Next have students read page 49. Ask: **Do you think that Duncan believes Walt can get the money? How can you tell?** (*Possible response: No, he asks if Walt thinks money falls from the sky. Then he tells him to give it up.*) **INTERPRET STORY EVENTS**

Pages 50–51

Have students read page 50 to find out what happens next. Ask: **What does Walt do to earn the money?** (*He sings and puts out his hat to collect money from people who walk by.*) **NOTE DETAILS**

Ask two volunteers to read aloud the parts on page 51. If students have difficulty reading as suggested by the directions, model using the use decoding/phonics strategy:

> **MODEL** On page 51, I notice the word *elated*. I'm not sure how to pronounce it. If I break the word into syllables, *e-la-ted*, I can pronounce each syllable. First, I say it with the stress on the first syllable, but that doesn't sound right. So I put the stress on the second syllable. That sounds right. **Focus Strategy USE DECODING/PHONICS**

After students read page 51, ask: **Why is Walt called the Can-Do Kid?** (Possible response: *because he was able to do what he said he would do*) **INTERPRET THEME**

Then ask: **Why does the CD man want to sell tapes of Walt singing?** (*People like his singing, so he is good for business. Also, Walt told the man he would get the money, and he did what he said he would— showing he was trustworthy.*) **Focus Skill CAUSE AND EFFECT**

INTERVENTION
PRACTICE
BOOK

page 25

Summarize the selection. Have students share what they think about the way Walt earned the money for the CD. Then invite them to complete *Intervention Practice Book* page 25 and summarize the selection.

Answers to *Think About It* Questions

1. He doesn't have enough money to buy the CD that he wants. He sings for people who are walking by and collects money from them in his hat. **NOTE DETAILS**

2. Possible response: Adjectives that describe Walt are *persistent, brave,* and *lucky.* He is persistent because he didn't give up when he didn't have enough money. He is brave because he was willing to sing in front of strangers, and he was lucky that he made enough money to buy the CD. **MAKE JUDGMENTS**

3. Accept reasonable responses. Students should number their list. **WRITE A LIST**

Skill Review
pages 172–173

USE SKILL CARD 6B

Cause and Effect

RETEACH **the skill.** Invite students to look at **side B of Skill Card 6: Cause and Effect.** Read the skill reminder with them, and have volunteers read each of the four sentences aloud. Discuss the cause and effect in each sentence.

Have a volunteer read aloud the next set of directions. Have students work with partners to create their own charts. Remind them to write one cause and one effect on each line of the chart.

After students have completed their charts, have them display their answers to discuss with the entire group. Point out that students will find examples of cause and effect in the play "The Baker's Neighbor."

FLUENCY BUILDER Have students look at their copy of *Intervention Practice Book* page 23. Explain that now students will work with a partner to practice reading the sentences at the bottom of the page. Point out that each sentence is written as if someone is speaking it. Encourage students to pretend they are in a play. Have them read aloud each sentence using a different expression or emotion. Invite each student to read aloud all the sentences at least three times.

INTERVENTION PRACTICE BOOK

page 23

Expository Writing: How-to Paragraph

Build on prior knowledge. Tell students that they are going to write about fire safety. Display the following information:

> **Fire Safety Tips**
> 1. Make an escape plan for your home in case of a fire.
> 2. If you smell smoke, drop to the floor and crawl.
> 3. Don't open the door until you check to see if the doorknob is hot.
> 4. Have a safe place outside for your family to meet.

Construct the text. "Share the pen" with students in a collaborative writing effort. As students dictate words and phrases, guide them in expressing the main idea of the paragraph in the form of a topic sentence.

- Reread with students each of the detail sentences listed above. Ask: **What will the main idea of our paragraph be?** (*things your family can do to prepare in case of a fire*)

- Guide students in formulating a main idea sentence for this paragraph. For example: *Follow these steps to help your family practice fire safety.*

- Have students add informative sentences from the Fire Safety Tips on the board. Remind them to use their own words to create their paragraph about fire safety.

Revisit the text. Go back and read the Fire Safety Tips together. Remind students to check that their ideas are in a specific order. Tell them to check that each sentence starts with a capital letter and ends with proper punctuation. Have students read the completed paragraph aloud.

> **On Your Own**
>
> Have students look through their writing portfolio to find a paragraph that needs a better topic sentence. Tell them to write at least two different topic sentences for this paragraph.

Connect Spelling and Phonics

RETEACH **vowel variant /ôl/al, all.** Write the word *tall* on the board. Tell students that you will be saying some words with the /ôl/ sound spelled *all*. Then write the word *salt* on the board. Have students notice the spelling of the /ôl/ sound here. Tell students that some of the words you will say have this same sound, spelled *al* as in *salt*. Dictate each word below. Have students write the words and then correct their work together. Give students a chance to correct any misspellings.

I. stall*	2. fall*	3. halt	4. palm*
5. wall*	6. bald	7. scald	8. smallest

Word appears in "Can-Do Kid."

Dictate the following sentence for students to write: *Kim came to a halt in the hall.*

Build and Read Longer Words

Write the word *baseball* on the board. Tell students that some words, such as *baseball*, are made up of two smaller words. Explain that a word made up of two smaller words is called a compound word. Cover the word *ball*, and have students read the remaining word, *base*. Then cover the word *base,* and have students read the remaining word, *ball*. Finally, draw your hand under the entire word as students read it. Then write *basketball* and *wallpaper* on the board. Ask volunteers to read the words and to explain how they figured them out.

Display the words *out*, *over*, and *under* in a pocket chart or on the board. Invite students to build onto these words to create as many new compound words as they can. Compile a class list from their suggestions.

INTERVENTION
ASSESSMENT
BOOK

FLUENCY BUILDER Have students choose a passage from "Can-Do Kid" to read aloud to a partner. You may have students choose passages that they found particularly interesting, or have them choose one of the following options:

- Read pages 47–48. (Total: 107 words)
- Read pages 50–51. (Total: 107 words)

Encourage students to read the selected passage aloud to their partners three times. Have the student rate his or her own reading on a scale from 1 to 4.

Review Vocabulary

To revisit Vocabulary Words prior to the weekly assessment, use these sentence frames. Have volunteers take turns reading aloud the frames and choices. Students identify the correct choice and explain why that choice makes sense in the sentence.

1. If you enjoy a privilege, you have
   a. more responsibility.   b. a special benefit.

2. A luxury might be a
   a. DVD player.   b. bed.

3. If you are elated, you are
   a. thrilled.   b. sad.

4. If someone gives his or her assent, they are
   a. disagreeing.   b. agreeing.

5. If you ad lib, you
   a. make up a line.   b. rehearse a part.

6. A shiftless person is
   a. ambitious.   b. lazy.

7. If you react indignantly, you are
   a. delighted.   b. angry.

8. A person who acts shamefacedly has done something
   a. bad.   b. good.

Correct responses: lb, 2a, 3a, 4b, 5a, 6b, 7b, 8a.

You may want to display the Vocabulary Words and definitions on page 59, and have students copy them to use when they study for the vocabulary test.

INTERVENTION PRACTICE BOOK

page 26

(Focus Skill) Review Cause and Effect

Discuss *Intervention Practice Book* page 26 to review cause and effect before the weekly assessment. Select volunteers to read the sentences aloud. Tell students to listen carefully to identify the cause and effect in each sentence. Guide students to complete the chart.

Review Test Prep

Invite students to turn to page 173 of the *Pupil Edition.* Read aloud and review the two tips for answering questions. Tell students that reading the question carefully is important.

LEAD THE WAY

page 173

INTERVENTION ASSESSMENT BOOK

✔

In Question 1, they need to carefully read each choice in order to find the action that is *not* a cause. Remind students that when they are trying to find a cause, it is helpful to ask *why did this happen?*

Self-Selected Reading

Have students select their own books to read independently. They might choose books from the classroom library shelf, or you may wish to offer a group of appropriate books from which students can choose. Titles might include:

- *How to Be a Friend* by Laurie Krasny-Brown and Marc Brown. Little, Brown, 1998

- *Zinnia and Dot* by Lisa Campbell Ernst. Viking Penguin, 1992

- *Because You're Lucky* by Irene Smalls. Little, Brown, 1997

You may also wish to choose additional books that are the same genre, by the same author, or that have the same kind of text structure as the selection.

After students have chosen their books, give each student a copy of My Reading Log, which can be found on page R38 in the back of the *Teacher's Edition*. Have students fill in the information at the top of their form. Then have them use the log to keep track of their reading and to record their responses to the literature.

Conduct student-teacher conferences. Invite students to meet with you one-on-one for a conference to discuss their self-selected reading choice. Encourage them to share their Reading Logs with you and to select a favorite passage to read aloud to you. Ask questions about the content of the book and why the student selected it. Discuss the characters, their actions and emotions, and the setting and the plot.

FLUENCY PERFORMANCE Invite students to read aloud to you the passage they practiced from "Can-Do Kid." Keep track of the number of words each student reads correctly and incorrectly. Ask the student to rate his or her own performance on a scale from 1 to 4. Give students the opportunity to reread aloud the passage to you again and again until they are satisfied with their performance.

See *Oral Reading Fluency Assessment* for monitoring progress.

LESSON 7

"The Emperor and the Kite"

BEFORE

Building Background and Vocabulary

Review Phonics: Short Vowel /a/*a*; Long Vowel /ā/*ai, ay*

Identify the sounds. Have students repeat the following sentence aloud three times: *Gail plays with Dan's train set.* Ask students to identify the words with the /a/ sound they hear in *mat.* (*Dan*) Then ask students to name the words with the /ā/ sound they hear in *stay.* (*Gail, plays, train*)

Associate letters to sounds. Write the above sentence on the board. Circle the word *Dan.* Remind students that words with this pattern of letters, a single vowel between consonants, usually have a short vowel sound. Have students read the word aloud. Underline the letters *ay* in *plays.* Point out that in this word, the letters *ay* stand for the /ā/, or the long *a* vowel sound. Then underline the *ai* in *Gail* and *train,* and tell students that the letters *ai* also can stand for the long *a* vowel sound.

Word blending. Model how to blend and read *stain.* Slide your hand under the letters as you elongate the sounds /sstāānn/. Then read the word naturally—*stain.* Repeat the procedure with *grand, play,* and *brain.*

Apply the skill. *Letter Substitution* Write the following words on the board, and have students read each aloud. Make the changes necessary to form the words in parentheses. Have students read each new word aloud.

INTERVENTION PRACTICE BOOK

page 28

mad (may)	**gram** (gray)	**bran** (brain)	**Sal** (sail)
trap (tray)	**rag** (ray)	**plan** (plain)	**Bat** (bait)

Introduce Vocabulary

PRETEACH **lesson vocabulary.** Tell students that they are going to learn eight new words that they will see again when they read a story called "The Emperor and the Kite." Teach each Vocabulary Word using the following process.

Use the following suggestions or similar ideas to give the meaning or context.

plotting	This is a multiple-meaning word. Relate to planning to do something secretly.
loyal	Relate to other positive character traits, such as honest and trustworthy.
neglected	Point out the *-ed* ending. Relate to ignoring.
insignificant	Point out the prefix *in-* meaning "not." Relate the root word

> Write the word.
> Say the word.
> Track the word and have students repeat it.
> Give the meaning or context.

significant to important. Put the meanings together.

encircling	Demonstrate by walking around the group of students.
unyielding	Relate to stopping. Then explain that *un-* means "not."
steely	Relate to being hard and cold.
twined	Demonstrate by twisting a piece of twine.

For vocabulary activities, see Vocabulary Games on pages 2–7.

Vocabulary Words

plotting planning in secret to do something

loyal constant and faithful

neglected failed to care for or attend to

insignificant lacking in importance, meaning, size, or worth

encircling forming a circle around

unyielding constant and never-ending

steely like steel, as in strength, hardness, or coldness

twined twisted around

AFTER

Building Background and Vocabulary

Apply Vocabulary Strategies

Use affixes and root words. Write the word *encircling* on chart paper. Tell students that sometimes they can find the meaning of an unfamiliar word by looking for prefixes, suffixes, roots, and root words. Model using the strategy.

> **MODEL** This is a word I do not recognize. I notice the prefix *en-*, which means "to go into." I also know the root word is *circle*, which is something that is round. When I combine *en-* and *circle* with the suffix *-ing*, I have a word meaning "forming a circle around."

Guide students in using a similar procedure with the words *insignificant* and *unyielding*.

RETEACH lesson vocabulary. Provide a set of word cards for each student or pair of students. Read aloud or write on the board the meaning of one of the Vocabulary Words and the first letter or two of the word. Students match the correct word card to the definition. Continue until students have matched all the words.

FLUENCY BUILDER Using the *Intervention Practice Book* page 27, read each word in the first column aloud, and have students repeat it. Then have students work in pairs to read the words in the first column aloud to each other. Follow the same procedure with each of the remaining columns. After partners have practiced reading aloud the words in each column separately, have them practice the entire list.

INTERVENTION PRACTICE BOOK

page 27

⭐ (Focus Skill) Narrative Elements

PRETEACH **the skill.** Review narrative elements by discussing those from a fairy tale. Discuss how the story would be different if any of the narrative elements were changed. Have students look at **side A of Skill Card 7: Narrative Elements.** Read the definition of narrative elements. Next, read the paragraph aloud. Now call attention to the story map and have volunteers take turns reading each box aloud. Ask: **How is the setting important to the story?** (Possible answer: *The setting leads to the story problem.*) **How might the story be different if Teresa's watch did not break?** (Responses will vary.)

Explain that recognizing the narrative elements will help students understand the story.

Prepare to Read: "The Emperor and the Kite"

Preview. Tell students they are going to read "The Emperor and the Kite," a folktale. Tell them that folktales were first told orally and passed down from one generation to the next. They usually teach a lesson. Preview the selection.

LEAD THE WAY

pages 176–195

- **Pages 176–177:** I see the title and the names of the author and the illustrator. I think the picture on these two pages is the kite mentioned in the title.

- **Pages 178–179:** I see a girl making a kite. Maybe she is a main character. I see three older girls. They might be her sisters.

- **Pages 180–181:** The girl is flying her kite and talking to a man. He might be important.

- **Pages 182–183:** There are several men. The man in the fancy clothes is the Emperor. It looks like the others may be trying to hurt him or take him somewhere.

- **Pages 184–185:** Here is the girl again and she is waving to the man from the previous page. She is flying her kite.

- **Pages 186–191:** First, the Emperor grabs the kite. Then, he climbs down the kite string. Finally, he is on the ground. He seems to be thanking the girl. Maybe she is his daughter.

- **Pages 192–193:** The Emperor seems to be punishing the men.

- **Pages 194–195:** The Emperor is on his throne and the girl is next to him. Many people are coming to give them gifts.

Set purpose. Model setting a purpose for reading the story.

MODEL From my preview, I know the story is about how a girl uses her kite to save the Emperor from evil men. My purpose will be to find out what lesson this folktale teaches.

Reread and Summarize

Have students reread and summarize "The Emperor and the Kite" in sections, as described in the chart below.

Pages 178–179

Let's reread pages 178–179 to recall how Djeow Seow was viewed by her family.

Summary: Djeow Seow was so small that she was seen as insignificant. Her brothers and sisters were older, bigger, and stronger, and sometimes her father, the Emperor, forgot all about her.

Pages 180–181

Now let's reread pages 180–183 to find how Djeow Seow used her size to help her father.

Summary: Djeow Seow hid from the evil men who took the Emperor and followed the men to the tower where they held him. Then she used her kite every day to give him food.

Pages 184–189

As we reread pages 184–189, let's find out how Djeow Seow used her kite to help her father escape from the tower.

Summary: Djeow Seow took a clue from the monk and made a thick, heavy twine on which to fly her kite. Then she flew the kite to the window where her father was being held prisoner. He grabbed the kite string and carefully slid down to the ground.

Pages 190–194

Let's reread pages 190–194 to recall the lesson the Emperor learned after being saved by Djeow Seow.

Summary: The Emperor learned that size is not important. He never again neglected another person—big or small.

FLUENCY BUILDER Redirect students to the *Intervention Practice Book* page 27. Invite them to look at the sentences on the bottom half of the page. Model reading with appropriate expression, pace, and phrasing. Have students echo each sentence after you. Continue the exercise by inviting the students to echo read the sentences three more times.

INTERVENTION PRACTICE BOOK

page 27

Directed Reading: "Small but Brave," pp. 54–61

Pages 54–55

Have a volunteer read aloud the title of the story. Have students predict what they think the story might be about. (*a character who is brave even though he or she is little*) **MAKE PREDICTIONS**

MOVING
AHEAD
pp. 54–61

Have students read to find out the two main characters in this story. (*Ray and his dog, Loyal*) **NOTE DETAILS**

Ask: **How does Ray seem to feel about his dog, Loyal? How can you tell?** (Possible response: *Ray loves his dog very much. He named him Loyal and gave him a warm, cozy place to sleep and a place to play. They spend time together.*) **DETERMINE CHARACTERS' EMOTIONS**

Ask: **How do you know that Loyal is not cruel?** (*Loyal likes to chase things, but he does not hurt them.*) **IMPORTANT DETAILS**

Then ask: **Why does Loyal feel important?** (Possible response: *He feels important because Ray cares about him and says that he is brave.*) **ANALYZE CHARACTERS' EMOTIONS**

Pages 56–57

Have students read to find out why Loyal wants to be the bravest dog in the world. (Possible response: *Loyal wants to be the bravest dog in the world so Ray will be proud of him.*) **CAUSE-EFFECT**

Ask a volunteer to read aloud the second paragraph on page 56 while students listen to find out what Loyal thinks he should do. Model using the self-question strategy:

> **MODEL** As I read this page, I am confused by why Loyal thinks he needs to leave home to find out if he is brave. I ask myself questions such as *Can Loyal prove he is brave when he is home? What might he do when he leaves to prove that he is brave?* These questions help me to see that Loyal might think he needs to leave his safe home to show that he is not afraid. Only then will he be able to prove that he is truly brave. **Focus Strategy SELF-QUESTION**

Then ask: **What do you think will happen next?** (Responses will vary.) **MAKE PREDICTIONS**

Have students read page 57 to confirm their predictions. Then ask: **How does Loyal show that he is brave when he meets the dog?** (Possible answer: *Loyal speaks up for himself even though a bigger dog is making fun of him.*) **ANALYZE CHARACTERS**

Pages 58–59

Have students read pages 58–59 silently. Ask: **Why do you think Loyal's new job was the loneliest of all?** (*He was alone with the chickens and had no one to play with.*) **SPECULATE**

Then ask: **What does Loyal do all night?** (*He trots around the pen all night encircling the hens and protecting them from the fox.*) **SUMMARIZE**

Ask: **How did Loyal react when the fox came for the hens? How do you know?** (*He was brave. He continued to fight even when the fox grabbed* *his legs.*) **SUMMARIZE/ANALYZE CHARACTERS**

Then ask: **What is Loyal's problem?** (*He is sad and lonely.*)
NARRATIVE ELEMENTS

Ask: **What do you think Loyal will do next? Why?** (*He will go home to Ray because he has proved that he is brave.*) **MAKE PREDICTIONS/SPECU-LATE**

After students have read page 60, ask: **What is the lesson in this story?** (Possible response: *Having a best friend is more important than being brave.*) **DETERMINE THEME**

Summarize the selection. Ask students to think about what happened to Loyal in this story. Then have them complete *Intervention Practice Book* page 29 and summarize the story.

Page 60

INTERVENTION PRACTICE BOOK

page 29

Page 61

Answers to *Think About It* Questions

1. Loyal decides to leave home. First, he stands up for himself against a bigger dog. Then, he fights a fox and protects hens on a farm. **SUMMARY**

2. Possible response: He loves Loyal and believes that he is brave. He shows Loyal this by taking good care of him and praising him. **INTERPRETATION**

3. Paragraphs should include an opinion of whether a best friend is more important than being brave and reasons to justify the answer. **WRITE AN OPINION**

 **Narrative Elements**

AFTER

Skill Review *pages 204–205*

USE SKILL CARD 7B

RETEACH **the skill.** Have students look at **side B of Skill Card 7: Narrative Elements**. Read the skill reminder aloud. Then invite volunteers to explain each of the elements in their own words.

Have a volunteer read aloud the next set of directions. Explain that students will be creating their own story map to identify the narrative elements for this story. Invite them to share their completed graphic organizers with the group, and discuss any differences between the students' work.

 FLUENCY BUILDER Make sure all students have a copy of *Intervention Practice Book* page 27. Tell students that they will be focusing on the sentences at the bottom half of the page. Pair each student with a partner. Then have partners take turns reading each sentence aloud to each other. Encourage students to read each sentence several times. Have partners critique their performances after each reading, discussing tone, inflection, and pace.

INTERVENTION PRACTICE BOOK

page 27

Written Directions: Using Time-Order Words

Build on prior knowledge. Tell students that they are going to work together to write directions for making a peanut butter and jelly sandwich using a variety of time-order words and phrases. Display the following chart.

Time-Order Words and Phrases		
after	until	soon
before	meanwhile	later
during	today	finally
first	tomorrow	then
second	yesterday	as soon as
third	next	when
		lastly

Construct the text. "Share the pen" with students in a collaborative group writing effort. Ask them to think about the steps necessary to make a peanut butter and jelly sandwich. Guide them in creating sentences using the following steps:

- List the steps used to make a sandwich.

- Check to make sure the steps are in the correct order.

- Add time-order words or phrases in each sentence to connect the steps to one another.

- Use a variety of sequence words from the chart. For example: *after, as soon as, meanwhile, later.*

- Guide students in identifying and adding any missing steps.

- Encourage them to add time-order words to make their steps clearer.

- Have students read aloud their sentences to see if they flow together smoothly.

Revisit the text. Have students review the steps for making a sandwich. Invite them to check their sentences for correct beginning and end punctuation, spelling, and grammar.

On Your Own

Ask students to think of something they do very well. Then have them write a set of directions using some of the sequence words from the chart. Tell them to include three or four steps in their directions.

Connect Spelling and Phonics

RETEACH **short vowel /a/a; long vowel /ā/ai, ay.** Write the word *tan* on the board. Tell students that you will be saying some words with the /a/ sound. Then write *stay* on the board. Have students notice that in this word, the letters *ay* stand for the long *a* vowel sound. Tell students that some of the words you will say have this sound. Then write *braid* on the board, and point out that the long *a* vowel sound can also be spelled *ai*. Dictate each word below. Have students write the words and then correct their work together. Give them a chance to correct any misspellings.

I. black*	2. camp	3. always*	4. payment
5. gray*	6. praise*	7. paint	8. waited*

*Word appears in "Small but Brave."

Dictate the following sentence for students to write: *May has her hair in long braids.*

Build and Read Longer Words

Write the word *painful* on the board. Have students identify two consonants next to each other. (*nf*) Remind students that two-syllable words that have this pattern are often divided between the two middle consonants. Have students read each syllable and then the whole word. Repeat with the words *random, rabbit, pancake, magnet, daytime, payment*, and *ponytail*.

Remind students to look for similar patterns with longer unfamiliar words with the short *a* vowel sound and the long *a* vowel sound spelled *ai* and *ay*. Encourage them to break the words into syllables and to read each part, and then the whole word.

INTERVENTION
ASSESSMENT
BOOK

FLUENCY BUILDER Have students select a passage from "Small but Brave" to read aloud to a partner. You may have students choose passages that they found particularly interesting, or have them choose one of the following options:

- Read page 56 and the first paragraph on page 57. (Total: 101 words)

- Read the last paragraph on page 59 and all of page 60. (Total: 118 words.)

Encourage students to read the selected passage aloud to their partner three times. Have the student rate his or her own reading on the four-point scale.

Review Vocabulary

Review the Vocabulary Words before the weekly assessment. Invite students to write each Vocabulary Word on a separate index card. Have them place their cards face-up in front of them. Tell students that you will read a definition and they should raise the word card that matches. Check the accuracy of their responses. Invite students to place the words they correctly match in one pile and those they miss in a different pile. Play the game several times, and challenge students to improve the number of correct answers.

INTERVENTION PRACTICE BOOK

page 30

⭐(Focus Skill) Review Narrative Elements

Distribute *Intervention Practice Book* page 30 to review narrative elements before the weekly assessment. Invite a volunteer to read the paragraph aloud. Tell students to listen and look for the characters, the setting, and the plot (including the problem, important events, and the solution). Guide students through completing the chart with these elements.

Review Test Prep

Have students turn to page 205 of the *Pupil Edition*. Call attention to the tips for answering the test questions. Tell students that paying attention to these tips can help them answer not only the test questions on this page, but also other test questions like these.

LEAD THE WAY

page 205

Have students follow along as you read aloud each test question and the tip that goes with it. Discuss how the words *plot change* in question I signal a need to identify an important event in the story that would be different.

INTERVENTION ASSESSMENT BOOK

✔

Self-Selected Reading

Have students select their own books to read independently. They might choose books from the classroom library shelf, or you may wish to offer a group of appropriate books from which students can choose. Titles might include:

- *Sammy, Dog Detective* by Colleen Stanley Bare. Cobblehill, 1998

- *The Story of the Little Black Dog* by J. B. Spooner. Arcade, 1994

- *The Bravest Dog Ever: The True Story of Balto* by Natalie Standiford. Random House, 1998

You may also wish to choose additional books that are the same genre or by the same author, or that have the same kind of text structure as the selection.

After students have chosen their books, give each student a copy of My Reading Log, which can be found on page R38 in the back of the *Teacher's Edition*. Have students fill in the information at the top of the form. Then have them use the log to keep track of their reading and to record their responses to the literature.

Conduct student-teacher conferences. Plan to conference one-on-one with each student about his or her self-selected reading. Be sure that students bring their Reading Log to share with you at the conference. Ask students questions about their books to generate discussion. For example, ask students if this book reminds them of anything in their own lives, or ask them to share their favorite part of the story.

FLUENCY PERFORMANCE Have students read aloud to you the passage from "Small but Brave" that they selected and practiced earlier. Keep track of the number of words they read correctly and incorrectly. Ask students what rating they would give themselves on the 1 to 4 scale. Give them the opportunity to reread the passage to you until they are happy and satisfied with their performance.

See *Oral Reading Fluency Assessment* for monitoring progress.

Use with

"Nights of the Pufflings"

Review Phonics: Digraphs /th/*th*; /sh/*sh*; /ch/*ch, tch*

Identify the sounds. Have students repeat this sentence three times: *I think my broth is too thick.* Ask which words have the /th/ sound. (*think, broth, thick*) Then follow a similar procedure for the /sh/ sound, using this sentence: *She wished she had a fish on a dish.* Do the same for the /ch/ sound, using this sentence: *Did Chen catch a frog in the ditch?*

Associate letters to sounds. Write the sentence *I think my broth is too thick* on the board, and underline the letters *th* in *think* and *broth*. Tell students that the letters *th* can stand for the /th/ sound they hear at the beginning of *think* and at the end of *broth*. Follow a similar procedure to introduce the letters *sh* and the /sh/ sound and the letters *ch/tch* and the /ch/ sound, using the two sentences above as examples. After introducing the /ch/ sound, point out that the letters *tch* are not used to begin a word; the /ch/ sound at the beginning of a word is usually spelled *ch*.

Word blending. Model how to blend and read the word *catch*. Slide your hand under the whole word as you elongate the sounds /kaach/. Then read the word naturally—*catch*. Follow a similar procedure for the words *fish, ditch*, and *broth*.

INTERVENTION
PRACTICE
BOOK
page 32

Apply the skill. *Consonant Substitution* Write the following words on the board, and have students read each aloud. Make the changes necessary to form the word in parentheses.

tin (thin)	**pat** (path)	**clap** (chap)	**hat** (hatch)	**sell** (shell)
tick (thick)	**sun** (such)	**rest** (chest)	**bat** (batch)	**least** (leash)

Introduce Vocabulary

PRETEACH **lesson vocabulary.** Tell students that they are going to learn six new words that they will see again when they read "Nights of the Pufflings." Teach each Vocabulary Word using the following process.

Use the following suggestions or similar ideas to give the meaning or context.

uninhabited	Point out the root word *inhabit* and the prefix *un-*. If your house is uninhabited, no one lives there.
burrows	Relate to the homes of moles.
venture	Describe as going to an unfamiliar place such as a dark cave.
stranded	Point out the *-ed* ending. Relate to being left helpless somewhere.

> Write the word.
> Say the word.
> Track the word and have students repeat it.
> Give the meaning or context.

nestles	Demonstrate by holding a stuffed animal close to you.
instinctively	Point out the root word *instinct*. Relate to the natural tendency of animals to care for their young.

For vocabulary activities, see Vocabulary Games on pages 2–7.

For vocabulary activities, see Vocabulary Games on pages 2–7.

AFTER

Building Background and Vocabulary

Apply Vocabulary Strategies

Use sentence and word context. Write this sentence on chart paper: *They stay safely hidden in the long dark tunnels of their burrows.* Explain that sometimes students can figure out the meaning of a word from the way it is used in a sentence. Model using the strategy.

> **MODEL** When I read this sentence, I am unsure what the word *burrows* means. I look back at the words *long dark tunnels* and *safely hidden*. I think these context clues will help me determine that *burrows* must be "safe places in the ground."

Guide students in using a similar procedure to find the meaning of the words *instinctively*, *nestles*, and *venture*.

RETEACH lesson vocabulary. List the Vocabulary Words on chart paper. Have students listen to each sentence and raise their hand when they know the Vocabulary Word that completes each sentence. Then have volunteers read the word aloud.

1. The explorer decided to _____ out into the forest. (*venture*)
2. Mother animals _____ know how to care for their young. (*instinctively*)
3. Rabbits made _____ in our yard for shelter. (*burrows*)
4. The _____ island was filled with plants. (*uninhabited*)
5. The baby _____ next to his mother during the storm. (*nestles*)
6. We were _____ after our car broke down. (*stranded*)

Vocabulary Words

uninhabited having no people living there

burrows holes in the ground made by animals

venture go out into a dangerous place

stranded left behind or in a helpless situation

nestles moves snugly next to

instinctively without thinking; in a way that is natural

FLUENCY BUILDER Distribute copies of *Intervention Practice Book* page 31. Read each word in the first column aloud, and have students repeat it. Then organize students into small groups. Invite each student to read the words in the list aloud while the rest of the group listens. Follow this same procedure for the remaining columns. Finish this activity by inviting the class to do a choral reading of all the words.

INTERVENTION PRACTICE BOOK
page 31

(Focus Skill) Summarize

PRETEACH **the skill.** Explain that a good summary tells the most important details of a story. Model a summary using a familiar book or movie. Discuss why it is important to only include the main ideas.

Have students look at **side A of Skill Card 8: Summarize.** Read the definition for summarize. Next, have students look at the fact sheet and diagram and read the information.

Now call attention to the chart, and have volunteers read the information. Ask:

- **What information did the student learn from the diagram?**
  (*Dolphins have a dorsal fin, two flippers, and a fluke.*)

- **How is the information in the chart different from the information on the fact sheet?** (*Possible answer: It includes the main idea, facts, and a summary in the student's own words.*)

Explain that a summary should be brief, include only the most important information, and be told or written in the student's own words.

Prepare to Read: "Nights of the Pufflings"

**LEAD
THE WAY**
pages
208–219

Preview. Explain to students that they are going to read "Nights of the Pufflings" which is a nonfiction selection. Explain that it gives information about how some children help baby birds called pufflings. Preview the selection.

- **Pages 208–209:** I see the title and the names of the author and photo illustrator, Bruce McMillan. I also notice the picture on page 209 is of a kind of bird. This must be a puffin.

- **Pages 210–211:** The picture on page 210 shows the birds flying in from the sea. There is a picture of a child on page 211, who is watching the birds.

- **Pages 212–213:** There are two birds that look to be a pair. They will probably tend to an egg. On page 213 it looks as if one of the birds is catching fish.

- **Pages 214–217:** I see children helping the birds. It looks as if the birds are lost and need help flying to the water. From the pictures I can tell that the children are able to help the young birds.

Set purpose. Model setting a purpose for reading the selection.

MODEL From my preview, I think I will be learning about puffins and their young as well as how the young birds grow and make their way back to the water. I will read to find out what happens to baby pufflings after they hatch.

Reread and Summarize

Have students reread and summarize "Nights of the Pufflings" in sections, as described in the chart below.

Page 211

Let's reread page 211 to recall what the children on the island are waiting for.

Summary: The children are waiting for the puffins to return to the island so they can lay their eggs and raise their pufflings.

Pages 212–213

Now let's reread pages 212–213 to find out how the adult puffins take care of the chicks.

Summary: The adult puffins find fish and feed the chicks many times a day. The adults protect the chicks by keeping them safely hidden in their burrows.

Pages 214–215

As we reread pages 214–215, let's find out how the children help the young pufflings.

Summary: Sometimes pufflings become confused and are unable to fly out to the water. The children rescue them and protect them from the cats and dogs.

Pages 216–217

Let's reread the final two pages of the story, pages 216 and 217, to recall what happens to the pufflings that are caught by the children.

Summary: The children release the pufflings by throwing them up into the air near the water. The pufflings and the adult puffins swim away for the winter.

FLUENCY BUILDER Make sure that students have a copy of *Intervention Practice Book* page 31. Focus attention on the sentences at the bottom of the page. Read each sentence and model appropriate phrasing, pace, and expression. Then have students read the sentences after you. Finally, organize students into small groups and have each read the sentences three times.

INTERVENTION
PRACTICE
BOOK
page 31

Making Connections
pages 226–227

Pages 62–63

Directed Reading: "Bringing Back the Puffins" pp. 62–68

Read aloud the title of the selection, and have students view the illustrations on pages 62 and 63. Tell students that puffins are seabirds that come to shore to nest.

MOVING AHEAD
pp. 62–68

Ask: **How can you tell that puffins once nested on Egg Rock?** (Possible response: *The selection says that Kress wants to bring them back.*) **DRAW CONCLUSIONS**

Ask students to predict what Kress and the other scientists did to bring the puffins back to Egg Rock. After students have read the pages, ask: **What did the scientists do?** (Possible responses: *They went to another land where puffins still live, they collected some puffin chicks, and they brought them back to Egg Rock.*) **SEQUENCE**

Ask: **Do you think it was right to take the young puffins? Why or why not?** (*Responses will vary.*) **MAKE JUDGMENTS**

Pages 64–65

Have students read to find out how Kress and the other scientists cared for the puffin chicks.

> **MODEL** The first time I read this page I noticed there was a lot of information to remember. I was not sure if I would remember everything because I had read the page rather quickly. I asked myself how I could keep track of all this new information. Then I decided to reread the page, but this time I read it more slowly. By adjusting my reading rate, I was able to understand and remember the important information about the puffins. **ADJUST READING RATE**

Ask: **Do you agree that the scientists made good parents to the puffin chicks? Why or why not?** (Possible response: *Yes, because they made the chicks homes to live in, they fed them, and they kept the gulls away.*) **INTERPRET STORY EVENTS**

Ask: **What did the puffins do when they came out of their village of burrows?** (Possible response: *They flew off into the sea.*) **NOTE DETAILS**

Pages 66–67

Read aloud the first sentence, then ask students what kinds of dangers they think the young puffins face at sea. Have them read page 66 to check their predictions. (Possible response: *Puffins can be eaten by gulls, stranded in fishing nets, or harmed by waves.*) **SUMMARIZE**

Ask: **In what ways are puffins made for sea life?** (*Possible response: The puffins are made for sea life because their bodies are shaped to help them swim fast and dive deep. They also have sharp beaks for catching fish.*) **SUMMARIZE**

Why did Steve Kress leap to his feet when he saw the returning puffins? (*Possible response: He had waited for them and worried about them for such a long time that he was probably thrilled to see them return.*) **CAUSE/EFFECT**

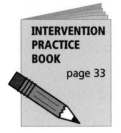

INTERVENTION PRACTICE BOOK

page 33

Page 68

Summarize the selection. Ask students to share their responses to the selection and to tell whether or not they liked it. Then have them complete *Intervention Practice Book* page 33.

Answers to *Think About It* Questions

1. They collected chicks from another spot. At Egg Rock, they acted as parents to those chicks. They fed them and kept them safe. **SUMMARY**

2. Possible response: Instinct made them go back to the spot where they grew up. **INTERPRETATION**

3. Accept reasonable responses. **CREATE QUESTIONS**

Skill Review
pages 228–229

USE SKILL CARD 8B

(Focus Skill) **Summarizing**

RETEACH the skill. Invite students to look at **side B of Skill Card 8: Summarize.** Read the skill reminder with them, and have a volunteer read the paragraph aloud.

Read aloud the next set of directions while students follow along. Tell students they will now work independently to create their own chart like the one at the bottom of this card. Review each heading in the chart. Remind them to write the information in their own words.

After students have completed their charts, have them explain their chart to a partner. Invite the pair to discuss the information they summarized.

FLUENCY BUILDER Be sure students have copies of *Intervention Practice Book* page 31. Explain that students will be practicing the sentences at the bottom of the page using echo reading. Begin by reading the first sentence aloud. Invite students to repeat the sentence, following the words on their own papers. Read and echo each sentence three times to give students practice. Follow the same procedure for each of the remaining sentences.

INTERVENTION PRACTICE BOOK

page 31

Informative Writing: Summary

Build on prior knowledge. Tell students that they are going to read information about penguins and then write a summary together.

Copy the following paragraph onto a piece of chart paper for display.

Emperor Penguins

The Emperor penguin is the <u>largest kind of penguin</u>. It can grow to be <u>3 or 4 feet tall</u>. These birds <u>live near Antarctica</u>, where the waters are icy. They <u>eat many kinds of fish and squid</u>. One interesting fact about penguins is that <u>both the mother and father birds take turns keeping their egg warm</u>.

Read the paragraph with students. Invite them to suggest what they think are the most important ideas. Use a colored marker to underline those ideas. (Suggested answers are underlined above.)

Construct the text. "Share the pen" with students in a collaborative group writing effort. As students dictate words and phrases, use these steps to guide students in writing a summary.

- Have students read one phrase about Emperor penguins.

- Call on students to write the phrase as a sentence in their own words.

- Repeat with other important phrases from the paragraph.

- Have students read the sentences. If necessary, rearrange the sentences in a logical order.

Revisit the text. Invite students to review the summary they wrote about Emperor penguins. Ask: **Have I used the most important ideas and stated them in my own words?** Guide them to edit and proofread the summary for proper punctuation, spelling, and grammar. Then have students read the completed summary aloud.

On Your Own

Have students select a paragraph from their science book. Tell them to read it carefully, and write a short summary. Remind them to include phrases with only the most important information and write sentences in their own words.

Connect Spelling and Phonics

RETEACH digraphs /th/*th*; /sh/*sh*; /ch/*ch, tch*. Write the word *thing* on the board. Point out the /th/ sound. Tell students you will be saying three more words with the /th/ sound. Have students write each word as you read it. After they write each one, display the correct spelling so students can proofread their work. Then on the board, write the word *push* to point out the letters that stand for the /sh/ sound and the words *pitch* and *chip* to point out the letters that stand for the /ch/ sound spelled *ch/tch*. Follow the same procedure to have students practice spelling the words listed below.

1. thump	2. thimble	3. path	4. shave
5. fresh*	6. chicks*	7. catch*	8. watches*

***Word appears in "Bringing Back the Puffins."**

Dictate the following sentence and have students write it: *A chimp snatched a brush from Beth.*

Build and Read Longer Words

Remind students that they have learned how to decode words with the /th/ sound spelled *th*, the /sh/ sound spelled *sh*, and the /ch/ sound spelled *ch/tch*. Explain that now they will use what they have learned to read longer words.

Write the word *hatchling* on the board. Ask students what consonants come together to make the /ch/ sound in this word. (*tch*) Tell students that when dividing a word in which the letters *tch* stand for the /ch/ sound, the *tch* always stays together. Demonstrate by drawing a line between the two syllables in the word *hatchling*. (*hatch/ling*) Cover the *ling* and have a volunteer read the word *hatch*. Then cover *hatch* and have a volunteer read the ending *ling*. Have students blend the word parts to read the longer word *hatchling*. Follow a similar procedure for the words *bathrobe*, *wishful*, and *punching*.

INTERVENTION
ASSESSMENT
BOOK

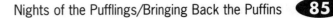

FLUENCY BUILDER Have students choose a passage from "Bringing Back the Puffins" to read aloud to a partner. You may have students choose passages that they found particularly interesting, or have them choose one of the following options:

- Read pages 62–63. (From *Spring has come . . .* through . . . *back to Egg Rock.* Total: 98 words)
- Read pages 64–65. (From *Steve Kress and his team . . .* through . . . *instinctively do this.* Total: 107 words)

Encourage students to read the selected passage aloud to their partner three times. Have the student rate his or her reading on a scale from 1 to 4.

Review Vocabulary

Review the weekly Vocabulary Words with students. Invite students to carefully evaluate each sentence as you read it aloud and demonstrate "thumbs up" if true and "thumbs down" if false. Remind students to consider if the Vocabulary Word is used correctly in the sentence.

1. An **uninhabited** island is filled with people. (false)

2. A baby may **nestle** against its mother. (true)

3. A brave person would not **venture** into the woods. (false)

4. If all roads closed during a snowstorm, you might be **stranded** at home. (true)

5. A gardener would not want **burrows** in his vegetable patch. (true)

6. A mother bear **instinctively** cares for her cub. (true)

(Focus Skill) Review Summarizing

To review summarizing before the weekly assessment, distribute *Intervention Practice Book* page 34. Call attention to the K-W-L chart at the bottom of the page. Guide students through completing the first two columns on the chart. Then invite them to read the paragraph. Tell students to summarize this information and complete the last column of the chart. Remind students to include only the most important information written in their own words.

INTERVENTION PRACTICE BOOK
page 34

Review Test Prep

Ask students to turn to page 229 of the *Pupil Edition*. Call attention to the tips for answering test questions. Tell students that paying attention to these tips can help them answer not only the test questions on this page but also other test questions like these.

LEAD THE WAY
page 229

Invite students to follow along as you read each test question and the tip that goes with it. Discuss why the choice *Manatees are threatened or endangered* is the most important sentence to include in a summary of the article. Explain that this sentence is the subject or topic of the paragraph. Remind students that a good summary includes only the most important information from the passage and is written in their own words.

INTERVENTION ASSESSMENT BOOK

Self-Selected Reading

Have students select their own books to read independently. They might choose books from the classroom library shelf, or you may wish to offer a group of appropriate books from which students can choose. Titles might include:

- *Sea Turtle Journey* by Lorrain A. Jay. Smithsonian Institution, 1995
- *Song of the Swallows* by Leo Politi. Atheneum, 1987
- *Penguins!* by Gail Gibbons. Holiday House, 1998

You may also wish to choose additional books that are the same genre or by the same author, or that have the same kind of text structure as the selection.

After students have chosen their books, give each student a copy of My Reading Log, which can be found on page R38 in the back of the *Teacher's Edition*. Have students fill in the information at the top of the form. Then have them use the log to keep track of their reading and to record their responses to the literature.

Conduct student-teacher conferences. Plan a conference with each student to discuss his or her self-selected reading. Use the student's Reading Log as a guide for the conference. Try beginning the conference by allowing the student to share his or her own reactions, questions, and interpretations of the selection with you. Follow up on those comments with more in-depth questions. For example, with nonfiction text you might ask what information the student learned from the selection, what further study the student might be interested in pursuing, how the author structured the text, or how illustrations and diagrams help to make the text clearer.

FLUENCY PERFORMANCE Invite students to read aloud the passage from "Bringing Back the Puffins" that they selected and practiced earlier. Record the number of words each student reads correctly. Then ask the student to rate his or her own performance on a scale of 1 to 4. Always allow the student the opportunity for additional practice if he or she is not happy with his or her performance. Provide another opportunity for the student to read to you at a later time.

See *Oral Reading Fluency Assessment* for monitoring progress.

BEFORE

Building
Background
and Vocabulary

INTERVENTION
PRACTICE
BOOK

page 36

Use with

"The Garden of Happiness"

Review Phonics: *R*-controlled Vowel /är/*ar*

Identify the sound. Have the students repeat the following sentence aloud three times: *Please park the car next to the market.* Ask students which words have the same /är/ sound as in *dark.* (*park, car, market*)

Associate letters to sound. Write the sentence from above on the board. Circle *park, car,* and *market* and ask students how these words are alike. (/ar/ sound; the letters *ar*) Tell students that in each of these words, the letters *ar* stand for the /är/ sound they hear in *park.*

Word blending. Model how to blend and read *park.* Slide your hand under the entire word as you elongate the sounds /pärrk/. Then say the word naturally—*park.* Follow a similar procedure with *car* and *market.*

Apply the skill. *Consonant Substitution* Write the following words on the board, and have students read each aloud. Make the changes necessary to form the words in parentheses. Have students read each new word aloud.

back (bark)	**lack** (lark)	**cat** (cart)	**packing** (parking)
ham (harm)	**tap** (tarp)	**Stan** (star)	**tact** (tart)

Introduce Vocabulary

PRETEACH **lesson vocabulary.** Tell students that they are going to learn five new words that they will see again when they read a story called "The Garden of Happiness." Teach each Vocabulary Word using this process.

Use the following suggestions or similar ideas to give the meaning or context.

> Write the word.
>
> Say the word.
>
> Track the word and have students repeat it.
>
> Give the meaning or context.

lavender   Point out the short vowel sounds. Show students a sample of the color lavender.

haze   Point out the long *a* sound, spelled *a-e.* Show students a picture or painting of a foggy day. Explain that *haze* is similar to fog.

inhaled   Point out the prefix *in-.* Demonstrate by taking a deep breath.

mural   Relate to a large painting. Associate with any murals in your school or community.

skidded   Point out the short *i* sound. Demonstrate skidding across the floor.

For vocabulary activities, see Vocabulary Games on pages 2–7.

Apply Vocabulary Strategies

Use reference sources. Write the sentence *She wore a lavender dress* on the board. Tell students that one way to figure out the meaning of an unfamiliar word is to use reference sources such as the dictionary. Model using the strategy to confirm the meaning of *lavender*.

> **MODEL** When I look up *lavender* in a dictionary, I find the definition *a pale purplish color*. When I substitute *purple* for *lavender* in the sentence, it makes sense. So *lavender* must mean "purplish color."

Have students use a dictionary to determine the meaning of other words.

RETEACH **lesson vocabulary.** Have students write each of the Vocabulary Words on a separate index card. Read each of the riddles below. Students should hold up the card that correctly answers each riddle.

1. I am a thing. I have the /ā/ sound. I can make it difficult for people to see where they are going. I am sometimes called a *mist*. (*haze*)

2. I can be a thing or a describing word. I have the /a/ sound. Some people call me *purple*. (*lavender*)

3. I am an action word in the past tense. I am what happened when someone stopped fast on a slippery surface. (*skidded*)

4. I am a thing. I require art supplies. I am large. (*mural*)

5. I am an action word in the past tense. I am something you did when you breathed. (*inhaled*)

Vocabulary Words

lavender a light purple color

haze mist; fog

inhaled breathed in

mural a large painting on a wall

skidded slid or slipped across

FLUENCY BUILDER Using *Intervention Practice Book* page 35, read each word in the first column aloud. Then invite students to do a choral reading of these words with you. Repeat the choral reading two more times. Follow this procedure for the remaining two columns. Then pair students with a partner, and invite them to read all the words aloud to each other, listening for correct pronunciation.

INTERVENTION PRACTICE BOOK

page 35

⭐ (Focus Skill) Cause and Effect

PRETEACH **the skill.** Point out to students that a cause is why something happens and an effect is what happens as a result of the cause. Give an example such as rain causing a picnic to be cancelled.

Have students look at **side A of Skill Card 9: Cause and Effect.** Read the definition of cause and effect. Have them look at the pictures and describe what is happening. Discuss the cause-and-effect relationship between the two pictures.

Now call attention to the cause-and-effect chart at the bottom of the card. Invite a volunteer to read aloud the sentences in each box. Ask:

- **Why is there an arrow between the *Cause* and *Effect* boxes?** (*Possible answer: The arrow shows that the cause in the first box leads to the effect in the second box.*)
- **Why is the sentence *The snowman melted* shown as both a cause and an effect?** (*Possible answer: An effect can cause something else to happen. The sun caused the snowman to melt and the melted snowman caused the hat to get wet.*)

Explain that when events in a story have cause-and-effect relationships, we say the text is organized this way.

Prepare to Read: "The Garden of Happiness"

Preview. Tell students that they are going to read "The Garden of Happiness." Explain that this is realistic fiction, which has characters and events that are like people and events in real life. Then preview the selection.

LEAD THE WAY
pages 232–243

- **Pages 232–233:** I see the title and the names of the author and the illustrator. The picture is showing a garden in the city.
- **Pages 234–237:** I see a piece of the garden. Across the street, I see people looking at a wall. Maybe they are going to make the wall a part of the garden. On page 236, a girl seems to be planting a seed in a crack.
- **Pages 238–241:** These pages show the garden after it has grown. There is a very large sunflower. The pictures show people working in the garden. I notice that the sunflower looks like it may be dying. I can guess that it is the end of the summer.
- **Pages 242–243:** These pages show the wall that was across from the garden. I think someone painted pictures of sunflowers like the one that was growing in the garden.

Set purpose. Model setting a purpose for reading "The Garden of Happiness."

MODEL From my preview, I know that the story has to do with people who plant and grow a garden. People also paint a picture of the sunflowers in the garden. I will read to find out why they painted a mural of sunflowers on the wall.

Reread and Summarize

Have students reread and summarize "The Garden of Happiness"
in sections, as described in the chart below.

Pages 232–235

**Let's reread pages 232–235 to recall what is happening to the empty
lot on Marisol's block.**

Summary: Marisol and her neighbors are cleaning up the empty lot and
planting a garden. Some teenagers are also going to paint a mural on
the wall across the street from the lot.

Pages 236–237

**Now let's reread pages 236–237 to find out how Marisol gets
involved with the garden project.**

Summary: Marisol takes one of the seeds that Mrs. Garcia is feeding to
the birds and plants it in the small crack in the sidewalk. She takes care
of the seed by watering it and pulling weeds that grow near it.

Pages 238–240

**As we reread pages 238–240, let's remember what Marisol learned
about sunflowers.**

Summary: After Marisol's sunflower bloomed, the people from her
neighborhood told her how sunflowers grew in their native countries.
She learned that sunflowers had many different names and grew in
many different places.

Pages 241–242

**Let's reread pages 241–242 to recall how Marisol felt at the end of
the summer.**

Summary: First Marisol was sad because her sunflower had died. Then
she was happy because the teenagers painted beautiful sunflowers on
the wall across from the lot.

FLUENCY BUILDER Be sure that students
have copies of *Intervention Practice Book* page 35.
Invite them to look at the sentences at the bottom
of the page. Read each sentence aloud and model
the appropriate pace and phrasing. Then have
students practice reading each sentence aloud to
a partner.

INTERVENTION
PRACTICE
BOOK

page 35

Directed Reading: "Green Tomatoes," pp. 70–77

Pages 70–71

Read aloud the title of the story. Have students look at the illustrations on pages 70–71. Ask: **Where does the story take place?** (*a backyard garden with a vegetable stand out front*) **IMPORTANT DETAILS**

Have students read to find out whose garden it is and what is grown there. (*It is Nick's garden; he grows green beans, tomatoes, cucumbers, and carrots.*) Ask: **How do you know it is Nick's garden?** (*Nick is running the stand, and Martin refers to it as Nick's garden.*) **DRAW CONCLUSIONS**

Ask: **What are Carla and Lil going to make?** (*pickles*) Explain that pickles are cucumbers or other vegetables preserved in vinegar or salt water.

Pages 72–73

Ask: **What does Nick like to do in his garden?** (*Possible response: He enjoys working on his mural, feeding his fish, and tending to his plants.*) **SUMMARIZE**

Ask: **Why do you think Nick is upset that someone has taken his tomatoes while they were still small and green?** (*Possible response: The tomatoes weren't ripe yet; now Nick will have fewer ripe tomatoes to sell.*) **SPECULATE**

Invite students to make predictions about what Nick will do. Have them read page 73 to find out how Nick plans to solve the mystery of the missing tomatoes. Model using the make and confirm predictions strategy:

> **MODEL** As I read this page, I wonder what Nick will do. I think he will want to know what happened to his tomatoes, so I would guess that he will try to find the person who took them. He might ask some of his neighbors if they have seen the tomatoes. (Focus Strategy) **MAKE AND CONFIRM PREDICTIONS**

Pages 74–75

Ask: **What is Lil doing with Nick's tomatoes? Why did she take them?** (*She is hitting them with the bat; she took them because green is her favorite color.*) **CHARACTERS' MOTIVATIONS**

Ask: **How does Nick seem to feel? How do you know?** (*Possible response: He feels sad. I can tell because he sniffs and blinks, as if he's trying not to cry.*) **DETERMINE CHARACTER'S EMOTIONS**

Ask: **Why do you think Nick feels sad?** (*Possible response: Nick feels sad because Lil picked his green tomatoes.*) (Focus Skill) **CAUSE-EFFECT**

Page 76

Have students look at the illustration on page 76. Ask: **What did Carla and Lil bring for Nick?** (*Possible response: a jar of green tomatoes*) **NOTE DETAILS**

Have students read page 76 to confirm their predictions. Ask: **Do you think Carla's idea was a good one? Why or why not?** (*Responses will vary.*) **What do Nick's actions tell you about him?** (*His actions show that he is forgiving and kind.*) **MAKE JUDGMENTS**

INTERVENTION
PRACTICE
BOOK

page 37

Page 77

Summarize the selection. Ask students to describe Nick and then to summarize the main problem in the story and its solution. Then have students complete *Intervention Practice Book* page 37.

Answers to *Think About It* Questions

1. Lil picks the tomatoes and uses them to play ball. Carla feels bad about this and pickles the green tomatoes for Nick to sell.
   SUMMARY

2. Possible response: Nick wants to let some of the tomatoes get ripe.
   INTERPRETATION

3. Posters should be designed to attract attention and should give information about what is available at the vegetable stand.
   MAKE A POSTER

AFTER

Skill Review
pages 250–251

USE SKILL CARD 9B

(Focus Skill) Cause and Effect

RETEACH **the skill.** Have students look at **side B of Skill Card 9: Cause and Effect.** Read the skill reminder with them, and then have a volunteer read the paragraph aloud. Ask students to think about cause-and-effect relationships as you read the paragraph aloud again.

Ask a volunteer to read aloud the next set of directions. Invite children to work in small groups to create their own cause-and-effect chart. Remind them that the cause is written in the left-hand column and the related effect is written directly across from the cause in the right-hand column.

After students have completed their charts, invite them to meet with another group to share their work. Point out that the selection "The Garden of Happiness" has many examples of cause and effect. It tells the story of how an empty lot changes because of the efforts of many people.

FLUENCY BUILDER Make sure that students have copies of *Intervention Practice Book* page 35. Explain that students will be practicing the sentences at the bottom of the page by reading them aloud on tape. Assign each student a partner. Have students take turns reading the sentences aloud to each other and then reading them on tape. After listening to the tape, have students tell how well they think they read each sentence. Then have them read the sentences aloud on the tape a second time, with improved pacing and tone.

INTERVENTION
PRACTICE
BOOK

page 35

Expository Writing: How-To Paragraph

Build on prior knowledge. Tell students that they are going to talk and write about how to plant a seed. Display the following information:

> **Task: plant a seed**
>
> **Materials needed:**
>
> 1. seed
> 2. pot
> 3. dirt
> 4. water

Ask students to think about how each of these materials is used in the task of planting a seed. Write their suggestions on the board or on chart paper. For example: Use the pot to hold the dirt.

Construct the text. "Share the pen" with students in a collaborative writing effort. Assist them in using the sentences from the chart to write a draft about how to plant a seed. Use the following steps as you guide students through the process:

- Read each sentence from the chart aloud with students.

- Have students add any steps for planting seeds that a reader would need to know to complete the task.

- Ask them to consider whether the steps are in the correct order.

Revisit the text. Have students read the completed how-to paragraph for clarity. Guide them to add time-order words to signal the sequence of events, such as *first, then, next,* and *finally*. Remind them to check for errors in spelling and punctuation.

On Your Own

Ask students to write a set of directions for something that they would like to do. Tell them to include at least three steps in their directions.

Connect Spelling and Phonics

RETEACH *R*-controlled vowel /är/*ar*. Write the word *carp* on the board. Underline the letters *ar*. Read the word aloud, and emphasize the /är/ sound. Explain that you will say seven more words with this same sound. Invite students to write each word as you say it. Proofread their work together.

1. carp*	2. yard*	3. farmed	4. lark
5. bark	6. darling	7. sparkle	8. harvest*

*Word appears in "Green Tomatoes."

Dictate the following sentence and have students write it: *I heard the dog bark at the lark that flew through the yard.*

Build and Read Longer Words

Review the words that students have learned with the /är/ sound spelled *ar*. Explain that now students will be reading longer words with this same spelling pattern.

INTERVENTION ASSESSMENT BOOK

Write *target* on the board. Have students identify two consonants next to each other. (*rg*) Draw a line between *r* and *g*, and tell students that two-syllable words with this pattern are usually divided between the two consonants that are next to each other. Frame *tar* in *target*, and ask a volunteer to read it. Repeat with the remaining part, *get*. Then draw your hand under the entire word as students read it. Follow a similar procedure with the words *garden*, *starling*, and *barter*. Ask students to read each word and explain how they were able to figure it out.

FLUENCY BUILDER Have students choose a passage from "Green Tomatoes" to read aloud to a partner. You may have students choose passages that they found particularly interesting, or have them choose one of the following options:

- Read page 71. (From *Carla and Lil got . . . season for garden visits.* Total: 85 words)

- Read pages 75–76. (From *Nick held up a . . . But not all of them!* Total: 116 words)

Encourage students to read the selected passage aloud to their partners three times. Have the student rate his or her own reading on a scale from 1 to 4.

Vocabulary Review

To revisit Vocabulary Words prior to the weekly assessment, use these sentence frames. Have volunteers take turns reading aloud the sentence stems and choices. Students identify the correct choice and explain why it makes sense in the sentence.

I. A **mural** might take up
   a. a large part of a wall.   b. a small part of a wall.

2. The car **skidded** on a
   a. deserted road.   b. wet road.

3. The color of **lavender** is
   a. red.   b. purple.

4. If you just **inhaled**, you
   a. took a breath.   b. went to sleep.

5. If you walk outside when there is a **haze**, you might be walking in a
   a. fog.   b. puddle.

Correct responses: la, 2b, 3b, 4a, 5a.

Display the Vocabulary Words and definitions on page 89 and have students copy them to use when they study for the vocabulary test.

(Focus Skill) Review Cause and Effect

INTERVENTION
PRACTICE
BOOK

page 38

To review cause and effect before the weekly assessment, distribute copies of *Intervention Practice Book* page 38. Point out the Cause and Effect chart on the bottom half of the page. Have volunteers read aloud the directions and the sentences. Remind students of the definitions of cause and effect to assist them in identifying each kind of statement. Have students use this information to sort the statements into the appropriate boxes on the chart.

Review Test Prep

Ask students to turn to page 251 of the *Pupil Edition*. Call attention to the tips for answering test questions. Tell students that paying attention to these tips can help them answer not only the questions on this page but also other test questions like these.

LEAD
THE WAY

page 251

INTERVENTION
ASSESSMENT
BOOK

Have students follow along as you read aloud each test question and the tip that goes with it. Read through each answer choice and discuss how the first two choices indicate things that happen after he plants his garden. Guide students to see that only the last choice tells why he planted it. Then ask students how the words *as a result* in question 2 give us a clue to the answer. (*Possible answer: They tell us to look for the effect the flowers had on people who saw them.*)

Self-Selected Reading

Have students select their own books to read independently. Suggest that they choose books from the classroom library shelf, or you may wish to offer a group of appropriate books from which students can choose.

- *Why Do Leaves Change Colors?* by Betsy Maestro. HarperCollins, 1994

- *Garden* by Robert Maass. Henry Holt, 1998

- *Dear Rebecca, Winter Is Here* by Jean Craighead George. HarperCollins, 1993

You may also wish to choose selections within the genre of realistic fiction, by the same author, or that have a similar text structure as the selection.

After students have chosen their books, give each student a copy of My Reading Log, which can be found on page R38 in the back of the *Teacher's Edition*. Have students fill in the information at the top of the form. Then have them use the log to keep track of their reading and to record their responses to the literature.

Conduct student-teacher conferences. Set up a conference with each student in which you will have him or her share entries from his or her Reading Log. Have each student bring his or her Reading Log to the conference. You may begin by posing a question about the story to stimulate discussion. Students might also wish to share their favorite part of the selection.

FLUENCY PERFORMANCE Invite students to read aloud the passage from "Green Tomatoes" that they selected and practiced earlier. Keep track of how many words the student reads correctly. Then invite the student to rate his or her performance on a scale of 1 to 4. Allow the student an opportunity to have additional practice time if he or she is unhappy with the reading. Then invite the student to read the passage to you again at a later time.

See *Oral Reading Fluency Assessment* for monitoring progress.

Use with

"How to Babysit an Orangutan"

Review Phonics: Long Vowel /ō/*oa, ow*

Identify the sound. Have students repeat the following sentence aloud twice: *Rob got a pet goat at the show.* Ask them to identify the words that have the /ō/ sound they hear in *boat* or *row*. (*goat, show*)

Associate letters to sound. Write the above sentence on the board. Underline the letters *oa* in *goat*. Tell students that the letters *oa* stand for the /ō/ sound. Remind students that when two vowels come together between consonants, they often stand for a long vowel sound. Then underline the letters *ow* in *show*. Tell students that the letters *ow* also can stand for the /ō/ sound. Read the sentence aloud as you point to each word.

Word blending. Model how to blend and read the word *sown*. Slide your hand under the letters as you elongate the sounds /ssōōnn/. Then read the word naturally—*sown*. Follow a similar procedure with *float*.

Apply the skill. *Letter Substitution* Write the following words on the board, and have students read each aloud. Make the changes necessary to form the words in parentheses. Have volunteers read the new words aloud.

INTERVENTION
PRACTICE
BOOK

page 40

rod (road)	**snob** (snow)	**blot** (bloat)	**shop** (show)
cots (coats)	**top** (tow)	**clock** (cloak)	**glob** (glow)

Introduce Vocabulary

PRETEACH **lesson vocabulary.** Tell students they are going to learn six new words that they will see again when they read "How to Babysit an Orangutan." Teach each Vocabulary Word using the following process.

Use the following suggestions and ideas to introduce the new vocabulary.

> Write the word.
> Say the word.
> Track the word and have students repeat it.
> Give the meaning or context.

displeasure   Point out the root word *pleasure* and the prefix *dis-*. Relate to unhappiness.

jealous   Relate to feelings that siblings may have toward each other, or to envy toward a friend over a desired possession.

endangered   Point out the root word *danger*. Relate to how some animals are protected because they are in danger of dying out.

smuggled   Relate to secretly bringing illegal items somewhere.

facial   Point out the root word *face*. Explain that *facial* relates to the face.

coordination Ask a student to stand on one foot and raise both arms over his or her head. Explain that this action requires coordination, or parts of the body working together.

For vocabulary activities, see Vocabulary Games on pages 2–7.

Apply Vocabulary Strategies

Use word origins and derivations. Write the word *facial* on chart paper. Tell students that one way to find the meaning of an unfamiliar word is to determine if the word is related to or comes from a familiar word. Model using the strategy.

> **MODEL** The word *facial* reminds me of the word *face*. I think *face* can provide me with a clue to the meaning of *facial*. In fact, I think the word *facial* means "related to the face."

Guide students in using a similar procedure to find the meanings of the words *endangered* and *coordination*.

RETEACH **lesson vocabulary.** Draw a continuum on the board with the words *Most Surprised* and *Least Surprised* at either end. Read the following scenarios aloud. Ask volunteers to stand next to the place on the continuum that shows their reaction to each statement.

How surprised would you be if . . .

1. your mother showed **displeasure** at your getting an *A* on a test? (*Most Surprised*)
2. your friend was **jealous** of your punishment? (*Most Surprised*)
3. you saw an **endangered** animal on the street? (*Most Surprised*)
4. it took great **coordination** to juggle three bowling balls? (*Least Surprised*)
5. your teacher had a strange **facial** expression when you came to class barefoot? (*Least Surprised*)
6. someone **smuggled** a dog on the bus? (*Answers may vary.*)

Vocabulary Words

displeasure the feeling of being displeased; dissatisfaction

jealous full of envy

endangered in danger of dying out

smuggled taken out of a place illegally

facial having to do with the face

coordination the ability to make the parts of the body work together smoothly

FLUENCY BUILDER Give each student a copy of the *Intervention Practice Book* page 39. Read the words in the first column aloud. Then organize students into small groups. Have students take turns reading the entire first column to the members of their group. Follow the same procedure for each of the remaining two columns. After the groups have finished reading the final column, invite the entire group to do a choral reading of all the words.

INTERVENTION PRACTICE BOOK

page 39

(Focus Skill) Summarize

PRETEACH the skill. Explain that a summary retells the most important points of the story in the correct sequence. Give an example, such as what happened on your way to school. Discuss how you shared only the most important information in the correct order.

Have students look at **side A of Skill Card 10: Summarize.** Read the story aloud. Invite students to look at the chart and read the information. Ask:

- **How can summarizing help readers?** (*It makes readers recall the most important events.*)

- **What other information should be included in a summary?** (*Possible response: events and details that support the main idea.*)

- **Why should the ideas be restated in the correct order?** (*So the events will make sense.*)

Explain that good readers summarize after reading each section to help them remember what they have read.

Prepare to Read: "How to Babysit an Orangutan"

Preview. Tell students that they are going to read a selection called "How to Babysit an Orangutan." Explain that this selection is nonfiction. Remind them that a nonfiction selection includes facts and details about a subject. It may also include photos with captions. Tell students that "How to Babysit an Orangutan" is about someone who takes care of baby orangutans in the rain forest when they are left without mothers. Then preview the selection.

LEAD THE WAY
pages 254–267

- **Pages 254–255:** I see the title and the names of the authors and photographers. The picture must be of an orangutan.

- **Pages 256–259:** The picture on page 256 shows a woman. I think she may be one of the orangutan babysitters. I notice that the other pictures on these pages have captions. The captions tell some of the things the babies like to do.

- **Pages 260–261:** The photographs show more baby orangutans. I see two things that the babies love to do—eat bananas and slurp soap. The picture at the top of page 261 shows a baby using a leaf to keep the rain off its head.

- **Pages 262–264:** The photographs show baby orangutans in the trees. The babies are climbing and hanging on a tree trunk. It looks like the babies sleep and play in the trees because the photograph on page 263 shows a baby learning to make a nest.

Set purpose. Model setting a purpose for reading the selection.

MODEL From what I have seen in my preview, I can see that I will probably learn how people take care of baby orangutans in the rain forest. I think I will also learn many things about how baby orangutans behave. I will read to find out how humans babysit orphaned orangutans.

Reread and Summarize

Have students reread and summarize "How to Babysit an Orangutan" in sections, as described in the chart below.

Pages 256–257

Let's reread pages 256–257 to recall why humans are needed to babysit some orangutans.

Summary: The mothers of some baby orangutans are killed. People need to take care of the babies and keep them safe from harm until they are old enough to care for themselves.

Page 258

Now let's read page 258 to find why people want to smuggle baby orangutans out of Borneo and Sumatra.

Summary: People think the apes are cute and would make good pets, so animal dealers can get a lot of money for them. Some of the babies are also put in the circus or private zoos, or they are used by movie trainers.

Pages 259–263

As we reread pages 259–263, let's find out some of the things babysitters must do for baby orangutans.

Summary: The babysitters feed, bathe, and play with the babies. They also help them develop balance and coordination so they can live in the trees where they belong.

Pages 264–265

Let's reread pages 264–265 to recall how adult orangutans help the babies.

Summary: Some adult orangutans come to visit the babies at the camp. They are good role models and teach the babies how to make nests in the trees.

FLUENCY BUILDER Be sure that students have a copy of the *Intervention Practice Book* page 39. Have students look at the sentences on the bottom half of the page. Tell students that their goal is to read each phrase or unit smoothly. Model appropriate phrasing, pace, and expression by reading each sentence and having students repeat it after you. Then call on each student individually to read selected sentences using the phrasing technique. Give students an opportunity to read their sentences more than once.

INTERVENTION PRACTICE BOOK

page 39

Directed Reading: "A Day with the Orangutans" pp. 78–85

MOVING
AHEAD
pp. 78–85

Pages 78–79

Ask a volunteer to read aloud the title. Help students identify the setting. Ask: **Where are the baby orangutans found?** (*up in trees; deep in the rain forest of Borneo*) **IMPORTANT DETAILS**

Ask: **Why are baby orangutans endangered?** (*Some are caught and sold as pets; some lose their parents to smugglers; some lose their homes when trees are cut down.*) **CAUSE/EFFECT**

Pages 80–81

Have students look at the photo on page 80. After they read, ask: **How are baby orangutans like human children? How are they different?** (*Possible response: Alike—They stay close to their moms. They depend on their moms for care and teaching. Different—They live in trees. They depend on their moms for only eight years.*) **COMPARE AND CONTRAST**

Ask: **Why shouldn't you try to coax a baby orangutan to come to you?** (*Orangutans like to be left alone.*) **CAUSE/EFFECT**

Ask: **How does a baby orangutan show it is upset?** (*It uses facial expressions, or it may throw a tantrum.*) **IMPORTANT DETAILS**

Pages 82–83

Have students read to find out what is special about an orangutan's hands and feet. Ask: **How do an orangutan's hands and feet help it in the rain forest?** (*They are just right for gripping tree branches.*) **NOTE DETAILS**

Ask: **Why is it important for orangutans to have good coordination?** (*Possible response: Orangutans need good coordination so they can swing in the treetops where they will be safe.*) (Focus Skill) **SUMMARIZE**

Ask a volunteer to read aloud page 83. Model using the use text structure and format strategy:

> **MODEL** I notice that the first sentence in the paragraph gives me a preview of what I will learn in the rest of the paragraph. This is the topic sentence. I see that the other sentences give details to support it. I think the author organized the story this way to help me remember what I am learning. (Focus Strategy) **USE TEXT STRUCTURE AND FORMAT**

Invite students to look at other paragraphs in the story to see if they are organized in the same way.

Page 84

INTERVENTION
PRACTICE
BOOK

page 41

Have students read page 84 to discover why some people want to save the rain forest of Borneo. Ask: **Why do some people care about the rain forest?** (*Possible response: They care about the orangutans that live in the forest.*) **CAUSE/EFFECT**

Then ask students to tell whether or not they think the rain forest should be protected, and why. (*Responses will vary.*) **MAKE JUDGMENTS/ EXPRESS PERSONAL OPINIONS**

Summarize the selection. Ask students to share the facts that they found most interesting about baby orangutans. Then have them complete *Intervention Practice Book* page 41 and summarize the selection.

Page 85

Answers to *Think About It* Questions

1. A baby orangutan lives with its mother for about eight years. It learns special skills such as building a nest. Its life is in danger from hunters. **SUMMARY**

2. Possible response: It makes the reader feel as if he or she is taking part in the adventure. It makes it more exciting. **INTERPRETATION**

3. Letters should describe the excitement of seeing orangutans in the rain forest. **WRITE A LETTER**

AFTER

Skill Review
pages 270–271

USE SKILL CARD 10B

(Focus Skill) **Summarize**

RETEACH the skill. Have students look at **side B of Skill Card 10: Summarize.** Read the skill reminder with them, and have a volunteer read the paragraph aloud. Encourage the rest of the group to listen for important information.

Read aloud the next set of directions. Allow students to work with a partner to create their own charts. Remind them to write one summary sentence for the box that has the most important idea.

After students have completed their work, allow some time for sharing. Invite them to explain why they filled in the charts as they did. Encourage them to refer to the paragraph when justifying their responses. Discuss any differences among students' charts.

FLUENCY BUILDER Be sure students have copies of *Intervention Practice Book* page 39. Have them work with a partner and practice reading the sentences to each other. Invite students to use expression when reading each sentence. Tell them to try experimenting with different emotions as they read. For example, they can read the first sentence as if they were excited, and then they could read it again as if they were sad. Remind students to try and improve their pacing and tone with each reading.

INTERVENTION PRACTICE BOOK

page 39

Expository Writing: Summary Sentence

Build on prior knowledge. Tell students that they are going to work together to write a summary sentence about the solar system. Explain that sometimes during a test, they may be given a specific length of time to complete their writing. Then explain that they will be using an idea web to organize the information. Display the following paragraph.

Our Solar System

Our solar system is made up of nine planets. All the planets orbit, or move around the sun. The Sun is the brightest and largest star in our solar system. It provides light and heat for Earth. There are many other stars in our solar system. Some of these stars are often viewed in groups called constellations.

Read the paragraph aloud, and clarify any unfamiliar vocabulary with students.

Construct the text. "Share the pen" with students in a collaborative writing effort. Guide students in using the information from the paragraph to complete an idea web and then to write a summary sentence.

- **What is the main topic of the paragraph?** (*the solar system*) Write it in the center of the idea web.

- Point out that the paragraph provides information about planets, the sun, and other stars. Guide students to add these three subtopics as spokes in the web.

- Help students pick out important information about planets, the sun, and other stars to include as notes in the three bubbles.

- Guide students in writing a sentence that summarizes the paragraph. Use the idea web for guidance.

Revisit the text. Go back and read the summary sentence together. Ask: **Is the main idea found in the summary sentence?**

- Guide students to check for beginning and end punctuation, spelling, and grammar to ensure that the text is clear.

- Have students read their sentences aloud.

On Your Own

Encourage students to select a paragraph from their social studies book. Tell them to create an idea web to organize the information from the paragraph.

AFTER

Spelling Lesson
pages 271G–271H

Connect Spelling and Phonics

RETEACH **long vowel /ō/ oa, ow.** Write the word *oats* on the board. Explain that you will say four words in which the /ō/ sound is spelled *oa*. Dictate words 1–4, and have students write them. After they write each one, display the correct word so students can proofread their work. Then write the word *slow* on the board, and tell students that in the last four words you say, the /ō/ sound is spelled *ow* as in *slow*. Dictate words 5–8, and have students proofread as before.

| 1. goal | 2. road* | 3. coax* | 4. roaming* |
| 5. own* | 6. throw* | 7. grown* | 8. yellow |

*****Word appears in "A Day with the Orangutans."**

Dictate the following sentence and have students write it: *A bowl of oatmeal will help you grow.*

Build and Read Longer Words

Remind students that they have learned to decode words with the long *o* vowel sound spelled *oa* and *ow*. Tell students that now they will use what they have learned to help them read some longer words.

Write the word *showtime* on the board. Remind students that when they come to a longer word, they should see if it is made up of two smaller words. Cover *time* and ask students to read the word *show*. Point out that *show* has the long *o* vowel sound spelled *ow*. Then cover the word *show* and have them read *time*. Draw your hand under the entire word as students read it aloud. Then write these words on the board: *tugboat*, *grown-up*, *snowball*, *goalkeeper*, *rainbow*, and *slowpoke*. Encourage students to read these words.

INTERVENTION
ASSESSMENT
BOOK

FLUENCY BUILDER Have students choose a passage from "A Day with the Orangutans" to read aloud to a partner. You may have students choose passages they found particularly interesting, or have them choose one of the following options:

- Read pages 79–80 of the selection. (Total: 96 words)
- Read pages 83–84. (Total: 117 words)

Students should read the selected passage aloud to their partners three times. Have the student rate his or her own reading on a scale from 1 to 4.

Vocabulary Review

Give each student two index cards with the letter *A* on one card and the letter *B* on the other. Then read each of the following sentence starters followed by the two ending choices. Invite students to hold up the card that represents the choice that makes the most sense to complete the statement. Discuss each sentence and have students justify their answers.

I. If your mother's face showed **displeasure**, she would be
   a. smiling.
   b. frowning.

2. **Facial** hair is located on your
   a. arms and legs.
   b. face.

3. An **endangered** animal would be
   a. protected and left in the wild.
   b. hunted for pleasure.

4. If a child feels **jealous** about another child's toy, he would
   a. throw a tantrum and be upset.
   b. smile and offer hugs and kisses.

5. A sign of good **coordination** would be
   a. tripping over a crack in the sidewalk.
   b. walking on a beam with a book on your head.

6. If a criminal **smuggled** an item into the room, she would
   a. carry it proudly for everyone to see.
   b. hide it in her coat.

Correct Responses: Ib, 2b, 3a, 4a, 5b, 6b.

(Focus Skill) Summarize

INTERVENTION
PRACTICE
BOOK

page 42

To review summarizing before the weekly assessment, distribute *Intervention Practice Book* page 42. Select a volunteer to read the paragraph. Ask students to summarize the information from the paragraph and help them complete the chart. Review that a summary includes only the most important information and that it is written in the student's own words.

Review Test Prep

INTERVENTION
ASSESSMENT
BOOK

✓

Ask students to turn to page 271 of the *Pupil Edition*. Call attention to the tips for answering the test questions. Tell students that paying attention to these tips can help them answer not only the test questions on this page but also other test questions like these. Point out that the title is one clue to the main idea of the passage. Also note that the sentences in the passage are details that support this main idea.

LEAD
THE WAY

page 271

Self-Selected Reading

Have students select their own books to read independently. They might choose books from the classroom library shelf, or you may wish to offer a group of appropriate books from which students can choose.

- *Animal Fact/Animal Fable* by Seymour Simon. Crown, 1987

- *Snakes are Hunters* by Patricia Lauber. HarperCollins, 1988

- *Trees and Plants in the Rain Forest* by Saviour Pirotta. Steck-Vaughn, 1999

You may also wish to choose additional books that are the same genre or by the same author, or that have the same kind of text structure as the selection.

After students have chosen their books, give each student a copy of My Reading Log, which can be found on page R38 in the back of the *Teacher's Edition*. Have students fill in the information at the top of the form. Then have them use the log to keep track of their reading and to record their responses to the literature.

Conduct student-teacher conferences. Arrange time for each student to meet with you individually about his or her self-selected reading. Have students bring their Reading Logs to the conference. Begin the conference by posing a question to students that will spark a discussion, or by inviting students to share ideas they have about what they read. You may also focus on the text structure to provide students with additional instruction on a particular genre.

FLUENCY PERFORMANCE Invite students to read aloud the passage that they have selected from "A Day with the Orangutans." As they read, keep track of the number of words each student reads correctly. Ask the student to rate his or her own performance on the 1 to 4 scale. If students are not happy with their oral reading, give them an opportunity to continue practicing and then read the passage to you again.

See *Oral Reading Fluency Assessment* for monitoring progress.

Use with

"Sarah, Plain and Tall"

Review Phonics: *R*-controlled Vowels /ôr/*or, oor, ore, oar, our*

Identify the sound. Have students repeat the following questions aloud three times: *Can you ignore the storm's roar? Will the rain pour in the worn door?* Have students identify the words that have the /ôr/ sound. (*ignore, storm's, roar, pour, worn, door*)

Associate letters to sound. Write the questions from above on the board. Underline the letters *ore, or, oar, our,* and *oor* in the words in which they appear. Tell students that when one of these groups of letters appears in a word, the letters often stand for the /ôr/ sound they hear in *roar.*

Word blending. Write *fort* on the board. Model blending letters and sounds to read *fort.* Touch *f* and say /f/. Draw your hand under *or* and say /ôr/. Touch *t* and say /t/. Slide your hand under the whole word as you elongate the sounds /ffôrt/. Then read the word naturally—*fort.* Repeat the process for *gourd, store, board,* and *floor.*

INTERVENTION
PRACTICE
BOOK

page 44

Apply the skill. *Letter Substitution* Write the following words on the board, and have students read each aloud. Make the changes necessary to form the words in parentheses. Have a volunteer read aloud each word.

flop (floor)	**barn** (born)	**roam** (roar)	**farm** (form)
share (shore)	**spot** (sport)	**boat** (boar)	**cart** (court)

Introduce Vocabulary

PRETEACH **lesson vocabulary.** Tell students that they are going to learn five new words that they will see again when they read "Sarah, Plain and Tall." Teach each Vocabulary Word using the following process.

Use the following suggestions or similar ideas to give the meaning or context.

> Write the word.
> Say the word.
> Track the word and have students repeat it.
> Give the meaning or context.

windbreak	Relate to a "windbreaker" jacket. Tall trees can "break" or stop the wind.
rustle	Rhymes with *muscle.* Rub palms together to make a rustling sound.
alarmed	Point out the *-ed* ending. Relate to the feeling students get when they hear a fire alarm or alarm clock.
paddock	Show a picture of a fenced-in area. Relate to a farm.

conch   Can be pronounced /känk/ or
               /känch/. Relate to other shells or
               items found in or near the
               ocean.

For vocabulary activities, see Vocabulary Games on pages 2–7.

Building Background and Vocabulary

Apply Vocabulary Strategies

Use familiar word parts. Write the word *windbreak* on chart paper. Tell students that they can sometimes figure out the meanings of words by looking for smaller words that make up a larger word. Model using the strategy.

> **MODEL** When I read the compound word *windbreak*, I notice two smaller words, *wind* and *break*. I know *wind* can blow things and that *break* is a word that can mean "end" or "stop." I think *windbreak* must mean "something that stops the wind."

Guide students in using a similar procedure to determine the meanings of other words.

RETEACH **lesson vocabulary.** Read each of these statements aloud. Have students answer *true* or *false* to each statement. Then have them give reasons for their answers by discussing the meanings of the Vocabulary Words.

    1. A person could get **alarmed** if caught outside in a thunderstorm. (*true*)

    2. You would find a **conch** on a mountain. (*false*)

    3. You could raise pet mice in a **paddock**. (*false*)

    4. A **windbreak** would provide shade on a sunny day. (*true*)

    5. Curtains can **rustle** in the breeze. (*true*)

Vocabulary Words

windbreak row of trees used to block the wind

rustle a soft sound made by things rubbing together

alarmed frightened or worried

paddock a fenced-in piece of land usually used for grazing horses

conch large spiral shell

FLUENCY BUILDER Distribute *Intervention Practice Book* page 43. Read each word in the first column aloud and have students echo the word after you read it. Repeat this procedure with each of the other two columns. Then have each student practice reading aloud the words in each column separately while you listen. Finally, have each student practice reading the whole list aloud.

INTERVENTION PRACTICE BOOK

page 43

BEFORE

Reading "Sarah,
Plain and Tall"
pages 276–287

USE SKILL CARD 11A

⭐ (Focus Skill) Draw Conclusions

PRETEACH the skill. Help students understand that they can use their own experiences to help them figure something out. Ask them to tell what game they would be playing in gym class if they saw this equipment set up: ball, bat, bases. (*baseball; softball*) Discuss how students were able to draw that conclusion.

Have students look at **side A of Skill Card 11: Draw Conclusions.** Read the definition. Then, read the passage aloud as students follow along. Discuss the story information and the personal experiences of the students that help them figure out where Meg and Dad are going.

Draw attention to the chart and have students take turns reading the information in each box aloud. Ask:

- **How do your experiences relate to the story information?** (*Possible response: They help you picture something that you might have already done or read about before.*)

- **What other conclusions could you draw about Meg and Dad?** (*They have fun together. They both enjoy camping.*)

Explain to students that using prior experiences and story information will help them draw conclusions about what they read.

Prepare to Read: "Sarah, Plain and Tall"

Preview. Tell students that they are going to read a selection called "Sarah, Plain and Tall." Explain that it is historical fiction. In historical fiction, the characters are not real people, but the times and places mentioned in the story actually did exist. Tell students that they will be reading about a family that lived on a farm over a century ago. Then preview the selection.

LEAD THE WAY

pages 276–287

- **Pages 276–279:** I see the title, "Sarah, Plain and Tall," and the name of the author. The clothes on the people in the picture seem to be from long ago.

- **Pages 280–283:** On page 281 there is a woman showing the little boy a seashell. On pages 282 and 283, I see pictures of the ocean and a conch shell. I wonder what these pictures have to do with life on a prairie farm?

- **Pages 284–287:** The picture of the flowers on page 284 is on the wall in the big picture on page 285. It looks like the boy is dancing while his family watches.

Set purpose. Model setting a purpose for reading "Sarah, Plain and Tall."

MODEL From my preview, I know that the story will be about the experiences of a family that lived on a farm on the prairie. I will read to find out what it was like to live on a prairie farm in the past.

Reread and Summarize

Have students reread and summarize "Sarah, Plain and Tall" in sections, as described in the chart below.

Pages 276–279

Let's reread pages 276–279 to recall how Caleb and Anna feel about Sarah coming to visit.

Summary: Caleb and Anna are nervous about meeting Sarah. They busy themselves by doing their chores as they anxiously wait for Papa to return with Sarah.

Pages 280–281

Now let's reread page 280 to find out what Sarah does when she first arrives.

Summary: She lets her cat out of its case and then gives Caleb something from the sea—a shell.

Pages 282–283

As we reread pages 282 and 283, let's recall how the prairie reminds Sarah of her home in Maine.

Summary: The rolling prairie grass makes Sarah think of the ocean waves near her home.

Pages 284–285

Let's reread page 284 to recall how the story ends.

Summary: Sarah decorates their home with flowers, and now the children are pretty sure that Sarah will marry their Papa and become their new mother.

FLUENCY BUILDER Be sure students have copies of *Intervention Practice Book* page 43. Have students locate the sentences on the bottom half of the page. Model the appropriate pace and expression as you read the marked phrases in each sentence. Have students echo your reading style. Then have students reread sentences until fluency is gained.

INTERVENTION PRACTICE BOOK

page 43

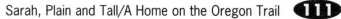

Directed Reading: "A Home on the Oregon Trail," pp. 86–92

Pages 86–87

Ask a volunteer to read the title of the story. Help students identify Kate, Jed, and the traveler. After students read page 86, ask: **How is Kate feeling, and why?** (*Possible response: She feels lonely because she misses the sea and her old home.*) **IDENTIFY CHARACTERS' EMOTIONS**

MOVING
AHEAD
pp. 86–92

Have students read page 87. Ask: **Who comes to visit the family?** (*Patrick Guthrey, a traveling man who takes pictures*) Ask: **How does Kate feel about the visitor? How do you know?** (*Possible response: She is happy to see him. She welcomes him and smiles.*) **DETERMINE CHARACTERS' EMOTIONS**

Pages 88–89

Have students read the first paragraph on page 88. Ask: **Why do you think Kate's parents were pleased to meet Patrick?** (*From the story I know travelers are welcome on the trail. From my own experience I know most people treat their guests courteously.*) (Focus Skill) **DRAW CONCLUSIONS**

Have students read the rest of page 88 and 89. Ask: **Why does Patrick run back into the house alarmed?** Model using the read ahead strategy:

> **MODEL** To find out why Patrick is alarmed, I can read ahead to find the reason. I read that there is a grass fire. I know I would be alarmed if I spied a fire, so that must be why Patrick is alarmed. (Focus Strategy) **READ AHEAD**

Have students reread the last paragraph on page 89 to identify the sentence that states the cause of the glow outside. Ask: **What does the family do after they learn about the fire?** (*The men try to beat back the fire while the others try to save their possessions and the animals.*) **SEQUENCE**

Pages 90–91

Have students read page 90. Ask: **What damage does the fire do?** (*Possible response: It blackens all the landscape, but does not damage the home.*) **DRAW CONCLUSIONS**

INTERVENTION
PRACTICE
BOOK

page 45

Have students read page 91 to find out how the story ends. Ask: **Why does Kate think the visit was perfect?** (*Possible response: She has a new friend.*) **DRAW CONCLUSIONS**

Summarize the selection. Ask students to think about the events that happened in "A Home on the Oregon Trail." Then have them complete *Intervention Practice Book* page 45.

Answers to *Think About It* Questions

1. Patrick travels the Oregon Trail, taking pictures. He goes to Kate's home to see if the family wants to pose for a portrait. **SUMMARY**

2. They have not had visitors for a long time and they miss their friends in Baltimore. **INTERPRETATION**

3. Lists and paragraphs should show student's understanding of Kate as lonely and sad at first, but happier at the end. **WRITE LISTS AND PARAGRAPHS**

(Focus Skill) Draw Conclusions

RETEACH the skill. Have students look at **side B of Skill Card 11: Draw Conclusions.** Read the skill reminder with them, and then have a volunteer read the passage aloud.

Read aloud the next set of directions. Explain that students can now create their own chart like the one on the card. Instruct them to fill in information from the story and their own experiences and to draw a conclusion about what the boys are doing.

After students complete their charts, have them take turns reading the information they wrote in each box. Ask them to explain how this information helped them figure out that Jake and Jimmy were going on a long bike ride.

FLUENCY BUILDER Be sure students have copies of *Intervention Practice Book* page 43. Explain that students will work as pairs to practice aloud the sentences on the bottom half of the page. Assign one student to be the Reader and one student to be the Listener. Tell the Reader to read a sentence aloud three times and self-evaluate his or her reading. After the third reading, the Listener notes how the reader improved. The Reader and Listener switch roles after each sentence.

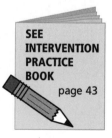

SEE INTERVENTION PRACTICE BOOK page 43

Informative Writing: Cause-and-Effect Statement

Build on prior knowledge. Have students think about what it would be like to move to a new town. Recreate this chart on the board and ask students to read the effects this change would bring about. Add their ideas to the chart.

Cause	Effects
Move to a new town	Find a place to live
	Go to a different school
	Make new friends

Remind students that one cause can have more than one effect. Encourage students to add other effects to the chart.

Construct the text. "Share the pen" with students in a collaborative group writing effort. Guide them to combine a cause and one of the effects from the chart. Use these steps to think aloud the process:

- Write the cause and write one effect from the chart.

- Then combine these two sentences into one sentence.

- Add phrases and words like *as a result* and *because* to join the two sentences.

Have students read the sentence aloud and then write it on paper.

Revisit the text. Invite students to review their cause-and-effect statement. Encourage them to check the draft for spelling, grammar, and punctuation errors. When they are satisfied with their sentence, call on a volunteer to write the final draft of the cause-and-effect sentence on the chart.

On Your Own

Ask students to pretend that an older relative or a new baby comes to live in their home. Tell them to write three sentences that tell about the effects this change would have on them and their family.

Connect Spelling and Phonics

RETEACH **R-controlled vowels /ôr/ *or, oor, ore, oar, our.*** Write the words *store, roar, bore,* and *floor* on the board. Ask students what these four words have in common. (the /ôr/ sound)

Have students number a sheet of paper 1–8. Write *port* on the board, and tell students that in the first two words you will say, the /ôr/ sound is spelled *or* as in *port.* Dictate words 1–2, and have students write them. After they write each one, display the correct spelling so students can proofread their work. Follow the same procedure for the remaining words below by writing *store, soar, floor,* or *pour* on the board before dictating the words with the matching spelling of /ôr/.

1. porch*	2. thorn	3. wore*	4. before*
5. roared*	6. door	7. your*	8. court

*Word appears in "A Home on the Oregon Trail."

Dictate the following sentence and have students write it: *Store the food for your horse behind the door.*

Build and Read Longer Words

Remind students that they have learned how to decode words with the /ôr/ sound spelled *or, oor, ore, oar,* and *our.* Explain that now they will use what they have learned to help them read some longer words.

Write these words on the board: *forbid, yourself, shoreline, flooring, boarder.* Ask students to identify which letters stand for the /ôr/ sound in each word. Explain that when the letters *or, our, ore, oor,* or *oar* stand for the /ôr/ sound, these letter combinations usually stay together when the word is divided into syllables. Model dividing *forbid* into syllables. Frame *for* and read it aloud; frame *bid* and read it aloud; then read the entire word. Call on students to read aloud the remaining words and to tell how they were able to figure them out.

INTERVENTION ASSESSMENT BOOK

FLUENCY BUILDER Have students choose a passage from "A Home on the Oregon Trail" to read aloud to a partner. You may have students choose passages that they found particularly interesting, or have them choose one of the following options:

- Read all of page 86 and the first paragraph on page 87. (From *Kate felt . . . through . . . needs a meal.* Total: 104 words)

- Read all of page 90 and the first two paragraphs of page 91. (From *Then everyone . . .* through *. . . share our harvest?* Total: 102 words)

Have students read the selected passage aloud to their partners three times. Have the student rate his or her own reading on a scale of 1 to 4.

Vocabulary Review

To revisit Vocabulary Words prior to the weekly assessment, use these sentence frames. Have volunteers take turns reading aloud the sentence stems and choices. Students identify the correct choice and explain why that choice makes sense in the sentence.

1. A **windbreak** might protect a house from
   a. waves.   b. strong winds.

2. If you hear a **rustle**, you are hearing something that is
   a. loud.   b. soft.

3. If you are **alarmed** about something, you are
   a. worried.   b. excited.

4. If a horse gets out of the **paddock**, it means
   a. the fence was closed.   b. the fence was left open.

5. A **conch** is likely to be found on a
   a. beach.   b. mountain.

Correct responses: lb, 2b, 3a, 4b, 5a.

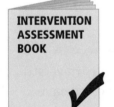

INTERVENTION PRACTICE BOOK

page 46

(Focus Skill) Review Draw Conclusions

To review the focus skill of drawing conclusions, distribute *Intervention Practice Book* page 46. Have volunteers read the passage aloud. Then have students list story information and personal experiences in the chart that help them draw the conclusion that Hannah is afraid of the water and is trying to teach herself how to swim.

Review Test Prep

Ask students to turn to page 299 of the *Pupil Edition*. Call attention to the tips for answering test questions. Remind students that the conclusions they draw about passages they read should make sense and come from information in the story and facts that they already know. Tell students to apply these tips to test questions like the ones found on this page.

LEAD THE WAY

page 299

Read aloud the passage. Then have students follow along as you read aloud each test question and the tip that goes with it. Discuss students' feelings before they answer question 1. Then have students identify story information that can help them figure out the answer to question 2.

INTERVENTION ASSESSMENT BOOK

Self-Selected Reading

Have students select their own books to read independently. They might choose books from the classroom library shelf, or you may wish to offer a group of appropriate books from which students can choose.

- *Everett Anderson's Friend* by Lucille Clifton. Henry Holt, 1976

- *Hey, New Kid!* by Betsy Duffey. Viking Penguin, 1996

- *Too Many Tamales* by Gary Soto. Putnam, 1993

You may also wish to choose additional books that are the same genre or by the same author, or that have the same kind of text structure as the selection.

After students have chosen their books, give each student a copy of My Reading Log, which can be found on page R38 in the back of the *Teacher's Edition*. Have students fill in the information at the top of the form. Then have them use the log to keep track of their reading and to record their responses to the literature.

Conduct student-teacher conferences. Schedule time to meet with each student individually to discuss his or her self-selected reading and Reading Log. Have students choose a passage from their book to read aloud to you and then summarize what their book was about. Ask questions about the book designed to stimulate discussion. For example, you might ask about how the setting in the book compares to your own community, facts students learned from reading nonfiction books, or how illustrations helped students understand the plot of the story.

FLUENCY PERFORMANCE Ask students to read their selected passages from "A Home on the Oregon Trail" aloud to you. Keep a record of the number of words the student reads correctly. Have the student rate his or her own performance using the 1 to 4 scale. Give students who are not satisfied with their oral reading another opportunity to read their passage aloud to you after they have practiced it several more times.

See *Oral Reading Fluency Assessment* for monitoring progress.

BEFORE

Building
Background
and Vocabulary

Use with

"Stealing Home"

Review Phonics: *R*-controlled Vowels /ûr/*er, ear, ur, or, ir*

Identify the sound. Have students repeat the following limerick three times: *There once was a pearl with a curl. / It was seen by a sweet young girl. / She went to work / in a shop as a clerk / so she could buy that colorful swirl.* Ask students to identify the words that have the same vowel sound as in *twirl.* (*pearl, curl, girl, work, clerk, colorful, swirl*)

Associate letters to sound. Write the limerick from above on the board. Underline the letters that stand for the /ûr/ sound: p<u>ear</u>l, c<u>ur</u>l, g<u>ir</u>l, w<u>or</u>k, cl<u>er</u>k, col<u>or</u>ful, sw<u>ir</u>l. Tell students that the underlined letters can all stand for the /ûr/ sound they hear in *word.*

Word blending. Model how to blend and read *swirl.* Slide your hand under the whole word as you read it aloud, elongating the sounds: /sswwûrll/. Then say the word naturally—*swirl.*

Apply the skill. *Letter Substitution* Write these words on the board, and have students read each aloud. Make the changes necessary to form the words in parentheses. Have a volunteer read aloud each new word.

INTERVENTION
PRACTICE
BOOK

page 48

still (stir)	**parson** (person)	**chip** (chirp)	**hen** (her)	**peck** (perk)
peel (pearl)	**lunch** (lurch)	**blunt** (blurt)	**lean** (learn)	**warm** (worm)

Introduce Vocabulary

PRETEACH **lesson vocabulary.** Tell students that they are going to learn eight new words that they will see again when they read a story called "Stealing Home." Teach each Vocabulary Word using the following process.

Use the following suggestions or similar ideas to give the meaning or context.

pastimes	Relate to fun ways of passing time such as sports, reading, and crafts.
tutor	Explain that some teachers tutor, or teach students individually, after school.
disposition	Relate to words like *cheerful, grumpy, mean.*
glumly	Point out the suffix. Make a gloomy face.
irritably	Relate to how students act when they don't get enough sleep.

> Write the word.
>
> Say the word.
>
> Track the word and have students repeat it.
>
> Give the meaning or context.

bicker	Relate to students arguing with a brother or sister.
impose	Explain that to impose makes someone else's life more difficult, for example, asking a friend to do your chores.
grudge	Point out the final /j/ sound. Relate to not being able to forgive.

For vocabulary activities, see Vocabulary Games on pages 2–7.

Vocabulary Words

pastimes pleasant ways of passing time

tutor to teach privately

disposition one's usual way of acting; temperament

glumly in a gloomy way

irritably grumpily, crossly

bicker to disagree in a quarrelsome way

impose to put an unwanted burden on

grudge ill will toward someone

AFTER

Building Background and Vocabulary

Apply Vocabulary Strategies

Use sentence and word context. Write this sentence on the board: *My brother and I always bicker and yell about who gets to go first.* Remind students that when they come to an unfamiliar word, they can look at the rest of the sentence to figure out its meaning. Model using the strategy.

> **MODEL** The word *bicker* doesn't look familiar. When I read the rest of the sentence, it says that the speaker and the brother "yell about who gets to go first." That's what my brother and I used to fight or argue about. *Bicker* must mean "to argue."

Guide students to use this strategy for other unfamiliar words.

RETEACH lesson vocabulary. Have students complete each sentence with their own ending. Then discuss how the Vocabulary Word in each sentence influenced their choice of endings.

1. Will held a **grudge** against his sister because _____ .
2. Kate will **impose** on Jill when she asks her to _____ .
3. Juan sat inside **glumly** looking outside at _____ .
4. My grandfather and I share the favorite **pastime** of _____ .
5. I need you to **tutor** me in _____ .
6. The woman and the clerk began to **bicker** about _____ .
7. Her cheerful **disposition** is perfect for the job of _____ .
8. The tired athlete talked **irritably** about _____ .

FLUENCY BUILDER Distribute *Intervention Practice Book* page 47. Read each word in the first column aloud, and have students repeat it three times after you say it. Repeat this procedure with each of the other two columns. Then have partners take turns reading aloud the words in each column and listening for increased speed on each reading.

INTERVENTION PRACTICE BOOK

page 47

(Focus Skill) Compare and Contrast

PRETEACH **the skill.** Display a pencil and piece of chalk. Ask students to compare these two items. Explain that when they read they should think about how the narrative elements are alike and different.

Have students look at **side A of Skill Card 12: Compare and Contrast.** Read the definitions of *compare* and *contrast*. Next, read the passage aloud as students follow along. Discuss how the twins in the passage are alike and different.

Point to the chart. Ask:

■ **What words help you know the ways in which the girls are alike?** (*both* and *also*)

■ **What words help you know the ways in which the girls are different?** (*rather* and *but*)

Explain to students that comparing and contrasting can help them better understand the characters, settings, and plot of a story.

Prepare to Read: "Stealing Home"

Preview. Tell students that they are going to read a realistic fiction story, "Stealing Home." Explain that the characters are not real, but the events could really happen. Tell them that the story is about a boy, his grandfather, and a person who moves into their home. Then preview the selection.

LEAD
THE WAY
pages
302–318

■ **Pages 302–305:** I see the title and the name of the author. "Stealing home" is a term used in baseball. I see from the picture on page 302 that a cat and a woman are in this story. It looks like two boys are talking to each other.

■ **Pages 306–315:** On page 306 I read the quote, "She's cleaning the whole place." I wonder if the woman is doing a good or a bad thing. The quote on page 309 says " . . . two strikes, a man on first with two out . . ." Here is another mention of baseball. The people on pages 310 and 311 look angry. The quotes on pages 313 and 314 make me think the woman is neat and a good cook.

■ **Pages 316–318:** On pages 316–317, the boy is playing a game of Scrabble with the older man. The cat from the first page is all curled up and sleeping on page 318. The cat looks peaceful.

Set Purpose. Model setting a purpose for reading "Stealing Home."

MODEL From my preview, I know that I will be reading about how the lives of a boy and his grandfather change when a woman comes to live with them. My purpose for reading will be to find out how the boy's life changes and how he learns to live with these changes.

Reread and Summarize

Have students reread and summarize "Stealing Home" in sections, as described in the chart below.

Pages 302–308

Let's reread pages 302–308 to recall what happens when Aunt Linzy first moves in.

Summary: Aunt Linzy takes over Thomas's room and moves many boxes into his home. She cleans the house and disturbs the games that Thomas and Grandfather like to play. Thomas talks to his friend Donny about how unhappy he is with the situation.

Pages 309–312

Now let's reread pages 309–312 to find out how Aunt Linzy uses baseball to annoy Grandfather and Thomas.

Summary: She tries to learn about baseball terms and teams, but she gets them confused. Grandfather and Thomas think she might be making fun of their favorite pastime.

Pages 313–314

As we reread pages 313–314, let's recall what Aunt Linzy does to make life more pleasant for Grandfather and Thomas.

Summary: She irons for them and sews new curtains and slipcovers. She is cheerful and is a very good cook.

Pages 315–318

Let's reread pages 315–318 to recall first how Thomas disappoints Grandfather and then how they both feel about Aunt Linzy in the end.

Summary: Grandfather thinks Thomas is being selfish about not being able to appreciate Aunt Linzy. He thinks Thomas needs to care more about her even if it changes the way Thomas has to live. Thomas admits that he will try harder and begins to see that change can be good.

FLUENCY BUILDER Be sure students have copies of *Intervention Practice Book* page 47. Have students identify the sentences on the bottom half of the page. Model appropriate pace, expression, and phrasing as you read, and have students echo each sentence after you. Then have pairs of students practice reading each sentence aloud together three times.

INTERVENTION PRACTICE BOOK

page 47

Directed Reading: "Sisters Forever," pp. 94–101

MOVING
AHEAD
pp. 94–101

Pages 94–95

Read the title of the story aloud. Point out that the girl in the illustration on pages 94–95 is Pearl, the main character. Draw students' attention to the photograph Pearl is looking at. Have students read page 94 to find out who is shown in the photograph. Ask: **How does Pearl feel about having a new stepsister? How can you tell?** (*Possible responses: She is not happy about it. She looks around glumly and makes sarcastic comments.*) **DETERMINE CHARACTERS' EMOTIONS**

Have students read page 95 to find out what happens when Pearl and LaVerne meet. (*Pearl thinks they have very different interests.*) Ask: **What are Pearl's opinions of LaVerne based on?** (*the way she looks*) **GENERALIZE**

Pages 96–97

Have students read the first paragraph on page 96. Ask: **What does it mean in the text when it says that LaVerne "cluttered the tidy shelf?"** Model using the use context to confirm meaning strategy:

> **MODEL** At first, I am not sure what *cluttered* means. It either means the same as or the opposite of *tidy*. Since the text says LaVerne put all of her books and possessions on one shelf, that would be a lot of things in a small space. *Cluttered* must mean the opposite of *tidy*, "to make messy." ★(Focus Strategy) **USE CONTEXT TO CONFIRM MEANING**

Ask students to describe the scene on pages 96–97, including the characters' moods. Then have them read the rest of page 96 and page 97. Ask: **How does LaVerne feel about Pearl?** (*no better than Pearl feels about her*) **DETERMINE CHARACTERS' EMOTIONS**

Ask: **Why do you think this is?** (*Possible response: Since Pearl does not like LaVerne, she is probably not treating her very well. This makes LaVerne dislike Pearl.*) **CAUSE/EFFECT**

Pages 98–99

After students read page 98, ask: **Why does Pearl sneak out when she goes to play soccer?** (*She does not want LaVerne to know she is going.*) **INTERPRET CHARACTERS' MOTIVATIONS**

Have students read page 99 to find out what happens next. Ask: **What activities do both girls like?** (*They both like sports and reading.*) ★(Focus Skill) **COMPARE AND CONTRAST**

Ask: **Do you think LaVerne and Pearl will become friends? Why or why not?** (*Possible response: Yes, because they are realizing that they have many things in common.*) **MAKE PREDICTIONS**

Page 100

INTERVENTION
PRACTICE
BOOK

page 49

Have students read page 100 to check their predictions. Ask: **Do you think the girls are becoming friends? How can you tell?** (*Yes, they joke and laugh together. They begin to like being sisters.*) **INTERPRET STORY EVENTS**

What is the message of the story? (*Possible response: Do not judge people too quickly.*) **INTERPRET THEME**

Summarize the selection. Ask students to think about the relationship between Pearl and LaVerne throughout "Sisters Forever." Then have them complete *Intervention Practice Book* page 49.

Page 101

Answers to *Think About It* Questions

1. LaVerne is Pearl's stepsister. She is spending the summer with Pearl. **SUMMARY**

2. Possible response: Pearl doesn't think that a girl with long, curly hair and lots of stuffed toys could be interested in sports. **INTERPRETATION**

3. The first paragraph should describe such similarities as the girls' interest in sports, reading, and games. The second paragraph should describe the differences in the girls' appearance; it might also mention that they live most of the year in different places. **WRITE PARAGRAPHS**

AFTER

Skill Review
pages 324–325

USE SKILL CARD 12B

⭐ (Focus Skill) Compare and Contrast

Have students look at **side B of Skill Card 12: Compare and Contrast.** Read the skill reminder with them, and have a volunteer read the passage aloud. Then have students take turns identifying ways that the city and country are alike and different.

Read aloud the next set of directions. Explain that students can now create their own chart like the one on the card. Remind them to list words and phrases from the text that describe how the city and country are alike and different.

After students finish their compare and contrast charts, have them take turns reading the information they wrote in each box.

FLUENCY BUILDER Be sure students have copies of *Intervention Practice Book* page 47. Explain that students will use buddy reading to practice the sentences on the bottom half of the page. Tell partners to take turns reading aloud alternate sentences three times each. When they finish, each person rereads the other sentences. Tell pairs to concentrate on their phrasing, pacing, and tone.

INTERVENTION
PRACTICE
BOOK

page 47

Stealing Home/Sisters Forever **123**

Expository Writing: How-to Paragraph

Build on prior knowledge. Tell students that together they are going to write a paragraph that explains how to play kickball. Ask what a person would need to know to play the game. Write their suggestions on the board. A model is shown as an example.

> Pick two teams.
>
> One team plays the outfield. The other team kicks.
>
> The pitcher rolls a ball to the kicker.
>
> The kicker kicks the ball out into the field.
>
> Kicker tries to run the bases while other team tries to tag the kicker out.
>
> There are three outs in one inning and nine innings.

Construct the text. "Share the pen" with students in a collaborative group writing effort. Guide them in using the suggestions and these steps to create a group paragraph that explains the process of playing kickball.

- Write an opening sentence that tells the reader what the process is about.

- Use a variety of sentence structures such as imperative, exclamatory, simple, and compound.

- Present the information in a logical order and use signal words such as *first, next,* and *finally*.

- Conclude by stating the desired outcome of the process, such as the team that crosses home plate most often wins.

Revisit the text. Have students read the completed draft aloud. As they read the paragraph, invite them to check for and correct any errors in grammar, usage, punctuation, and spelling.

On Your Own

Tell students to write steps that explain how to play their favorite game. Tell them to remember to include a title, an opening sentence, what happens in the game, and a closing sentence.

Connect Spelling and Phonics

RETEACH *R*-controlled vowels /ûr/*er, ear, ur, or, ir.* Write the word *bird* on the board, and tell students that in the first two words you will say, the /ûr/ sound is spelled *ir* as in *bird*. Dictate words 1–2, and have students write them on the board. After they write each one, write the correct spelling on the board so students can proofread their work. Follow the same procedure by writing *curb, her, word,* or *earn* on the board before dictating every two words below that have the matching spelling for /ûr/ .

1. dirt	2. girls*	3. burn	4. turn	5. clerk
6. herd	7. worse	8. world	9. learn	10. pearl*

*Word appears in "Stealing Home."

Dictate the following sentence and have students write it: *On Thursday, Mr. Sherman's third graders wore purple shirts.*

Build and Read Longer Words

INTERVENTION
ASSESSMENT
BOOK

Write the word *turkey* on the board. Ask students to identify the letters that stand for the /ûr/ sound. (*ur*) Remind students that in words in which *er, ear, ur, or,* or *ir* stand for the /ûr/ sound, these combinations of letters usually stay together when a word is broken into syllables. Frame *tur* and have students read it aloud. Do the same for *key.* Then draw your hand under the entire word as students read it aloud. Follow a similar procedure for *earnest, kernel, personnel, twirling, turnpike, workshop,* and *perfect.*

FLUENCY BUILDER Have students choose a passage from "Sisters Forever" to read aloud while a classmate tape-records them. Students may choose passages that they found particularly interesting, or have them choose one of the following options:

- Read all of page 95, and the first paragraph on page 96. (*From All the way . . .* through . . . *her possessions.* Total: 125 words)

- Read page 98. (From *The next morning . . .* through . . . *stuffed toys.* Total: 89 words)

Students read the selected passage aloud to their partners three times. Have the student rate his or her own readings on a scale from 1 to 4. After the third reading, have students listen to the readings on tape and note improvements from the first to the last reading.

Vocabulary Review

Have students demonstrate an understanding of the Vocabulary Words. First have them give a definition. Then students should answer the question that uses the word. Use these ideas as examples:

1. What are your favorite **pastimes**?
2. What subject could you **tutor**?
3. How would you describe the **disposition** of someone in your family?
4. What would cause you to act **glumly**?
5. With whom do you **bicker**?
6. Have you ever held a **grudge**? Why?
7. Have you ever **imposed** on a member of your family?
8. What do you do when you act **irritably**? Tell about it.

(Focus Skill) Review Compare and Contrast

INTERVENTION
PRACTICE
BOOK

page 50

To review the focus skill of compare and contrast, distribute *Intervention Practice Book* page 50. Have volunteers read the passage aloud. Then guide students to look for signal words like *both* and *instead* to help them find ways that desert animals and arctic animals are alike and different. Have students record these comparisons and contrasts in the appropriate boxes in the chart.

Review Test Prep

Ask students to turn to page 325 of the *Pupil Edition*. Point out the tips for answering test questions. Explain that following these tips will help them answer test questions about comparing and contrasting characters, events, and settings.

LEAD
THE WAY

page 325

INTERVENTION
ASSESSMENT
BOOK

Have students follow along as you read aloud each test question and the tip that goes with it. Point out that the tip for question 1 tells students how to look for differences between two characters. Then ask students how they would create a diagram that shows how "Stealing Home" and the story on this page are alike and different to help them answer question 2.

Self-Selected Reading

Have students select their own books to read independently. They might choose books from the classroom library shelf, or you may wish to offer a group of appropriate books from which students can choose.

- *Tanya's Reunion* by Valerie Flournoy. Dial, 1995

- *Zinnia and Dot* by Lisa Campbell Ernst. Viking Penguin, 1992

- *Arctic Son* by Jean Craighead George. Hyperion, 1997

You may also wish to choose additional books that are realistic fiction, contain similar themes, or provide opportunities for students to practice comparing and contrasting characters or settings.

After students have chosen their books, give each student a copy of My Reading Log, which can be found on page R38 in the back of the *Teacher's Edition*. Have students fill in the information at the top of the form. Then have them use the log to keep track of their reading and to record their responses to the literature.

Conduct student-teacher conferences. Arrange a conference with each student to discuss his or her self-selected reading and Reading Log. Suggest that students choose a passage from their book to read aloud to you and then summarize what their book was about. Ask questions about the book that will prompt students to compare and contrast the setting or characters in the story to places and people they are familiar with.

FLUENCY PERFORMANCE Ask students to read their selected passages from "Sisters Forever" aloud to you. Tally the number of words the student successfully reads. Have each student rate his or her own performance using the 1 to 4 scale. Students who are not satisfied with their oral reading can practice reading to each other before they reread their passage to you.

See *Oral Reading Fluency Assessment* for monitoring progress.

LESSON 13

BEFORE

Building Background and Vocabulary

Use with

"The Cricket in Times Square"

Review Phonics: Long Vowels
/ā/a; /ē/e, y; /ī/i, y; /ō/o; /(y)o͞o/u

Identify the sound. Ask students to repeat this sentence twice: *Even when the sky turned hazy, the cargo pilot put on his uniform.* Ask them to name the word with the /ā/ sound they hear in *baby*. (*hazy*) Follow the same procedure for words with the /ē/ sound (*even, hazy*), the /ī/ sound (*pilot, sky*), the /ō/ sound (*cargo*), and the /yo͞o/ sound (*uniform*).

Associate letters to sounds. Write the sentence from above on the board. Underline the letters that stand for the long vowel sounds as follows: <u>e</u>ven, sk<u>y</u>, h<u>a</u>z<u>y</u>, carg<u>o</u>, p<u>i</u>lot, <u>u</u>niform. Tell students that in some words, a single vowel can stand for a long vowel sound.

Word blending. Model how to blend and read the word *program*. Slide your hand under the first syllable as you elongate the sounds /pprro͞o/. Slide your hand under the second syllable as you elongate the sounds /grraamm/. Then read the whole word naturally—*program*. Repeat the procedure with the words *crazy, python,* and *final*.

Apply the skill. *Letter Substitution* Write these words on the board, and have students read each aloud. Make the changes necessary to form the words in parentheses. Have a volunteer read aloud each new word.

INTERVENTION PRACTICE BOOK

page 52

shell (she)   **army** (Amy)   **drip** (dry)

fin (find)   **Mom** (moment)   **dusty** (duty)

Introduce Vocabulary

PRETEACH **lesson vocabulary.** Tell students that they are going to learn seven new words that they will see again when they read "The Cricket in Times Square." Teach each Vocabulary Word using the following process.

Use the following suggestions or similar ideas to give the meaning or context.

> Write the word.
> Say the word.
> Track the word and have students repeat it.
> Give the meaning or context.

wistfully	Relate to remembering a special place and wishing you were there right now.
scrounging	Relate to a dog digging through a trash can for food.
acquaintance	Break into syllables. Anyone you know is an acquaintance.
excitable	Point out *excite*. Related words: The race would be *exciting*. Thinking about it made the child *excitable*.

eavesdropping	Role-play by putting your hand to your ear and listening to students who are talking with their backs to you.
sympathetically	Relate to how you act toward someone who is hurt or sad.
logical	Point out the short o sound. Related word: He used *logic* to solve the problem.

For vocabulary activities, see Vocabulary Games on pages 2–7.

For vocabulary activities, see Vocabulary Games on pages 2–7.

AFTER

Building Background and Vocabulary

Apply Vocabulary Strategies

Reference sources. Write *He made a logical choice* on chart paper. Tell students that when they come to a word whose meaning they want to confirm, they can use a thesaurus or a dictionary. Model using a thesaurus.

MODEL When I look up *logical* in a thesaurus, I find that the words *reasonable* and *sensible* have similar meanings. When I substitute these words for *logical* in the sentence, it makes sense. *Logical* must mean "reasonable" or "sensible."

Guide students to use reference sources to confirm the meanings of other words.

RETEACH lesson vocabulary. Write these endings on the board and read them aloud. Ask students to supply a beginning for each. Discuss how the meaning of the Vocabulary Word influenced their response.

1. . . . when I caught him **eavesdropping** on my phone conversation.
2. . . . and listened **sympathetically** to the crying lost child.
3. . . . would be the **logical** thing to do after she found the wallet.
4. . . . made John look **wistfully** out the window at the lake.
5. . . . after the bear was found **scrounging** through our camp.
6. . . . because she is a close **acquaintance** of mine.
7. . . . the **excitable** hamster ran around the cage.

Vocabulary Words

wistfully longingly; sadly remembering something nice

scrounging looking for scraps of food or abandoned materials

acquaintance knowing someone or something

excitable very emotional; easily excited

eavesdropping listening secretly to a conversation

sympathetically in a way that shows concern for someone else's feelings

logical reasonable; to be expected

FLUENCY BUILDER Using *Intervention Practice Book* page 51, read each word in the first column aloud and have pairs of students repeat it. Repeat with each of the other two columns. Then have students practice reading aloud the words in each column to each other. Finally, have each student practice reading the whole list, focusing on speed rather than accuracy.

INTERVENTION PRACTICE BOOK

page 51

USE SKILL CARD 13A

⭐ (Focus Skill) Draw Conclusions

PRETEACH **the skill.** Ask students what they would think about a person who welcomes a stray cat into his or her home. (*The person cares about animals.*) Discuss how they arrived at their conclusion. (*by watching how the person reacts to the cat and by using what they already know about people who act this way.*)

Have students look at **side A of Skill Card 13: Draw Conclusions**. Read the definition and the passage aloud. Discuss the story information and the personal experiences of the students that help them figure out why Mrs. Green sends Kim to the nurse.

Now call attention to the chart. Ask:

- **What information does the writer give you about Kim?** (*Her head is pounding. Her face is pale and she's thirsty.*)

- **What do you know about feeling like Kim does?** (*People who look and act like Kim does are usually sick.*)

- **What will probably happen when Kim goes to the nurse's office?** (*Possible response: The nurse will take her temperature, find it is above normal, and send Kim home.*)

Explain to students that using prior experiences and story information can help them draw conclusions about characters.

Prepare to Read: "The Cricket in Times Square"

Preview. Tell students that they are going to read a fantasy selection called "The Cricket in Times Square." Explain that a fantasy is a make-believe story. Tell them that this story is about a country cricket that gets taken to New York City. Then preview the selection.

LEAD THE WAY
pages 328–344

- **Pages 328–331:** On the title page I see a cat, a mouse, and a cricket. I also see the title and the name of the author. On page 331, it looks like the mouse is talking to the cricket.

- **Pages 332–335:** On page 333 the mouse is looking for something. On page 335 the mouse and the cricket are eating.

- **Pages 336–340:** I can't tell how the mouse, cat, and cricket feel about one another, but on page 340, they are sharing food.

- **Pages 341–343:** On page 343 the three creatures are standing on a city street. I wonder why they are doing that?

Set Purpose. Model setting a purpose for reading the story.

MODEL From my preview, I know this story is about the cricket, the mouse, and the cat in a place called Times Square. One purpose for reading is enjoyment. I'll read to find out whether the mouse, the cricket, and the cat become friends.

Reread and Summarize

Have students reread and summarize "The Cricket in Times Square" in sections, as described in the chart below.

> **Pages 328–333**
>
> **Let's reread pages 328–333 to recall what happens when Tucker and Chester first meet.**
>
> Summary: Chester begins to tell Tucker how he got to New York. Then Tucker shares some liverwurst with Chester as he listens to the story.
>
> **Pages 334–337**
>
> **Next let's reread pages 334–337 to find out how Chester got from Connecticut to New York.**
>
> Summary: Chester is trapped in a picnic basket of a family that takes the train back to their home in New York. He hops off the train and lands in his new home.
>
> **Pages 338–341**
>
> **As we reread pages 338 through 341, let's recall Chester's special talent.**
>
> Summary: Chester can make music by rubbing his wings together.
>
> **Pages 342–344**
>
> **Let's reread pages 342 to 344 to recall Chester's reaction to Times Square.**
>
> Summary: Chester is both scared and amazed at what he sees. But he feels comforted knowing that a star he looks at is the same star he looked at in his old home.

FLUENCY BUILDER Be sure students have copies of *Intervention Practice Book* page 51. Have students identify the sentences on the bottom half of the page. Sit slightly behind a student and read each sentence aloud as he or she tracks the print being read. Then have the students read aloud themselves as quickly and accurately as possible.

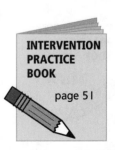

INTERVENTION PRACTICE BOOK

page 51

Directed Reading: "Oak Grove Picnic," pp. 102–108

Page 102

Ask volunteers to read the title of the selection and describe the illustration on page 102. Help students identify the season as late summer. Then have students read to find out what Bo and Ruben are doing. Ask: **What are the animals doing?** (*They are looking for food.*) **NOTE DETAILS**

MOVING
AHEAD
pp. 102–108

Why do you think the animals must look so hard? (*Possible response: Food is scarce because it's the end of summer and the land is dry.*) **SPECULATE**

Page 103

Have students read page 103 to find out what news Ruben the squirrel has and how he learned it. Ask: **What news does Ruben get? How does he get it?** (*He hears from the treehoppers that the acorns are falling.*) **IMPORTANT DETAILS**

Ask: **What are treehoppers?** (*bugs*) **How do you know this?** (*The story calls them insects that have a talent for finding things to eat. Bugs fit that description.*) **DRAW CONCLUSIONS**

Page 104

Help students identify Davis and Mavis (the jays) and the owls in the illustration. Then have them read page 104 to find out what the jays think of the news. Ask: **How can you tell that Davis is excitable?** Model using the create mental images strategy:

> **MODEL** Page 104 says that Davis is shouting, hopping, and flapping around the nest. When I picture this, I know the bird must be very excited. **CREATE MENTAL IMAGES**

Discuss whether students agree with your thinking and what they can picture as they read.

Page 105

Have students listen to find out what the owls want. Ask: **If owls don't eat acorns, why do you think they are interested in going to picnic day?** (*They hope to eat animals there.*) **SYNTHESIZE**

Page 106

Have students read page 106 to find out why the oak trees and acorns are so important to the animals of the woodland habitat. Ask: **What are some of the ways different animals make use of acorns and oak trees?** (*Possible response: Some eat the acorns right away; some store acorns for the winter; some make homes from twigs.*) **SUMMARIZE**

Page 107

INTERVENTION
PRACTICE
BOOK

page 53

Have students read page 107. Ask: **Why do the other animals relax when the owls go home?** (*Possible response: When the owls are around, the small animals have to watch out because owls might eat them.*) **SYNTHESIZE**

Summarize the selection. Ask students to think about the order of events in "Oak Grove Picnic." Then have them complete *Intervention Practice Book* page 53.

Answers to *Think About It* Questions

1. Picnic day is the day when the acorns in the oak trees ripen and fall. It comes at the end of summer. **SUMMARY**

2. All the animals have a hard time finding food at the end of the hot summer. Picnic day means they will have plenty of food to eat and to store for the winter. **INTERPRETATION**

3. Paragraphs should describe various animals eating and gathering food as well as explain the children's excitement and/or amazement at observing the activities of the picnic. **WRITE A PARAGRAPH**

AFTER

Skill Review
pages 348–349

USE SKILL CARD 13B

(Focus Skill) Draw Conclusions

RETEACH **the skill.** Have students look at **side B of Skill Card 13: Draw Conclusions**. Read the skill reminder with them, and have a volunteer read the passage aloud.

Read aloud the next set of directions. Explain that students can now create their own chart like the one on the card. Remind them to fill in information from the story and their own experiences that helps them draw a conclusion about how Chris feels.

After students complete their charts, have them take turns reading the information they included from the story and information they know from personal experience. Ask them to explain how this information helped them figure out that Chris was nervous about speaking in front of an audience. Point out that students can use this skill to help them draw conclusions about how characters act and feel in stories like "Stealing Home."

FLUENCY BUILDER Be sure students have copies of *Intervention Practice Book* page 51. Make a tape recording of the sentences on the bottom half of the page. Explain that students will work as pairs to practice reading these sentences aloud. Assign partners. Then have them play back each sentence and take turns reading the sentence independently. Students should try to match the expression and phrasing that they hear in the tape recording.

INTERVENTION PRACTICE BOOK

page 51

Expository Writing: Explanatory Paragraph

Build on prior knowledge. Tell students that together they are going to write a paragraph that explains why they like a certain subject in school. Ask students to agree on a subject and then list three reasons for their choice. Display the following example and lead students through each box.

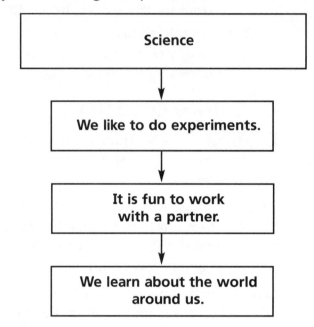

Construct the text. "Share the pen" with students in a collaborative group writing effort. Help them organize the answers to the questions below into a paragraph.

- What is your favorite subject?

- What are three reasons why you like this subject?

Revisit the text. Go back and read the paragraph together. Ask: **What could I add to my sentences to make them more interesting?** (*descriptive words*)

- Guide students to add details and descriptive words to their sentences.

- Have students read their completed paragraph aloud.

On Your Own

Have students think of a favorite activity that they would like to pursue. Tell them to write a paragraph explaining why they would like to pursue that activity. Remind them to include three reasons in their writing.

Spelling Lesson
pages 349G–349H

Connect Spelling and Phonics

RETEACH long vowels /ā/*a*; /ē/*e*, *y*; /ī/*i*, *y*; /ō/*o*; /(y)ōō/*u*. Tell students that in each word you will say, a single letter stands for each long vowel sound. Dictate the following words, and have students write them on the board. After they write each one, display the correct spelling so students can proofread their work.

I. find*	2. bold	3. clover*	4. acorns*
5. even	6. music	7. try	8. baby*

***Word appears in "Oak Grove Picnic."**

Dictate the following sentence and have students write it: *The pilot will open the hatch in a moment.*

Build and Read Longer Words

Remind students that they have learned that words with the CVC pattern, such as *trip* and *block*, usually have a short vowel sound. Tell them that in some words with more than one syllable, a vowel between two consonants can have the long vowel sound. Explain that when students come across such a word, they should try breaking it before the consonant. Write the word *tutor* on the board and read it aloud. Frame the word part *tu*, and have students repeat it after you. Do the same for the word part *tor*. Then draw your hand under the entire word as students read it aloud. Follow a similar procedure with these words: *favorite*, *nobility*, *minus*, *chosen*, *reviewing*, *moment*.

FLUENCY BUILDER Have students choose a passage from "Oak Grove Picnic" to read aloud to a partner. You may have students choose passages that they found particularly interesting, or have them choose one of the following options:

- Read all of page 103. (From *Bo looked* . . . through . . . *all eaten up.* Total: 91 words)

- Read all of page 105 and the first paragraph on page 106. (From *The owls* . . . through . . . *we'll have* . . ." Total: 119 words)

Students read the selected passage aloud to their partners three times. Have the student rate his or her own readings on a scale from 1 to 4.

Review Vocabulary

Have students review the meanings of Vocabulary Words by deciding which sentence ending in each pair below makes sense and which is nonsense.

    1. Taking the **logical** route home would
        a. get you home quickly.
        b. make you get lost.

    2. Listening **sympathetically** to a sad friend would
        a. make the friend feel worse.
        b. make the friend feel better.

    3. If an animal is **scrounging** for food, it is
        a. hungry.
        b. burying the food in the ground.

    4. When you are pleased to make someone's **acquaintance**, you say
        a. hello.
        b. goodbye.

Have students make up their own sensible and nonsense endings for sentences using *wistfully*, *excitable*, and *eavesdropping*.

**INTERVENTION
PRACTICE
BOOK**

page 54

(Focus Skill) Review Draw Conclusions

To review the focus skill of drawing conclusions, distribute *Intervention Practice Book* page 54. Have volunteers read the passage aloud. Then have students list in the chart story information and personal experiences that help them draw the conclusion that Matt didn't catch the ball, so Sam had time to get on base.

Review Test Prep

Ask students to turn to page 349 of the *Pupil Edition*. Call attention to the tips for answering test questions. Remind students that the conclusions they draw about passages they read should make sense and come from information in the story and facts that they already know. Tell students to apply these tips to test questions like the ones found on this page.

**LEAD
THE WAY**

page 349

Read aloud the passage. Then have students follow along as you read aloud each test question and the tip that goes with it. Discuss people students know who might act the same way as Selma Snail does in order to help them describe Selma's character for question 1. Then have students use the story information and their own knowledge to decide which answer in question 2 makes the most sense.

**INTERVENTION
ASSESSMENT
BOOK**

✔

Self-Selected Reading

Have students select their own books to read independently. They might choose books from the classroom library shelf, or you may wish to offer a group of appropriate books from which students can choose.

- *Dear Rebecca, Winter is Here* by Jean Craighead George. HarperCollins, 1993

- *Willie Takes a Hike* by Gloria Rand. Harcourt Brace, 1996

- *The Market Square Dog* by James Herriot. St. Martins, 1989

After students have chosen their books, give each student a copy of My Reading Log, which can be found on page R38 in the back of the *Teacher's Edition*. Have students fill in the information at the top of the form. Then have them use the log to keep track of their reading and to record their responses to the literature.

Conduct student-teacher conferences. Arrange time for each student to confer with you individually about his or her self-selected reading. Have students bring their Reading Log to share with you at the conference. Students might choose a favorite passage to read aloud to you. Look at the illustrations in the book together and ask the student to use the text to explain details found in the pictures. Encourage students to describe the traits, feelings, and actions of characters found in their book.

FLUENCY PERFORMANCE Ask students to read their selected passages from "Oak Grove Picnic" aloud to you. If possible, record the student's reading on tape. Keep track of the number of words the student reads correctly. Have the student rate his or her own performance using the 1 to 4 scale. Allow students who are not satisfied with their reading a chance to listen to themselves on tape and then practice the sections that they believe they can improve upon. Give students an opportunity to reread their passage to you.

See *Oral Reading Fluency Assessment* for monitoring progress.

LESSON 14

BEFORE

Building
Background
and Vocabulary

INTERVENTION
PRACTICE
BOOK

page 56

Use with

"Two Lands, One Heart"

Review Phonics: Long Vowel /ī/*igh, ie*

Identify the sound. Have students repeat the following sentence twice: *He tried to get the right pie.* Ask them to identify the words that have the /ī/ sound. (*tried, right, pie*)

Associate letters to sound. Write the above sentence on the board. Underline *igh* in *right* and *ie* in *tried* and *pie*. Explain that these letter combinations stand for the /ī/ sound. Point out that the letters *gh* in *right* are silent.

Word blending. Model how to blend and read the word *tried*. Slide your hand under the word as you elongate the sounds /trrīīd/. Then say the word naturally—*tried*. Follow a similar procedure with *might* and *tie*.

Apply the skill. *Letter Substitution* Write these words on the board, and have students read each aloud. Make the changes necessary to form the words in parentheses. Have a volunteer read aloud each new word.

fit (fight)	**sit** (sight)	**flit** (flight)	**Fred** (fried)
mitt (might)	**litter** (lighter)	**lip** (lie)	**slit** (slight)

Introduce Vocabulary

PRETEACH **lesson vocabulary.** Tell students that they are going to learn seven new words that they will see again when they read "Two Lands, One Heart." Teach each Vocabulary Word using the following process.

Use the following suggestions or similar ideas to give the meaning or context.

> Write the word.
> Say the word.
> Track the word and have students repeat it.
> Give the meaning or context.

equivalent   Point out related words: The punch has *equal* parts of juice and water. The amount of juice is *equivalent* to the amount of water.

interpreter   Point out the suffix *-er*. Say a word in a different language and ask a volunteer to translate the word.

irrigation   Draw a picture of a ditch going through a field. Demonstrate how water collects in the ditch and spreads to the plants.

occasionally   Relate to something that you do once in a while.

appetizing   Relate to foods that taste good.

overwhelm	Relate to the feeling you can get when seeing something beautiful.
hysterically	Role-play this sentence: The child cried hysterically after dropping his ice-cream cone.

For vocabulary activities, see Vocabulary Games on pages 2–7.

For vocabulary activities, see Vocabulary Games on pages 2–7.

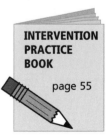

Vocabulary Words

equivalent equal in some way

interpreter a person who translates

irrigation furnishing water to land where crops are grown

occasionally sometimes; once in a while

appetizing appearing to be good to eat

overwhelm to overpower (with feelings)

hysterically with uncontrolled emotions

AFTER

Building Background and Vocabulary

Apply Vocabulary Strategies

Use sentence and word context. Write this sentence on the board: *My mouth began to water when I saw the appetizing foods.* Tell students that they can sometimes figure out the meaning of a word by thinking about the words around it. Model using the strategy.

MODEL I'm not sure what *appetizing* means so I reread the sentence. When my mouth waters, I am hungry. The appetizing foods would be ones that I like to eat. So *appetizing* must mean "appearing to be good to eat."

Guide students to use sentence and word context to figure out the meanings of other words.

RETEACH lesson vocabulary. Distribute Vocabulary Word cards to students. Then read each sentence and ask students to choose a Vocabulary Word that has a similar meaning to the underlined word or words in the sentence. Discuss the meaning of the Vocabulary Word that fits each sentence.

1. <u>Sometimes</u>, we go to the library after school. (*occasionally*)
2. The bright colors in the painting <u>overpower</u> me. (*overwhelm*)
3. That pizza sure looks <u>tasty</u>. (*appetizing*)
4. The baby cried <u>wildly</u> when she lost her toy. (*hysterically*)
5. The plants grew well because of the <u>watering system</u>. (*irrigation*)
6. Please ask the <u>translator</u> what this word means. (*interpreter*)
7. The two workers received <u>the same</u> pay. (*equivalent*)

FLUENCY BUILDER Distribute *Intervention Practice Book* page 55. Read each word in the first column aloud three times and have students echo you. Repeat for the other two columns. Then divide students into two groups and have one group read a column of words while the other group repeats it. Tell students to concentrate on reading the words as smoothly and quickly as they can.

INTERVENTION PRACTICE BOOK

page 55

⭐(Focus Skill) Compare and Contrast

PRETEACH the skill. Have students visualize their home and their classroom. Then have them tell how these two places are alike and different. Explain that they are making comparisons and contrasts about two places as authors often do in the stories they write.

Have students look at **side A of Skill Card 14: Compare and Contrast.** Read the definitions of compare and contrast. Next, read the passage aloud. Discuss how the sports of skiing and snowboarding are alike and different. Draw attention to the chart. Ask:

- **Does the word *both* signal a comparison or contrast?** (*a comparison because you are looking for how two sports are alike*)

- **What other activities can you do in the snow? How are they like skiing and snowboarding?** (*Possible response: Sledding is a fun activity where you ride something downhill just as you do when you ski or snowboard.*)

Explain to students that authors compare and contrast to show how unfamiliar topics are similar to and different from familiar topics.

Prepare to Read: "Two Lands, One Heart"

Preview. Tell students that they are going to read a nonfiction selection called "Two Lands, One Heart." Explain that nonfiction tells about real people, events, and places and that this story is about a boy who visits relatives in Vietnam. Preview the selection.

LEAD THE WAY
pages 352–366

- **Pages 352–355:** I see the title and the names of the authors. The text under the title tells me that this story is about a boy's journey to his mother's homeland, Vietnam. On page 355, I see a map of Southeast Asia and a map that shows the flight from Denver to Ho Chi Minh City. The boy must live in Denver.

- **Pages 356–361:** From page 356 I can tell that Vietnam borders water and has many fishing boats. On page 357, the boy looks happy. The pictures on pages 358 and 359 show me what a family meal is like. Getting water and taking a shower sure looks different in Vietnam than in the U.S.

- **Pages 362–366:** The pictures on pages 364 and 366 give me an idea of how children living on a farm help their family in this country.

Set purpose. Model setting a purpose for reading the story.

MODEL From my preview, I know I will probably learn about the experiences that the American family has when visiting a different culture. I'll read to find out how life in Vietnam is similar to and different from life in the United States.

Reread and Summarize

Have students reread and summarize "Two Lands, One Heart" in sections, as described in the chart below.

Pages 352–357

Let's reread pages 352–357 to recall how TJ and his family get to the family farm.

Summary: On the first day a bus takes them from a crowded city to the mountains by the sea. The next day they leave the mountains and travel to the farm located in the rice fields.

Pages 358–361

Now let's reread pages 358–361 to find out how TJ's aunts cook their food.

Summary: The aunts cook on a dirt floor using fireplaces. They do not have a stove, microwave oven, or a refrigerator. They use big kettles and woks.

Pages 362–363

As we reread pages 362–363, let's recall how TJ helps his Uncle Thao farm.

Summary: Uncle Thao leads the family oxen to the field. They pull the plow while Uncle Thao controls where it should go. TJ finds out how hard this is when he tries to control the plow.

Pages 364–366

Let's reread pages 364–366 to recall other new experiences TJ has on the family farm.

Summary: TJ pulls weeds from the rice fields, he knocks a coconut from a tree, and he takes a canoe ride down a river.

FLUENCY BUILDER Be sure students have copies of *Intervention Practice Book* page 55. Point out the sentences at the bottom of the page. Have students listen to you model reading each sentence aloud, focusing on phrasing and expression. Then have partners take turns reading the sentences three times each. Ask partners to provide positive feedback by describing the improvement they hear with each reading.

INTERVENTION
PRACTICE
BOOK

page 55

Directed Reading: "A Pen Pal in Vietnam," pp. 110–117

MOVING AHEAD
pp. 110–117

Page 110

Read the title of the story aloud. Explain that this story is made up of letters that a girl in America writes to her pen pal in Vietnam. Have students preview the illustrations and then predict what they might learn. Ask a volunteer to read the letter from Michelle on page 110. Ask: **How are Michelle and Kim alike and different?** (*They are both nine. Michelle lives in a small village, while Kim lives on a farm.*) (Focus Skill) **COMPARE AND CONTRAST**

Page 111

Ask students to read page 111. Ask: **What are the rice fields like?** (*Possible response: They are very muddy like the bottom of a lake.*) **IMPORTANT DETAILS**

Pages 112–113

Have volunteers read the letters on pages 112 and 113, focusing on the new things Michelle learns about Kim's culture. Ask: **How do Michelle and Kim both feel about visiting big cities?** Model using the Reread to Clarify strategy:

> **MODEL** I am not sure how they both feel, so I will reread the section about Ho Chi Minh City on page 112. Michelle says that she feels confused in a big city, too. That means that Kim must have mentioned this feeling in her previous letter to Michelle. They both feel confused by all of the people and places in a big city. (Focus Strategy) **REREAD TO CLARIFY**

Pages 114–115

Have students look at the illustrations and predict what they might read about on pages 114–115. Then have them read to confirm their predictions. Ask: **What did you find out about city traffic in Ho Chi Minh City?** (*Possible response: The streets are crowded with bicycles. One way people get around is on a taxi bike.*) **SUMMARIZE**

Page 116

INTERVENTION PRACTICE BOOK

page 57

Have students read page 116 to find out whether the pen pals will meet each other in person. Ask: **How does Michelle feel about the upcoming visit.** (*She is hysterically happy.*) **IDENTIFY CHARACTERS' EMOTIONS**

Summarize the selection. Help students create a Venn diagram summarizing the similarities and differences between Michelle and Kim. Then have them complete *Intervention Practice Book* page 57.

Page 117

Answers to *Think About It* Questions

1. Michelle and Kim are both nine, they both feel confused in a big city, and they both like to eat meat broth. Michelle lives in a small village while Kim lives on a farm. Kim has ridden in a canoe, but Michelle has ridden in a rowboat. Kim has been to a fish fry and Michelle has not. **COMPARE AND CONTRAST**

2. Possible response: Kim is probably just as excited as Michelle is to meet her in person because they have been writing letters to each other for a long time. **MAKE JUDGMENTS**

3. The letter should include a thank you and list activities that the two girls did on the visit. **WRITE A LETTER**

AFTER

Skill Review
pages 370–371

USE SKILL CARD 14B

(Focus Skill) Compare and Contrast

Have students look at **side B of Skill Card 14: Compare and Contrast.** Have a volunteer read the skill reminder aloud. Then read the passage aloud. Have students take turns identifying ways that Redwood National Park and Everglades National Park are alike and different.

Read aloud the next set of directions. Explain that students can now create their own Venn diagram like the one on the card. Remind them to list words and phrases from the text that describe how the two national parks are alike and different. Remind them to look for signal words that will help them discover similarities and differences. After students finish completing their Venn diagrams, have them take turns reading the information they wrote in each section. Have them explain how this information helped them to better understand the settings in the passage. Point out that the author of "Two Lands, One Heart" gives students many opportunities to compare and contrast two settings and the everyday life of the families who live there.

FLUENCY BUILDER Distribute copies of *Intervention Practice Book* page 55. Sit in a circle and have each student read the first sentence. Ask students to pretend they really have a pen pal that they will be writing to and add expression to their voices. After each student reads the sentence, point out something positive about the reading such as its phrasing, expression, or pace. Repeat this activity using all of the sentences on the page.

INTERVENTION PRACTICE BOOK

page 55

Expository Writing: Definition Paragraph

Build on prior knowledge. Tell students that they are going to write a paragraph that defines the concept of a good sport. Write *Good Sport* on the board and ask students to give their own definition of a good sport. For example:

Good Sport

- Someone who plays fairly.

- Someone who will not get mad if he or she does not win.

- Someone who does not change or make up rules to make the game go in his or her favor.

Then ask students to give examples of something a good sport would or would not do and record their ideas.

Construct the text. "Share the pen" with students in a collaborative group writing effort. Guide them in writing a definition for what makes a person a good sport.

- Write a sentence that introduces the topic of a good sport.

- Add sentences that define the concept. Use the list on the board for help.

- Next, write a concluding statement that summarizes the concept of a good sport.

Revisit the text. Have students read the definition paragraph aloud and add details, such as adjectives, to make their writing clearer to the reader.

On Your Own

Have students write a definition about what makes a good teacher. Tell them to remember to include examples or details that will help the reader understand their definition.

AFTER

Spelling Lesson
pages 371G–371H

Connect Spelling and Phonics

RETEACH **long vowel /ī/*igh, ie*.** Write the word *bright* on the board, and tell students that in the first four words you will say, the /ī/ sound is spelled *igh* as in *bright*. Dictate words 1–4, and have students write them. After they write each one, write the correct spelling on the board so students can proofread their work. They should draw a line through an incorrect word and write the correct spelling beside it. Then write the word *pie* on the board, and repeat the procedure for words 5–8. Have students proofread as before.

1. **fight***	2. **night***	3. **tight**	4. **right***
5. **spied**	6. **flies***	7. **lies**	8. **tried**

*Word appears in "A Pen Pal in Vietnam."

Dictate the following sentence for students to write: *By the time they got the tiger in the cage, it was only slightly frightened.*

Build and Read Longer Words

Write the word *overnight* on the board. Remind students that when they come to a longer word, they can check to see if it is made up of two shorter words. Cover *night* and have a volunteer read *over*. Reverse the procedure and have a volunteer read *night*. Have students blend the word parts to read the longer word *overnight*. Follow a similar procedure with these words: *daylight*, *highway*, and *watertight*.

INTERVENTION ASSESSMENT BOOK

FLUENCY BUILDER Tape students reading a passage from "A Pen Pal in Vietnam." Students may choose their own passage, or have them choose one of the following options:

- Read page 111. (Total: 103 words)
- Read all of page 114 and the first paragraph on page 115. (Total: 117 words)

Students read the selected passage aloud first with a partner and then to their partner. Together students can rate each reading on a scale from 1 to 4.

Review Vocabulary

Read the questions below. Have students answer *yes* or *no* to each one. Then have them use the meaning of the Vocabulary Word in the explanation of their answer.

1. Does an **interpreter** work with words? (*yes*)
2. Could a gardener use **irrigation**? (*yes*)
3. Would cat food be **appetizing** to a person? (*no*)
4. Can perfume **overwhelm** someone? (*yes*)
5. Is a bike **equivalent** to a truck? (*no*)
6. Do you **occasionally** brush your teeth? (*no*)
7. Do fans sometimes act **hysterically**? (*yes*)

INTERVENTION
PRACTICE
BOOK

page 58

(Focus Skill) Review Compare and Contrast

To review the focus skill of compare and contrast, distribute *Intervention Practice Book* page 58. Have volunteers read the passage aloud. Then guide students to look for signal words such as *all*, *but*, and *although* to help them find ways that the inventors in the passages are alike and different. Have students record these comparisons and contrasts in the appropriate areas of a Venn diagram.

Review Test Prep

Ask students to turn to page 371 of the *Pupil Edition*. Direct students to the tips for answering test questions. Explain that following these tips will help them answer test questions about comparing and contrasting people, places, events, or things.

LEAD
THE WAY

page 371

INTERVENTION
ASSESSMENT
BOOK

✔

Read each question and then have a volunteer read its tip aloud. Point out that the tip in question 1 suggests signal words that students can look for to find comparisons. Then tell students that the author chooses to use a compare and contrast pattern to give information about two Vietnamese plants. Have them write about how this text structure helps them understand the plants' similarities and differences.

Self-Selected Reading

Have students choose their own books to read independently. Allow them to select books from the classroom library shelf, or you may wish to offer a group of appropriate books from which students can choose.

- *What You Know First* by Patricia Maclachlan. HarperCollins, 1998
- *Grandmama's Joy* by Eloise Greenfield. Philomel, 1980
- *The Remembering Box* by Eth Clifford. Houghton Mifflin, 1985

You may also wish to choose additional books that are nonfiction, contain similar themes, or provide opportunities for students to practice comparing and contrasting characters, settings, and events.

After students have chosen their books, give each student a copy of My Reading Log, which can be found on page R38 in the back of the *Teacher's Edition*. Have students fill in the information at the top of the form. Then have them use the log to keep track of their reading and to record their responses to the literature.

Conduct student-teacher conferences. Set up a conference with each student to discuss the book they chose to read independently. Have them bring their Reading Logs to share with you. This is a good time for students to read a passage from their story aloud and discuss the parts that interested them the most. Ask questions about the book that prompt the student to compare and contrast the setting or characters in the story to places and people they are familiar with.

FLUENCY PERFORMANCE Ask students to read their selected passages from "A Pen Pal in Vietnam" aloud to you. Keep track of the number of words the student reads correctly. Have each student rate his or her own performance using the 1 to 4 scale. Suggest that students who are not satisfied with their oral reading record their reading on tape and then listen to it to find out where they can make improvements. Then let students reread their passages to you.

See *Oral Reading Fluency Assessment* for monitoring progress.

LESSON 15

BEFORE

Building Background and Vocabulary

INTERVENTION PRACTICE BOOK

page 60

Use with

"Look to the North"

Review Phonics: Vowel Diphthongs /ou/*ow, ou*

Identify the sound. Have students repeat the following sentence aloud three times: *The clown walked around town without making a sound.* Have students identify the words that have the /ou/ sound. (*clown, around, town, without, sound*)

Associate letters to sound. Write the above sentence on the board. Underline the letters *ou* in *around, without*, and *sound*. Tell students that the vowel combination *ou* can stand for the /ou/ sound in *around*. Then underline the letters *ow* in *clown* and *town*. Point out that the letters *ow* also can stand for the /ou/ sound.

Word blending. Model how to blend and read the word *cloud*. Slide your hand under the word as you elongate the sounds /klloud/. Then say the word naturally—*cloud*. Follow a similar procedure with *proud* and *frown*.

Apply the skill. *Letter Substitution* Write the following words on the board, and have students read each aloud. Make the changes necessary to form the words in parentheses. Have a student read aloud each new word.

tan (town)	**hill** (howl)	**moth** (mouth)	**or** (our)
fond (found)	**Don** (down)	**fall** (fowl)	**spot** (spout)

Introduce Vocabulary

PRETEACH **lesson vocabulary.** Tell students that they are going to learn six new words that they will see again when they read a story called "Look to the North." Teach each Vocabulary Word using the following process.

Use the following suggestions or similar ideas to give the meaning or context.

> Write the word.
> Say the word.
> Track the word and have students repeat it.
> Give the meaning or context.

ceases	Demonstrate by first telling students to talk. Then say, "All talking *ceases*."
tundra	Relate to a cold place with frozen ground and no trees.
abundant	Sound out the syllables. Show examples of abundant amounts of paper clips and books.
bonding	Related words: The two friends have a common *bond*. They are *bonding* when they play their instruments together.
piteously	Relate to the word *pity*. Demonstrate how a kitten would cry piteously for its mother.

surrender Relate to one side in a war "waving the white flag" to show giving up.

For vocabulary activities, see Vocabulary Games on pages 2–7.

Apply Vocabulary Strategies

Use reference sources. On chart paper, write the sentence *They explored the tundra, traveling in freezing conditions.* Tell students that they can find out the meaning of the word *tundra* by looking it up in a dictionary. Model using the strategy.

> **MODEL** When I look up the word *tundra* in a dictionary, I find the words "flat plain with no trees" and "arctic regions." When I substitute these words in the sentence, they make sense. I think *tundra* means "an area in the arctic that is flat."

Vocabulary Words

ceases stops

tundra area in arctic regions where there are no trees and where the ground is frozen all year

abundant in large amounts or numbers; more than enough

bonding establishing closer ties or friendships

piteously sorrowfully; in a way that makes others feel sorry for someone

surrender the act of giving up

Guide students to use this strategy to find the meanings of other Vocabulary Words.

RETEACH lesson vocabulary. Write a continuum on the board with the words **Least pleasing** and **Most pleasing** at either end. Then ask these questions and have students use it to indicate their answers. Have them discuss the meaning of each underlined word.

How pleased would you be if . . .

1. you began **bonding** with your favorite author?
2. an **abundant** amount of gold was found in your backyard?
3. your family moved to the **tundra**?
4. your brother or sister **ceases** to talk to you?
5. you were asked to **surrender** your favorite CD?
6. your best friend was acting **piteously**?

FLUENCY BUILDER Distribute *Intervention Practice Book* page 59. Read each word in the first column aloud and have students echo you. Follow the same procedure for the other two columns of words. Then have students work in groups of three or four. Ask pairs of students to read the words aloud while the other members listen. Remind students to focus on reading quickly and smoothly.

INTERVENTION PRACTICE BOOK

page 59

USE SKILL CARD 15A

(Focus Skill) Summarize

PRETEACH the skill. Ask a volunteer to retell the plot of a book he or she recently enjoyed. Explain that the student retold only the important parts; he or she did not retell everything that happened. Tell students that a brief retelling of a story is called a **summary**.

Have students look at **side A of Skill Card 15: Summarize**. Read aloud the definition. Next, read the passage aloud while students follow along. Discuss what the passage is mainly about (the life of Helen Keller) and then identify which facts will help students remember this main idea. Draw attention to the chart, and have students take turns reading the information in each box aloud. Ask:

- **Why wouldn't the part about Annie Sullivan be included in the summary?** (*Possible response: This part is a detail that doesn't really support the main idea.*)

- **How can you tell which details are important to include in your summary and which details are not?** (*Possible response: You have to judge which facts help support the main idea.*)

Explain that authors sometimes begin or end each section with a summary. This helps readers focus on the important parts of the selection.

Prepare to Read: "Look to the North"

Preview. Tell students that they are going to read "Look to the North." Explain that this is an informational narrative that presents facts. Tell students that "Look to the North" gives information about the lives of wolves. Then preview the selection.

LEAD
THE WAY

pages
374–389

- **Pages 374–377:** I see the title and the name of the author. Looking at pages 374–377, I see that each page tells about wolf pups at different ages.

- **Pages 378–383:** On pages 378–383, I can tell from the pictures that the wolf pups are getting older. Under each age, there are sentences in italics that include the words "look to the north." Maybe this is where the story gets its title.

- **Pages 384–389:** The pictures on pages 384–389 show that the pups are beginning to look like adult wolves. I see that the story ends when the pups are six months old.

Set purpose. Model setting a purpose for reading "Look to the North."

MODEL From my preview, I can tell that I will probably learn about how wolves grow and react to other wolves around them. I will read to find out what wolf pups can do during the first six months of their lives.

Reread and Summarize

Have students reread and summarize "Look to the North" in sections, as described in the chart below.

Pages 374–377

Let's reread pages 374–377 to recall what baby wolves are like during their first two weeks of life.

Summary: When wolves are born they can't see or hear. Their mother stays by them to keep them warm.

Pages 378–381

Now let's reread pages 378–381 to find out the roles of the pups in their pack.

Summary: Boulder is the alpha pup, Scree is his assistant, and Talus has the strongest sense of smell. He will help the pack find food.

Pages 382–385

As we reread pages 382–385, let's recall what the wolves learn from 10 weeks of age to 16 weeks of age.

Summary: The pups learn adult wolf talk, they play and bond with each other, and they practice their hunting skills.

Pages 386–389

Let's reread pages 386–389 to recall how the story ends.

Summary: The pack finds the injured beta wolf, brings it food, and settles by this fellow pack member until it gets well.

FLUENCY BUILDER Be sure students have copies of *Intervention Practice Book* page 59. Call attention to the sentences at the bottom of the page. Demonstrate how to read each sentence aloud, focusing on tone, phrasing, and expression. Then have students use choral reading and repeat each sentence after you. Provide time for students to practice reading each sentence aloud independently three times.

INTERVENTION
PRACTICE
BOOK

page 59

Directed Reading: "Wolf Pack: Sounds and Signals" pp. 118–125

MOVING
AHEAD
pp. 118–125

Page 118

Ask a volunteer to read aloud the title of the story. Have students read page 118. Ask: **Why do wolves howl?** (*It's one of the ways pack members talk to each other.*) **NOTE DETAILS**

Ask: **How does the author compare the wolf pack to a musical group?** (*The author says that each wolf is like a singer sounding a different note, so together, the wolves are like a musical group.*) **UNDERSTAND FIGURATIVE LANGUAGE**

Page 119

Have students read page 119 to find out more about why wolves howl. Ask: **What are five important reasons why wolves howl?** (*Wolves howl to call the pack together, to say "keep out," to call for help, to mourn, and to celebrate.*) (Focus Skill) **SUMMARIZE**

Page 120

Have students read page 120. Ask: **What are other ways wolves talk to each other?** (*Wolves growl when angry, squeak when bonding with each other, and bark when they're excited.*) (Focus Skill) **SUMMARIZE**

Pages 121–122

Ask a volunteer to read the pages aloud. Ask: **How do you think a wolf becomes a leader?** (*Possible response: by showing it is stronger than all the others in the pack*) **DRAW CONCLUSIONS**

Page 123

Before students read page 123, have them suggest some ways that wolves might show cooperation. (*Possible response: They may hunt or play together.*) **SPECULATE**

Then have students read page 123 to discover several ways that wolves show their cooperation with each other.

Page 124

Have students read page 124 to see what else they can learn about "wolf talk." Model the strategy of using Text Structure and Format:

INTERVENTION
PRACTICE
BOOK

page 61

> **MODEL** So far in the story, the photographs have helped me understand what the author is writing about. Because of the photograph on page 124, I know I will learn that wolf pups can howl or "talk" like the adults. If I read the text, I learn that the pups howl when they pick up a scent. (Focus Strategy) **USE TEXT STRUCTURE AND FORMAT**

Summarize the selection. Ask students to think about the different types of sounds and signals that wolves make and what the sounds and signals mean. Then have students complete *Intervention Practice Book* page 61 to write a summary statement about the selection.

Answers to *Think About It* Questions

1. Wolves communicate through sounds and body signals. Examples will vary. **SUMMARY**

2. Possible response: Strong leaders help keep the pack together so that all the wolves can be safe. **INTERPRETATION**

3. Paragraphs should describe students' personal reactions. **WRITE A PARAGRAPH**

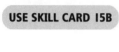

Skill Review
pages 396–397

USE SKILL CARD 15B

⭐ (Focus Skill) Summarize

RETEACH **the skill.** Have students look at **side B of Skill Card 15: Summarize.** Have a volunteer read the skill reminder aloud. Then read the passage aloud. Talk about what the passage is about and identify details that support the main idea.

Read aloud the next set of directions. Explain that students can now create their own chart like the one on the card. Remind them to write the main idea and then evaluate which details are important enough to include in a retelling of the passage. Tell students to try to keep their summaries to three sentences or less.

After students finish their summary charts, have them take turns reading the information they wrote in each box. Have them explain how creating a brief retelling of the passage helped them remember what it was about.

FLUENCY BUILDER Distribute copies of *Intervention Practice Book* page 59. Explain that partners will be buddy reading the sentences at the bottom of the page. Suggest that pairs take turns reading the odd- or even-numbered sentences so that they get a chance to read each one aloud. Tell students to read through the sentences at least three times, focusing on keeping an even tempo of words with no breaks or rests. Encourage partners to praise each other for using expression in their voices as they read about the mother wolf and the danger she faces.

INTERVENTION PRACTICE BOOK

page 59

Expository Writing: Explanatory Paragraph

Build on prior knowledge. Tell students that together they will write an explanatory paragraph about the importance of eating a balanced diet. Explain that sometimes during a test they may be asked to write in a certain amount of time. Remind students that they will need to organize their ideas before they actually begin writing. Display the following word web:

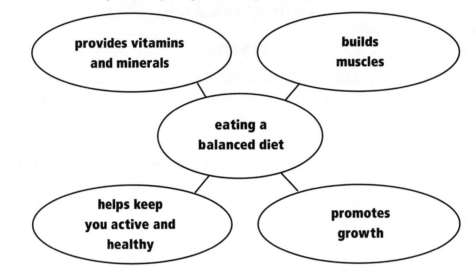

Invite students to brainstorm reasons why it is important to eat a balanced diet. Add their ideas to the word web.

Construct the text. "Share the pen" with students in a collaborative group writing effort. Guide them in using their ideas to create sentences that form an explanatory paragraph.

- Write an introductory main idea statement. Use the main idea sentence from the word web.

- Add two or three sentences based on the ideas recorded in the word web.

- Read the paragraph and add transition words to help the sentences flow from one to the next.

Revisit the text. Have students reread the paragraph again. This time, students should be looking for spelling errors and making sure that the words they used make sense.

On Your Own

Have students choose an animal that they think would make the perfect pet. Tell them to list their ideas in a word web. Then tell them to use their ideas to write sentences about the topic.

Connect Spelling and Phonics

RETEACH vowel diphthongs /ou/ *ow, ou*. Write the word *shout* on the board, read it aloud, and tell students that the first four words you will say have the same *ou* vowel pattern as in *shout*. Dictate words 1–4. After students write each one, display the correct spelling so that students can proofread their work. Then write the word *now* on the board and point out the *ow* vowel pattern that will appear in the next four words. Repeat the process.

| 1. sound* | 2. proud* | 3. snout* | 4. mouth* |
| 5. down* | 6. howling* | 7. growls* | 8. crowd |

*Word appears in "Wolf Pack: Sounds and Signals."

Dictate the following sentence for students to write: *Our brown hound was howling.*

Build and Read Longer Words

Write these words on the board: *tower, cloudless.* Tell students that when they read a longer word with the letters *ow* or *ou*, these letter combinations usually stay together when the word is broken into syllables. Ask students to identify which part of the first word sounds like /tou/ and which part sounds like /ər/. Then have students identify the two consonants that are next to each other in *cloudless.* (*dl*) Draw a line between *d* and *l*, and remind students that words that have this pattern are usually divided into syllables between the two consonants. Frame *cloud* and have students read it. Frame *less* and have students read it. Then have students read aloud the following words: *outdoors, chowder, outward, powder, townspeople, downtown.*

**INTERVENTION
ASSESSMENT
BOOK**

FLUENCY BUILDER Have students read aloud a passage from "Wolf Pack: Sounds and Signals" to a partner. Students may choose a passage that they found interesting, or they may choose one of the following options:

- Read all of page 121 and the first paragraph on page 122. (Total: 118 words)

- Read page 124. (Total: 94 words)

Students should read the selected passage aloud, first to themselves and then to a partner. Together students rate each reading on a scale from 1 to 4.

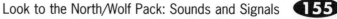

Review Vocabulary

Play the "Name Game" by asking students to name examples that answer the questions below. Record their ideas on the board and then go back and have students use the word meaning to explain their answer for each Vocabulary Word.

1. Name something that **ceases**.
2. Name something you would find in the **tundra**.
3. Name something that is **abundant** in your school.
4. Name two characters who are **bonding** with each other.
5. Name a reason why an animal would cry **piteously**.
6. Name a reason someone would **surrender** something.

 Review Summarize

To review the focus skill of summarizing, distribute *Intervention Practice Book* page 62. Have volunteers read the passage aloud. Then guide students to look for the main idea and important details that they can include in a summary of the passage about zebras. Have students record their ideas and write a summary of the passage in the appropriate boxes on the chart.

INTERVENTION
PRACTICE
BOOK

page 62

Review Test Prep

Ask students to turn to page 397 of the *Pupil Edition*. Direct students to the tips for answering test questions. Explain that the tips given at the bottom of the page will help them answer these questions as well as similar questions they may see on other tests.

LEAD
THE WAY

page 397

Read each question and then have a volunteer read its tip aloud. Point out that the tip in question 1 suggests that students choose the statement that tells the important idea. The other two answer choices support this important idea. Remind students to evaluate the details that they find in the story and include only the ones they want to remember as they write their summary.

INTERVENTION
ASSESSMENT
BOOK

✔

Self-Selected Reading

Have students select their own books to read independently. Students may choose from the classroom library shelf or you may wish to offer a group of appropriate books from which they can choose. Titles may include the following:

- *Dream Wolf* by Paul Goble. Bradbury, 1990.

- *The First Dog* by Jan Brett. Harcourt Brace, 1998.

- *Wild Babies* by Seymour Simon. HarperCollins, 1997.

After students have chosen their books, give each student a copy of My Reading Log, which can be found on page R38 in the back of the *Teacher's Edition*. Have students fill in the information at the top of the form. Then have them use the log to keep track of their reading and to record their responses to the literature.

Conduct student-teacher conferences. Arrange time for each student to confer with you individually about his or her self-selected reading. Have students share their Reading Logs with you and summarize sections of the book that they especially liked. Ask students to read a passage from the story aloud. Ask questions about the book that prompt the student to tell about the main ideas and details of various passages.

FLUENCY PERFORMANCE Have students read aloud to you the passage from "Wolf Pack: Sounds and Signals" that they selected and practiced with their partners. Tally the number of words the student reads correctly. Have the student rate his or her own performance using the 1 to 4 scale. Some students may wish to practice reading aloud with a new partner for more insights on how they can improve. When the student feels ready, ask him or her to reread the passage to you.

See *Oral Reading Fluency Assessment* for monitoring progress.

LESSON 16

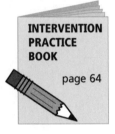

INTERVENTION
PRACTICE
BOOK

page 64

Use with

"The Kids' Invention Book"

Review Phonics: Consonant /s/ *ce, ci, cy*

Identify the sound. Have students repeat this sentence aloud three times: *In the center of the city was a giant cypress tree.* Ask them to identify the words that have the /s/ sound. (*center, city, cypress*)

Associate letters to sound. Write /s/ words (*center, city, cypress*) on the board. Ask volunteers to say each word and underline the letter that follows the *c*. Help students form a generalization about which vowels follow /s/*c*. (For example: When the letter *c* is followed by *e, i,* or *y,* it makes the /s/ sound.)

Word blending. Model how to blend and read the word *city.* Point to each letter as you say its sound. Slide your hand under the whole word as you elongate the sounds /ssiitēē/. Then say the word naturally—*city.*

Apply the skill. *Letter Substitution* Write these words on the board, and have students read each aloud. Make the changes necessary to form the words in parentheses. Ask volunteers to read the new words.

call (cell)   **curtain** (certain)   **slick** (slice)   **lake** (lace)   **fact** (face)

Introduce Vocabulary

PRETEACH lesson vocabulary. Tell students they are going to learn seven new words that they will see again when they read "The Kids' Invention Book." Teach each Vocabulary Word using this process.

Use the following suggestions or similar ideas to give the meaning or context.

> Write the word.
> Say the word.
> Track the word and have students repeat it.
> Give the meaning or context.

device	Provide examples of devices students use daily, such as a computer to write reports.
prosthetic	Relate to *prosthesis*, the name of a replaced body part.
disabilities	Explain that the prefix *dis-* can mean "not." *Disabilities* refers to not being able to completely use a particular ability.
document	Relate to the Declaration of Independence—an important document.
circular	Point out that many words that contain the letters *cir* have something to do with a circle.
modify	Provide synonyms for *modify*: *adjust, change, revise.*

scholarship Point out the suffix *-ship*, which means "the quality of." *Scholar* means "learner." So *scholarship* means "the qualities of a learner."

For vocabulary activities, see Vocabulary Games on pages 2–7.

For vocabulary activities, see Vocabulary Games on pages 2–7.

AFTER

Building Background and Vocabulary

Apply Vocabulary Strategies

Decode multisyllabic words. Write the word *prosthetic* on chart paper. Tell students that when they come to long or unfamiliar words, it may make reading easier to break them into syllables. Model using the strategy.

> **MODEL** I am unsure how to pronounce the word *prosthetic*. I notice that each syllable ends with a vowel followed by a consonant. I think the vowel sound is short as in the word *September*. When I break the word into syllables and say them with short vowel sounds, I pronounce the word *pros/thet/ic*.

Guide students to use this strategy with other multisyllabic words.

RETEACH lesson vocabulary. Have students listen as you read each statement. Ask them for "thumbs up" if it is true, "thumbs down" if false. Have them tell how false statements can be made true.

1. A sphere and a wheel are both **circular**. (*true*)
2. You can **modify** milk by adding chocolate to it. (*true*)
3. A printer is a **device** attached to a radio. (*false; A printer is a device attached to a computer.*)
4. People who have lost an arm or leg can sometimes have **prosthetic** surgery. (*true*)
5. A hearing aid is a **document**. (*false; A letter is a document.*)
6. Excellent **scholarship** includes hard work and determination. (*true*)
7. **Disabilities** always stop people from achieving. (*false; Many people with disabilities have achieved much in their lives.*)

Vocabulary Words

device something built for a purpose

prosthetic replacing a missing body part

disabilities conditions that make doing some things more difficult

document paper with important information

circular shaped like a circle

modify to change

scholarship the qualities of a student

FLUENCY BUILDER Use *Intervention Practice Book* page 63. Read a word from the first column aloud. Have students scan the list and point to the word. Then have students repeat the word. Next, partners take turns reading, finding, and repeating words from each list in the same manner— one student reads a word from the list and the partner finds it and repeats it. Finally, have each student practice reading an entire list as his or her partner listens.

INTERVENTION PRACTICE BOOK

page 63

BEFORE

Reading
"The Kids'
Invention Book"
pages 402–416

USE SKILL CARD 16A

(Focus Skill) **Main Idea and Details**

PRETEACH **the skill.** Explain that authors often link related details into one paragraph to make it easier for the reader to remember information.

Have students look at **side A of Skill Card 16: Main Ideas and Details**. Read the definition and the directions aloud. Next, read aloud the paragraph. Point out the main idea and the details.

Now call attention to the chart. Ask:

- **What questions do the details answer?** (*who invented and what they invented*)

- **Why might an author use main ideas and details to organize a selection?** (*Possible response: to make it easier for the reader to understand and remember*)

Explain to students that when they give a one-sentence summary of a selection, they are stating the main idea.

Prepare to Read: "The Kids' Invention Book"

Preview. Tell students that they are going to read "The Kids' Invention Book." Explain that this is a nonfiction selection because it tells about real people and events. Tell students that it is about four children who solved problems by inventing things. Then preview the selection.

LEAD THE WAY

pages 402–416

- **Pages 402–403:** The title and the pictures suggest that this will be an informational article about kids and inventions. We might learn who invented the Slinky® and the Koosh® Ball.

- **Pages 404–405:** The subhead suggests that this is an informational article. The caption under Chester Greenwood's photo suggests that we will read about his invention.

- **Pages 406–407:** I wonder what a "Prosthetic Catch and Throw Device" is. Maybe it has something to do with baseball.

- **Pages 408–409:** The photo on page 409 shows a girl winning a prize, probably for her invention.

- **Pages 410–411:** The photos show what this invention will look like. It's called a "Conserve Sprinkler," so it must save water.

- **Pages 412–416:** These eleven steps seem to be telling how to go about making an invention.

Set purpose. Model setting a purpose for reading the selection.

MODEL From my preview, I know I will be learning about some interesting inventions and their inventors. I will read to find out what problem was solved with each invention.

Reread and Summarize

Have students reread and summarize "The Kids' Invention Book" in sections, as described in the chart below.

Pages 404–405

Let's reread pages 404–405 to recall what Chester Greenwood invented and why.

Summary: Chester Greenwood had cold ears when he ice-skated, so he invented earmuffs.

Pages 406–407

As we reread pages 406–407, let's find out why Josh wanted to help his friend David.

Summary: Josh wanted to help David by inventing a device for him to throw a baseball so that he could be on a Little League team.

Pages 408–409

Let's reread pages 408–409 to remember what Reeba Daniel did to win several inventor prizes.

Summary: Reeba Daniel thought doing laundry took too many steps so she made drawings of how the step of moving clothes from the washer to the dryer could be automated.

Pages 410–411

As we reread pages 410–411, let's find out why Larry invented the "Conserve Sprinkler."

Summary: Larry thought there should be a way to save water and time when watering trees, so he invented the circular "Conserve Sprinkler."

Pages 412–416

Let's reread pages 412–416 to recall the steps the author suggests for creating an invention.

Summary: Arlene Erlbach suggests listing many problems and possible solutions before choosing one to draw and build.

FLUENCY BUILDER Be sure students have copies of *Intervention Practice Book* page 63. Point out the sentences on the bottom half of the page. As you read each marked phrase, model the appropriate expression and pace. Have students read each phrase after you, echoing the style. Then encourage them to practice by taking turns reading the sentences aloud with a partner.

INTERVENTION
PRACTICE
BOOK

page 63

Directed Reading: "Who Invented This?," pp. 126–132

Pages 126–127

Read the title of the selection. Tell students that on each page of this selection, they will read about a different invention. Have students read pages 126–127 before asking: **What invention is described on page 126?** (*pencils with erasers on them*) **NOTE DETAILS**

MOVING
AHEAD
pp. 126–132

What is the main idea of each page? What problems were solved with inventions? (Possible responses: *Two inventors solved the problem of not always having an eraser when using a pencil. A supermarket owner solved the problem of people only buying what they could put in their baskets by inventing the shopping cart.*) **MAIN IDEA AND DETAILS**

Pages 128–129

Read aloud page 128 quickly. Ask: **Where and when did Ernest Hamwi invent the ice-cream cone?** Then have a student read the page aloud slowly. Model using the adjust reading rate strategy:

> **MODEL** It wasn't until this page was read slowly that I was able to think about the importance of the details. When I took time to think about the setting, the World's Fair in the summer, I could picture the many hot people who would buy ice cream if they could. Since it was summer, the ice cream would melt and would have to be thrown away if it was not purchased. Reading slowly helped me understand why it was so important to solve the problem of running out of dishes. **ADJUST READING RATE**

Discuss whether students agree with your thinking. Have another volunteer read page 129 slowly while they listen to another solution to a problem. Ask: **What was the problem? How was it solved?** (*Possible response: A teacher wanted a better way to teach the countries of the world, so he invented puzzle maps for students to put together.*) **MAIN IDEA AND DETAILS**

Page 130

Ask students to use the speech balloon on page 130 to predict what they will read about. Then have them read to confirm their predictions. Ask: **Who kept the idea and the profits for Hunt's invention?** (*the man who gave him the wire*) **IMPORTANT DETAILS**

Page 131

After students read page 131, ask: **How are all the inventions you read about alike?** (*Possible responses: They all solve a problem, and they're simple.*) **MAIN IDEA**

INTERVENTION
PRACTICE
BOOK

page 65

Ask: **What makes someone a good inventor?** (*Possible response: being a problem solver*) **INTERPRET THEME**

Summarize the selection. Have students think about the different inventions they read about and what each does. Then have them complete *Intervention Practice Book* page 65 and summarize the story.

Answers to *Think About It* Questions

1. A person might invent something to solve a problem or to improve something. **SUMMARY**

2. Possible response: He may have felt proud of inventing something so useful, but unhappy that someone else got rich from his inventions. **INTERPRETATION**

3. News stories should tell the *who, what, when, where,* and *why* of the invention. **WRITE A NEWS STORY**

AFTER

Skill Review
pages 420–421

USE SKILL CARD 16B

(Focus Skill) **Main Idea and Details**

RETEACH the skill. Have students look at **side B of Skill Card 16: Main Idea and Details.** Read the skill reminder with them, and have a volunteer read the paragraph aloud. Then help students identify the first sentence as the main idea and the other sentences as supporting details.

Have a volunteer read aloud the next set of directions. Explain that students can now work with partners to create their own main idea and details chart. Remind them to write the main idea in the top row and the details below.

After students have completed their main idea and details charts, have them display and explain their work. Point out that the selection "The Kids' Invention Book" is organized by main ideas and their supporting details. It organizes information by grouping details that tell about each main idea. Each invention is introduced as a main idea followed by details about the invention.

FLUENCY BUILDER Be sure students have copies of *Intervention Practice Book* page 63. Explain that partners will practice the sentences on the bottom half of the page by reading them to each other twice. Have partners give feedback before the first and second reading and listen for improvement after the second reading.

INTERVENTION PRACTICE BOOK

page 63

Expository Writing: Sentences That Contrast

Build on prior knowledge. Tell students that they are going to write together about how two inventions are different. Display the following information:

Contrasting Two Inventions: Slinky® and Yo-yo	
Slinky®	**Yo-yo**
spiral	string sandwiched between two nonmoving circular parts
metal or plastic	metal, plastic, wood
stack and stretch	wrap string around axis
moves on its own once it is started	move wrist up and down

Construct the text. "Share the pen" with students in a collaborative group writing effort. Guide them to write sentences from the contrasting ideas they listed on the chart. Use these steps to think aloud the process:

- Write one phrase about the Slinky®.

- Add a contrasting phrase about the yo-yo.

- Put together the two phrases to create a complete sentence contrasting a Slinky® and a yo-yo.

- Repeat using other pairs of related phrases from the chart.

Revisit the text. Go back and read the sentences together. Ask: **Have we shown the differences between the two inventions? What could be added to help readers picture the differences?** (*exact words*)

- Guide students in adding exact words to show the contrasting ideas.

- Have students read the completed sentences aloud.

On Your Own

Have students choose two inventions in a certain category that they use, such as a pen and pencil or escalators and elevators. Tell them to write some phrases that describe each invention. Then have them use these phrases to write sentences that tell how these two inventions differ.

Connect Spelling and Phonics

RETEACH consonant /s/ *ce, ci, cy*. Write the words *celery, cider,* and *cylinder* on the board. Ask students what these three words have in common. (the /s/ sound) Tell students that for each word you say, the /s/ sound is spelled with a *c*. Dictate the following words. After students write each one, display the correct spelling so they can proofread their work.

I. cent	2. tricycle	3. city*	4. cement
5. face	6. ice*	7. celery*	8. pencil*

*Word appears in "Who Invented This?"

Dictate the following sentence and have students write it: *Tracy noticed the ceiling in the cinema was peeling.*

Build and Read Longer Words

INTERVENTION ASSESSMENT BOOK

Remind students that they have learned that words such as *final* and *program* have a long vowel sound in the first syllable; such words are divided right after the vowel in the first syllable. Then write *celery* on the board and read it aloud. Point out that *celery* has the same pattern of letters but is divided after the *l* because the first syllable has a short vowel sound. Explain to students that to figure out whether the first syllable has a long or short sound, they should try both and decide which one sounds right. Next, write these words on the board: *cinnamon, palace, cellular, recess.* Have volunteers read each one and tell how they figured it out.

FLUENCY BUILDER Have students choose a page from "Who Invented This?" to read aloud to a partner. You may have students choose a page that they found particularly interesting, or have them choose one of the following options:

- Read the first page of the selection on page 126, including the speech bubbles. (Total: 97 words)

- Read page 128, including the speech bubbles. (Total: 101 words)

- Read page 131, including the speech bubbles. (Total: 112 words)

Students read the selected passage aloud to their partner three times. Have each student rate his or her own reading on a scale from I to 4.

Review Vocabulary

List the Vocabulary Words on the board: *device*, *disabilities*, *prosthetic*, *scholarship*, *document*, *circular*, *modify*. Then write *noun*, *verb*, *adjective* at the top of three columns on the board. (Noun: *device, disabilities, document, scholarship*; Verb: *modify*; Adjective: *circular, prosthetic*.) After the lists are made, have students verbally create a sentence for each Vocabulary Word, beginning with each of the nouns.

You may want to display the Vocabulary Words and definitions on page 159. Have students copy them to use when they study for the vocabulary test.

(Focus Skill) Review Main Idea and Details

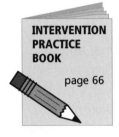

INTERVENTION
PRACTICE
BOOK

page 66

To review main idea and details before the weekly assessment, distribute *Intervention Practice Book* page 66. To begin, read aloud the direction line and guide students to underline the main idea statement when they figure it out. Have volunteers create a main idea table for the paragraph using the one found on the bottom of the page. Guide them to write the main idea statement in the top box and to write one detail in each box.

Review Test Prep

Ask students to turn to page 421 of the *Pupil Edition*. Call attention to the tips for answering the test questions. Tell students that paying attention to these tips can help them answer not only the test questions on this page but also other test questions like these.

LEAD
THE WAY

page 421

INTERVENTION
ASSESSMENT
BOOK

Have students follow along as you read aloud each test question and the tip that goes with it. Discuss why main ideas might be used in a retelling, but not the details. Read the second test question and tip. Explain how several details can be used to form a main idea. To find the main idea and details, you might also have students ask themselves if each question tells about one thing or everything in the paragraph.

Self-Selected Reading

Have students select their own books to read independently. They might choose books from the classroom library shelf, or you may wish to offer a group of appropriate books from which students can choose.

- *Inventing a Better Tomorrow.* (See page 42 IM of the *Teacher's Edition* for a lesson plan.)

- *Annie's Gifts* by Angela Shelf Medearis. Just Us Books, 1997

- *Max Malone Makes a Million* by Charlotte Herman. Henry Holt, 1992

You may also wish to choose additional books that are the same genre or by the same author, or that have the same kind of text structure as the selection.

After students have chosen their books, give each student a copy of My Reading Log, which can be found on page R38 in the back of the *Teacher's Edition*. Have students fill in the information at the top of the form. Then have them use the log to keep track of their reading and to record their responses to the literature.

Conduct student-teacher conferences. Arrange time for each student to confer with you individually about his or her self-selected reading. Have students share their Reading Logs with you at the conference. Ask them if they would like to choose a favorite passage to read aloud to you. Ask questions about the book designed to stimulate discussion. For example, you might ask how the illustrations and diagrams helped students understand the inventions topic.

FLUENCY PERFORMANCE Have students read aloud to you a passage previously selected from "Who Invented This?" The passage should be one that they have practiced with a partner. Track the number of words each student reads correctly. Ask the student to rate his or her own performance on the 1 to 4 scale. Students who are not happy with their oral reading should have another opportunity to continue practicing. Encourage them to reread the passage to you when ready.

See *Oral Reading Fluency Assessment* for monitoring progress.

LESSON 17

BEFORE
Building Background and Vocabulary

INTERVENTION PRACTICE BOOK

page 68

Use with

"The Case of Pablo's Nose"

Review Phonics: Consonant /j/ge, gi, gy, dge

Identify the sound. Have students repeat this sentence aloud three times: *The gentle giraffe eats leaves for energy.* Have them identify words that have the /j/ sound they hear in *hedge.* (*gentle, giraffe, energy*)

Associate letters to sound. Write the above sentence on the board. Underline the letter that follows the *g* in each word and explain that when *g* is followed by *e, i,* or *y,* it has the /j/ sound. Then write *hedge* on the board and underline the letters *dge.* Tell students that these letters also stand for the /j/ sound. Point out that when *g* is followed by other letters, it usually stands for the /g/ sound: *game, goat, gust.*

Word blending. Model blending *gentle.* Slide your hand under the word as you elongate each sound /jeenntəəll/. Then say the word naturally— *gentle.* Follow a similar procedure for the words *energy* and *hedge.*

Apply the skill. *Letter Substitution* Write the following words on the board and have students read each aloud. Make the changes necessary to form the words in parentheses.

cel (gel)	**stale** (stage)	**let** (ledge)	**but** (budge)
sum (gym)	**rate** (rage)	**bat** (badge)	**stint** (stingy)

Introduce Vocabulary

PRETEACH lesson vocabulary. Tell students they are going to learn six new words that they will see again when they read "The Case of Pablo's Nose." Teach each Vocabulary Word using the following process.

Use the following suggestions or similar ideas to give the meaning or context.

sculptor	Related words: The *sculpture* was made with plaster and metal. The *sculptor* used stone.
straightaway	Discuss how the meanings of *straight* and *away* combine to create a new word with a new meaning.
alibi	Provide synonyms for *alibi*: *excuse, explanation, reason.*
retorted	Point out the *-ed* ending and the prefix *re-,* meaning "to do again." Tell students that the root word *tort* means "to twist."
muttered	Demonstrate by speaking quietly and angrily with your lips partly closed.

> Write the word.
> Say the word.
> Track the word and have students repeat it.
> Give the meaning or context.

strengthening Point out the root word *strength*. Relate to materials added to things to make them stronger.

For vocabulary activities, see Vocabulary Games on pages 2–7.

AFTER
Building Background and Vocabulary

Apply Vocabulary Strategies

Use sentence and word context. Write on the board the sentence, *His alibi proved he was somewhere else during the robbery.* Tell students that they can use the words around an unfamiliar word to figure out its meaning. Model using the strategy.

> **MODEL** *Alibi* is a word I do not recognize. When I look at the surrounding text, I see the words "proved he was somewhere else." *Alibi* must be an excuse.

Guide students to use the strategy to figure out the meaning of other unfamiliar words.

RETEACH **lesson vocabulary.** Provide these sentence starters orally and ask volunteers to complete them.

1. The principal walked by the caged lion in our room and **muttered** . . . (*Possible response: "What is going on in there?"*)

2. Our fence needed **strengthening**, so we . . . (*Possible response: nailed new boards to it.*)

3. If the defendant's **alibi** was believable, then . . . (*Possible response: the jury would find him not guilty.*)

4. If I wanted to be a **sculptor**, I would start collecting . . . (*Possible response: pieces of metal, wire, nuts, bolts, and washers.*)

5. After Jan's sister criticized her messy room, Jan **retorted**, . . . (*Possible response: "Your room is messier!"*)

6. I will always come **straightaway** to a . . . (*Possible response: birthday party!*)

Vocabulary Words

sculptor artist who creates sculptures (three-dimensional works of art)

straightaway right away

alibi excuse that proves a person couldn't have committed a crime

retorted answered sharply

muttered said quietly and often angrily, with lips partly closed

strengthening having the ability to make someone or something stronger

FLUENCY BUILDER Use *Intervention Practice Book* page 67. Read the first column aloud and tell students that these words are from "The Case of Pablo's Nose." Have students repeat the list. Then read the second column aloud and say that these are all common words. Finally, read the third column aloud and tell students that these words all have the /j/ sound. Have partners take turns reading aloud the words in the second and third columns.

INTERVENTION PRACTICE BOOK
page 67

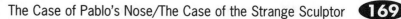

BEFORE

Reading
"The Case of
Pablo's Nose"
pages 424–430

USE SKILL CARD 17A

(Focus Skill) **Sequence**

PRETEACH the skill. Point out that events usually happen in a certain order, or sequence. Give an everyday example, such as choosing a book from the library, then reading the book, and finally sharing the book with a friend. Repeat the events in a different order and discuss why this sequence does not make sense.

Have students look at **side A of Skill Card 17: Sequence**. Read the definition of sequence. Next, have students look at the pictures and describe what is happening in each one. Now call attention to the diagram and have volunteers take turns reading the sentences aloud. Ask:

- **Why does the diagram show the sentences in this order?** (*This is the order in which the events happen.*)

- **Which words help you figure out the sequence of events?** (*then, soon, at last*)

- **What would happen if you put the sentences in a different order?** (*The sequence would not make sense.*)

Remind students that using signal words to show sequence of events is a good way to organize text to make their writing easy to understand.

Prepare to Read: "The Case of Pablo's Nose"

Preview. Tell students that they are going to read a mystery called "The Case of Pablo's Nose." Point out that noting clues in the order they are given can help the reader solve the mystery. Tell students that "The Case of Pablo's Nose" is the mystery of the nose Pablo Pizzaros sculpted that disappears before it can be entered in a contest. Then preview the selection.

LEAD
THE WAY
pages
424–430

- **Pages 424–425:** "The Case of Pablo's Nose" sounds like a mystery that has something to do with a nose. The title is written in a magnifying glass. Skimming the summary tells me that Encyclopedia Brown solves mysteries.

- **Pages 426–427:** The boy and girl on the left must be Encyclopedia Brown and Sally; the other boy must be their client.

- **Pages 428–429:** The caption tells me that Encyclopedia Brown figures out the mystery. The girl on the bicycle must have something to do with the solution.

- **Page 430:** I think the author wrote the solution upside down to keep me from reading it until I tried to figure it out.

Set purpose. Model setting a purpose for reading the story.

MODEL From my preview, I know this story is a mystery. I will read to understand each event in the order it occurs and to find the solution.

Reread and Summarize

Have students reread and summarize "The Case of Pablo's Nose" in sections, as described in the chart below.

Pages 424–425

Let's reread pages 424–425 to remind us what Encyclopedia Brown is famous for in his town.

Summary: Encyclopedia Brown, the son of the town's Chief of Police, is a young detective who is known for solving difficult cases.

Pages 426–427

As we reread pages 426–427, let's find out what the mystery is and whether there are any clues.

Summary: Pablo asks Encyclopedia Brown to solve the case of his missing sculpted nose that he thinks was stolen by a girl riding a purple bike.

Pages 428–429

Let's reread pages 428–429 to find clues that Encyclopedia Brown used to solve the mystery.

Summary: When the kids approach Desmoana, they find her purple bike hidden. She says that not only did she not take the nose, but she also hasn't ridden her bike in a year. However, Brown saw Desmoana doing tricks on her bike, which made him realize that she had lied about not riding her bike.

Page 430

Let's reread the solution on page 430 to recall the order of clues used to solve the case.

Summary: Brown solved the mystery by having Desmoana prove she hadn't ridden her bike in a year. In the process, she made it obvious that she had. She returned Pablo's nose, which won the contest.

FLUENCY BUILDER Have students look at the bottom of *Intervention Practice Book* page 67. As you read each sentence aloud, ask students to repeat after you. If they are having difficulty, read each phrase before students repeat it. Have them echo the appropriate pace, expression, and phrasing that you model. Then have students practice reading each sentence with a partner.

INTERVENTION
PRACTICE
BOOK

page 67

BEFORE

Making Connections
pages 434–435

Pages 134–135

Directed Reading: "The Case of the Strange Sculptor," pp. 134–141

Read aloud the title of the story. Have students read pages 134–135. Ask: **What has the crowd in the picture gathered to see?** (*Reggie Rodgers's statue of the Gentle Giant*) **IMPORTANT DETAILS**

> **MOVING AHEAD**
> pp. 134–141

Ask: **How does Al feel about seeing the statue? How can you tell?** (*Possible response: He is not eager to see it. He says he can't understand "what all the fuss is about."*) **DETERMINE CHARACTERS' EMOTIONS**

Ask: **What sequence of events leads up to Al's not liking Reggie?** (*Possible response: Reggie won first prize in last year's art show and he has been bragging ever since.*) **SEQUENCE**

Pages 136–137

Read page 136 aloud. Then ask: **Why does the crowd call Reggie Rodgers a "genius"?** (*Possible response: They think the statue is very lifelike.*) **INTERPRET CHARACTERS' MOTIVATIONS**

Ask a volunteer to read aloud page 137. Have other students listen to find out how Al reacts when he sees the statue. Ask: **What upset Al?** (*Possible response: He realizes that Reggie must have stolen his statue and is taking credit for his work.*) **DRAW CONCLUSIONS**

Pages 138–140

Have students read page 138. Ask: **Why does Gina believe Al is telling the truth?** (*Al has never told a lie and Gina has a feeling something isn't quite right with Reggie.*) **DRAW CONCLUSIONS**

Before students read page 139, ask: **What do you predict will happen?** (*Possible response: Al will find out that Reggie took his statue.*) Model using the read ahead strategy to confirm their predictions:

> **MODEL** I wanted to read ahead to find out whether Reggie stole the statue or not. I also wanted to see if the clues I wondered about would help me solve the case. **READ AHEAD**

Have students read pages 139 and 140, including the upside-down solution on page 140 to confirm their predictions and discover the solution.

INTERVENTION PRACTICE BOOK
page 69

Summarize the selection. Ask students to discuss whether they thought "The Case of the Strange Sculptor" was realistic. Then have them complete the *Intervention Practice Book* page 69 and summarize the story.

172 Lesson 17 • Intervention Teacher's Guide

Answers to *Think About It* Questions

1. Gina listens to Reggie's side of the story. He slips up twice, giving Gina clues that he is guilty. **SUMMARY**
2. Reggie may feel pleased with himself when the statue is revealed. He must feel scared when he sees Al and his friends hurrying toward him. **INTERPRETATION**
3. Students should continue the story and show how Al and Reggie react to the revelation. **WRITE A STORY**

AFTER

Skill Review
pages 436–437

USE SKILL CARD 17B

(Focus Skill) Sequence

RETEACH the skill. Have students look at **side B of Skill Card 17: Sequence**. Read the skill reminder with them, and have a volunteer read the paragraph aloud. Encourage the rest of the group to take note of different events and to listen closely for signal words.

Have a volunteer read aloud the next set of directions. Explain that students can now work with a partner to create their own diagrams. Remind them to write only one event per box to show the correct sequence.

After students have completed their sequence diagrams, invite them to display and explain their work. Point out that the selection "The Case of Pablo's Nose" is organized according to sequence. The story begins when Pablo hires Encyclopedia Brown to find his sculpture of a nose and follows each event leading up to Encyclopedia's solving the case.

FLUENCY BUILDER Be sure students have copies of *Intervention Practice Book* page 67. Point out the dialogue found in several of the sentences. Explain that small groups will listen to you read the dialogue from those sentences. Have students repeat each piece of dialogue, using their *Intervention Practice Book* page to guide them. Finally, read each sentence in its entirety and have students echo it after you. Encourage them to listen to each other and to try to make each rereading, especially of the dialogue, sound more like your model.

INTERVENTION PRACTICE BOOK

page 67

Expository Writing: Persuasive Paragraph

Build on prior knowledge. Tell students that they are going to work together to write a persuasive paragraph. Display the following reasons why students might want to go on a field trip:

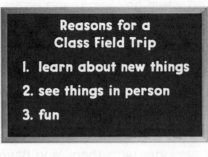

**Reasons for a
Class Field Trip**

1. learn about new things
2. see things in person
3. fun

Remind students that when you write to persuade, you want to convince your audience to feel the way that you feel.

Construct the text. "Share the pen" with students in a collaborative group writing effort. Guide them to create a short persuasive paragraph from the reasons listed on the chart. Use these steps to think aloud the process:

- Write an opinion statement about going on a field trip.

- Add details to support the opinion statement.

- Think about which opinion statement is the strongest. Arrange the sentences so the strongest statement comes at the end.

- Add a topic sentence—a sentence that tells why you are writing.

Revisit the text. Go back and read the persuasive paragraph together. Ask: **Have we included reasons and details to support our opinion? What could we add to make our opinion stronger?** (*emotional words*)

- Guide students to add emotional words such as "in our best interest," "to help students appreciate."

- Have students read the completed paragraph aloud.

On Your Own

Tell students to think of something that would improve their school. Have them make a list of reasons, write them into opinion statements, and support them with details. Remind them to arrange their sentences into a short paragraph, ending with the strongest opinion.

Connect Spelling and Phonics

RETEACH **consonant /j/** **ge, gi, gy, dge.** Write the word *gymnast* on the board and point out that since the *g* is followed by *y* it has the /j/ sound. Tell students they will now write words that have a *g* or *dge* in them. Dictate the following words and then display the correct spelling so students can proofread their own work.

I. gymnast	2. general	3. giant*	4. logical*
5. stage	6. genius*	7. fudge*	8. badge

*Word appears in "The Case of the Strange Sculptor."

Dictate the following sentence and have students write it: *The general's gym badge was on the stage.*

Build and Read Longer Words

Remind students that when a word with the VCCV pattern is broken into syllables, it is usually broken between the consonants.

Write the word *gymnast* on the board. Ask students which part of the word sounds like /jim/ and which part sounds like /nast/. Follow the same procedure with *stingy*, *surgical*, and *clergy*.

 FLUENCY BUILDER Have students choose a page from "The Case of the Strange Sculptor" to read aloud to a partner. You may have students choose a page that they found particularly interesting or have them choose one of the following options:

- Read the title and first page of the selection on page 134. (Total: 87 words)

- Read all of page 137. (Total: 85 words)

- Read all of page 139 through the first paragraph on page 140. (Total: 127 words)

Students should read the selected passages aloud to their partner several times. Have the listening partners rate each reading on a scale from I to 4.

Review Vocabulary

To revisit Vocabulary Words prior to the weekly assessment, use these sentence frames. Have volunteers take turns reading aloud the sentence stems and choices. Students identify the correct choice and explain why that choice makes sense in the sentence.

1. If you watch a **sculptor** working you are seeing
   a. an athlete.   b. an artist.

2. A poor **alibi** for not doing your homework is
   a. "My dog ate it."   b. "There was a family emergency."

3. If you go **straightaway** to school, you are going
   a. right away.   b. later.

4. The woman **retorted** because
   a. someone was rude to her. b. someone was kind to her.

5. He **muttered** the answer because
   a. he was confident.   b. he was unsure of it.

6. The house needed **strengthening** against
   a. strong winds.   b. gentle breezes.

Correct responses: lb, 2a, 3a, 4a, 5b, 6a

(Focus Skill) Review Sequence

To review sequence before the weekly assessment, distribute *Intervention Practice Book* page 70. Have volunteers read aloud the first direction line and the sentences. Guide students to use both signal words and text clues to put the sentences in the correct sequence on the diagram. Have them circle and identify the signal words in each sentence.

**INTERVENTION
PRACTICE
BOOK**

page 70

Review Test Prep

Ask students to turn to page 437 of the *Pupil Edition*.
Call attention to the tips for answering the test questions.
Tell students that paying attention to these tips can help
them answer not only the test questions on this page but
also other questions they will see on tests.

**LEAD
THE WAY**

page 437

Have students follow along as you read aloud each test question and the tip that goes with it. Discuss how signal words can help make sense of the clues. Discuss why someone might tell a story out of order. Then ask what words the person might use to help the listener understand the order of events.

**INTERVENTION
ASSESSMENT
BOOK**

Self-Selected Reading

Have students select their own books to read independently. They might choose books from the classroom library shelf, or you may wish to offer a group of appropriate books from which students can choose.

- *The Masterpiece*. (See page 437K of the *Teacher's Edition* for a lesson plan.)

- *The Time Machine and Other Cases* by Seymour Simon. Avon, 1997

- *Who Stole the Wizard of Oz?* by Avi. Knopf, 1990

You may also wish to choose additional books that are the same genre or by the same author, or that have the same kind of text structure as the selection.

After students have chosen their books, give each student a copy of My Reading Log, which can be found on page R38 in the back of the *Teacher's Edition*. Have students fill in the information at the top of the form. Then have them use the log to keep track of their reading and to record their responses to the literature.

Conduct student-teacher conferences. Arrange time for each student to confer with you individually about his or her self-selected reading. Have students bring their Reading Logs to share. Students might also like to choose a passage to read aloud to you during the conference. Ask questions about the passage they read and then about the entire book. For example, you might ask what the mystery is and what clues led to the solution.

FLUENCY PERFORMANCE Have students read the passage previously practiced from "The Case of the Strange Sculptor." Keep track of the number of words the students read correctly and incorrectly. Ask students what rating they would give themselves on the 1 to 4 scale. Give students the opportunity to reread the passage aloud until they are satisfied with their performance.

See *Oral Reading Fluency Assessment* for monitoring progress.

Use with

"In the Days of King Adobe"

Review Phonics: Vowel Diphthongs /oi/*oi, oy*

Identify the sound. Have students repeat the following sentence aloud three times: *Troy avoids oysters*. Have them identify the words that have the /oi/ sound. (*Troy, avoids, oysters*)

Associate letters to sound. Write the above sentence on the board. Underline the letters *oy* or *oi* in each word. Explain that these letter combinations stand for the /oi/ sound heard in *boy* and *soil*.

Word blending. Write *soil, broil, loyal,* and *boys* on the board. Model how to blend and read the word *soil*. Point to *s* and say /s/. Slide your hand under *o* and *i* and say /oi/. Point to *l* and say /l/. Draw your hand under the whole word as you elongate the sounds /ssoill/. Then say the word naturally—*soil*. Repeat the procedure with the remaining words.

Apply the skill. *Letter Substitution* Write the following words on the board and have students read them aloud. Then make the changes necessary to form the words in parentheses. Ask volunteers to read the new words aloud.

INTERVENTION
PRACTICE
BOOK

page 72

owl (oil)	**bay** (boy)	**fail** (foil)	**coal** (coil)
tray (Troy)	**Ron** (Roy)	**bail** (boil)	**sail** (soil)

Introduce Vocabulary

PRETEACH **lesson vocabulary.** Tell students they are going to learn five new words that they will see again when they read "In the Days of King Adobe." Teach each Vocabulary Word using the following process.

Use the following suggestions to give the meaning or context.

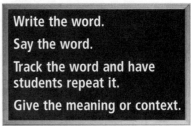

Write the word.
Say the word.
Track the word and have students repeat it.
Give the meaning or context.

thrifty   Point out the root word *thrift*. Work with students to make a list of ways to be careful with money.

generous   Relate to receiving a large portion of dessert.

roguish   Remind students that the suffix *-ish* turns a noun (*rogue*) into an adjective (*roguish*). Use *rogue* and *roguish* in phrases to show the different uses: *a mean rogue; a roguish man*.

rascally   Make a list of *rascally* characters in stories, such as the wolf in "Red Riding Hood."

fascinated   Relate to things that fascinate people such as good books, space exploration, and movie stars.

For vocabulary activities, see Vocabulary Games on pages 2–7.

AFTER

Building Background and Vocabulary

Apply Vocabulary Strategies

> **Vocabulary Words**
>
> **thrifty** careful in spending
>
> **generous** large; plentiful
>
> **roguish** treacherous; dishonest
>
> **rascally** naughty; dishonest
>
> **fascinated** amazed and intrigued

Use antonyms. Write the following sentences on chart paper: *The bank turned down Don's job application. They are looking for honest people and he is rather roguish.* Tell students that they can use antonyms as context clues to determine the meaning of a new word. Model using the strategy.

> **MODEL** I am unsure of the meaning of the word *roguish*. When I reread the sentences, I notice the phrase "honest people." Since Don doesn't get the job, he must not be honest. *Honest* and *roguish* must have opposite meanings. I think *roguish* must mean "dishonest."

Guide students to use a similar procedure to figure out the meaning of other Vocabulary Words.

RETEACH lesson vocabulary. Have students listen as you read each sentence starter followed by two possible endings. Have students choose *a* or *b* to indicate the most logical answer for each one.

1. Melanie was **fascinated** with her new computer game so she
   a. watched TV.   b. played it until bedtime.
2. Louis acted in a **roguish** way when he tried to
   a. collect everyone's trash.   b. steal everyone's lunch.
3. The best way to be **thrifty** is to
   a. save your money.   b. spend your money.
4. Most children would like a more **generous** helping of
   a. homework.   b. allowance.
5. The **rascally** friend
   a. played a prank.   b. offered to help with chores.

Correct Responses: 1b, 2b, 3a, 4b, 5a

FLUENCY BUILDER Have students look at *Intervention Practice Book* page 71. Read the words in the first column aloud. Invite students to track each word and repeat the words after you. Then have students work in pairs to read the words in the first column aloud to each other. Follow the same procedure with each of the remaining columns. After partners have practiced reading aloud the words in each of the columns, have them practice all of the words.

> **INTERVENTION PRACTICE BOOK**
>
> page 71

In the Days of King Adobe/Just Enough Is Plenty   **179**

USE SKILL CARD 18A

(Focus Skill) Main Idea and Details

PRETEACH **the skill.** Point out that every story has a main idea—what the selection is mostly about. Explain that details tell more about the main idea. Ask students to tell the main idea of a story they recently completed. Then explain that often the main idea is unstated.

Have students look at **side A of Skill Card 18: Main Idea and Details**. Read the definitions. Then read the paragraph aloud. Point out that the main idea is written in the center of the web and tells what the story is mainly about. Ask:

- **How do the details lead to the main idea?** (*Possible response: The details are clues to what the story is mainly about.*)

- **How does knowing how to identify the main idea help you understand the story?** (*Possible response: It helps me remember the story and focus on the most important parts.*)

Remind students that knowing the main idea and its supporting details can help them summarize and remember the story.

Prepare to Read: "In the Days of King Adobe"

Preview. Tell students that they are going to read a folktale called "In the Days of King Adobe." Explain that folktales are stories that were first told orally. They reflect the customs and beliefs of a culture. Then preview the selection.

LEAD THE WAY

pages
440–448

- **Pages 440–441:** I see the title and the names of the author and illustrator. The picture shows an old woman making something. I wonder what it is.

- **Pages 442–443:** The woman looks as though she might have a secret. The men look like they might be plotting something.

- **Pages 444–445:** The woman looks as if she is eavesdropping on something going on in the other room. She looks a bit surprised.

- **Pages 446–447:** The illustration makes me wonder if these men are thieves. They have a bag and they look as if they are hiding something. They also look surprised as they open the bag.

Set Purpose. Model setting a purpose for reading the story.

MODEL From my preview, I know this is a folktale. Folktales often teach a lesson. I will read to find out what lessons the characters learn.

Reread and Summarize

Have students reread and summarize "In the Days of King Adobe" in sections, as described in the chart below.

Page 441

Let's reread page 441 to recall what the woman is doing and why.

Summary: The woman is poor but she makes visitors welcome by sharing her food. She lets two young men spend the night.

Pages 442–443

As we reread pages 442–443, let's find how the woman and her guests treat one another.

Summary: The woman is generous to the young men but they plan to steal her special ham anyway.

Pages 444–445

Let's reread pages 444–445 to remember how the men steal the ham and how the woman tricks the men in return.

Summary: The woman wasn't asleep while the men were stealing the ham. She tricked them by replacing the ham with a brick.

Pages 446–447

As we reread pages 446–447, let's find out about the woman's dream and how the men discover they have been tricked.

Summary: The woman describes a dream to hint at the fact that she has switched the ham with an adobe brick. The men don't figure out what the dream really means until they discover the brick in their bag.

Page 448

Let's reread page 448 to see what the men did the next time they met a generous woman.

Summary: They learned their lesson and did not trick her.

FLUENCY BUILDER Redirect students to the *Intervention Practice Book* page 71. Model appropriate pace, expression, and phrasing as you read each sentence. Have students listen to the pacing and meaning of each sentence. Then ask them to read aloud simultaneously with you as you repeat each sentence. Students can gain further practice by reading the sentences aloud three times to a partner.

INTERVENTION PRACTICE BOOK

page 71

Directed Reading: "Just Enough Is Plenty," pp. 142–148

Pages 142–143

Read aloud the title of the selection. Have students preview the pictures. Have a volunteer read the first three paragraphs aloud. Ask: **What seems to be the main problem in the story?** (*The farmer is so fascinated with his riches that he annoys his friends.*) (focus Skill) **MAIN IDEA AND DETAILS**

> MOVING
> AHEAD
> pp. 142–148

Ask: **What do you think will happen next?** (*The friends will play a prank on the farmer.*) **MAKE PREDICTIONS**

Page 144

Reread the page aloud. Have students listen to confirm their predictions. Ask: **Why do you think the farmer buys extra land?** (*He doesn't want his friend to own more than he does.*) **DRAW CONCLUSIONS**

Page 145

Have students read the page silently. Ask: **How do you think the farmer feels after his friend tells him about his new pigs and hens?** (*jealous, envious*) **DETERMINE CHARACTERS' EMOTIONS**

Pages 146–147

Read aloud page 146. Ask: **Why do you think the friend suggests that the farmer needs a bigger house?** (*Possible response: to help the farmer realize that being rich doesn't always make you happy*) **DRAW CONCLUSIONS**

Ask a volunteer to read aloud page 147. Then have students reread it to clarify the lesson the farmer learns. Model using the Reread to Clarify strategy:

> **MODEL** If I am confused about what lesson the farmer learns, I can reread to clarify the information. When I read page 147 again, I understand that the lesson the farmer learns is that having more things is not the key to happiness. (focus Strategy) **REREAD TO CLARIFY**

Discuss whether students agree with your thinking.

INTERVENTION PRACTICE BOOK

page 73

Summarize the selection. Have students think about the folktale they read and what the lesson is. Then help them summarize the story in one sentence.

Answers to *Think About It* Questions

1. He buys more to show that he really is rich. At last, he gets tired of the extra work his riches give him and goes back to having just enough. **SUMMARY**

2. Possible response: He may feel happy having just enough and relieved that he no longer has to worry about keeping up with his tricky friend. **INTERPRETATION**

3. Conversations should express the neighbors' surprise and puzzlement at the farmer's actions. **WRITE A CONVERSATION**

AFTER

Skill Review
pages 452–453

USE SKILL CARD 18B

(Focus Skill) **Main Idea and Details**

RETEACH the skill. Have students look at **side B of Skill Card 18: Main Idea and Details**. Read the skill reminder with them and invite students to read along. Ask volunteers to describe the concepts of main idea and details in their own words.

Have students read the paragraph aloud with you. Direct students to create a chart that will help them identify the main idea and important details in this story. Remind students that authors don't always directly state the main idea. Often, readers have to use details as clues to figure out the main idea.

After students have identified the main idea and details of the story, have them share the chart with the group. Discuss any differences among students' charts.

FLUENCY BUILDER Tell students they will practice the sentences on the bottom of *Intervention Practice Book* page 71 that they worked with earlier. Ask students to work in pairs. One student will be the reader and one will be the listener. Have the reader read the sentences aloud to the listener three times. After the third reading, the listener notes how the reader improved. Have partners switch roles and repeat the exercise.

INTERVENTION PRACTICE BOOK

page 71

Expository Writing: Literature Response

Build on prior knowledge. Tell students that they are going to write a paragraph together that responds to literature. Display the following information:

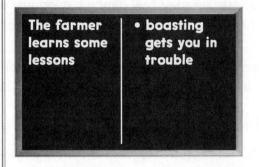

The farmer learns some lessons	• boasting gets you in trouble

Duplicate this chart on the board. Ask students to think about the lessons the farmer learns in "Just Enough is Plenty." Add their ideas to the second column in bullet form. Remind students to support their responses with evidence from the story.

Construct the text. "Share the pen" with students in a collaborative group writing effort. Guide them to create sentences from the responses listed in the chart.

- Write an introductory sentence that describes one of the lessons the farmer learns.

- Find evidence in the chart that proves the farmer learns the lesson.

- Write a sentence that focuses on this evidence.

- Conclude by restating the main idea of your paragraph in a final sentence.

Revisit the text. Reread the draft aloud with students. Ask: **Have we used reasons and details to support our response?**

- Guide students to provide supporting details as necessary.

- Have students read the completed paragraph aloud.

On Your Own

Have students choose a story that they have enjoyed and list three reasons why they liked it. Tell them to write a paragraph that includes their opinion and the three reasons that support it. Encourage them to write a main idea statement for their response and restate it at the end of the paragraph.

Connect Spelling and Phonics

RETEACH **vowel diphthongs /oi/oi, oy.** Write *boil* on the board, and tell students that the first four words you will say have the same *oi* vowel pattern as in *boil*. Dictate words 1–4 and have students record them. Then write the word *toy* on the board. Tell students that the next four words have the /oi/ sound spelled with the same *oy* pattern as in *toy*. Dictate words 5–8, and have students proofread as before.

1. coin*	2. toiling*	3. voice*	4. pointed*
5. annoyed*	6. decoy	7. boys	8. joyfully

*Word appears in "Just Enough Is Plenty."

Dictate the following sentences and have students write them: *The boys make a lot of noise. Leroy is overjoyed when the boys go home.*

Build and Read Longer Words

Write these words on the board: *pointlessly, joyless.* Draw students' attention to the word *pointlessly*, and have a volunteer identify the two vowels that together stand for the /oi/ sound. (*oi*) Then point to *joyless*, and ask students which letters stand for the /oi/ sound in this word. (*oy*) Underline the *oi* and *oy*, and tell students that these letter combinations usually stay together when a word is broken into syllables. Help students identify the syllables in *pointlessly* by asking: **Which letters sound like /point/? Which letters sound like /ləs/? Which letters sound like /lē/?** Then draw your hand under the entire word while students read it. Repeat for the words *voyage, royal,* and *employer.*

INTERVENTION ASSESSMENT BOOK

FLUENCY BUILDER Have students choose a passage from "Just Enough Is Plenty" to read aloud in a small group. They might choose their favorite part or you could suggest the following:

- Read all of page 144, which is about the plan. (Total: 102 words)

- Read all of page 146, which is about how the man reacts to being rich. (Total: 114 words)

Encourage partners to take turns reading a page or two aloud to each other. Ask students to focus on punctuation and expression of emotion as they read. Have the student rate each of his or her own readings on a scale from 1 to 4.

Review Vocabulary

List these Vocabulary Words on the board: *fascinated*, *thrifty*, *generous*, *roguish*, *rascally*. Have partners each choose a word secretly from the list. Have one student use his or her word in a question, such as **Why are people usually fascinated by new toys?** Have the partner answer the question, trying to use the word he or she chose in the answer. Then have partners switch places and eventually switch partners for additional practice.

INTERVENTION
PRACTICE
BOOK

page 74

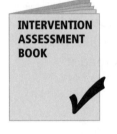

(Focus Skill) Review Main Idea and Details

To review main idea and details before the weekly assessment, distribute *Intervention Practice Book* page 74. Read aloud the paragraph and guide students to record the details of the story. Then have them write a main idea statement in the middle of the web to tell what the paragraph is mainly about.

Review Test Prep

Ask students to turn to page 453 of the *Pupil Edition*. Point out the two tips for answering questions. Remind students that knowing the details of a story can help them answer many questions about the story. These details can also help them to understand the main idea of the story.

LEAD
THE WAY

page 453

INTERVENTION
ASSESSMENT
BOOK

Have students follow along as you read aloud each test question and the tip that goes with it. Discuss how to identify the important details—those that lead to a main idea.

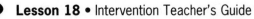

Self-Selected Reading

Have students select their own books to read independently. They might choose books from the classroom library shelf, or you may wish to offer a group of appropriate books from which students can choose.

- *The Emperor and the Peasant Boy.* (See page 453M of the *Teacher's Edition* for a lesson plan.)

- *Coyote Steals the Blanket* by Janet Stevens. Holiday House, 1997

- *The Old Woman Who Lived in a Vinegar Bottle* by Margaret Read Macdonald. August House, 1995

You may also wish to choose additional books that are the same genre, are by the same author, or have the same kind of text structure as the selection.

After students have chosen their books, give each student a copy of My Reading Log, which can be found on page R38 in the back of the *Teacher's Edition*. Have students fill in the information at the top of the form. Then have them use the log to keep track of their reading and to record their responses to the literature.

Conduct student-teacher conferences. Confer with students about their self-selected reading choices. Encourage students to share their Reading Log with you and to select a favorite passage to read aloud to you. Ask questions about the book to stimulate discussion. For example, you might ask what lesson was learned in a folktale or what details helped them understand parts of the story better.

FLUENCY PERFORMANCE Remind students that they practiced at least one passage from "Just Enough Is Plenty" earlier with a partner. Tell them that you would like to hear them read their passages aloud. Keep track of the number of words each student reads correctly. Ask the student to rate his or her own performance on the 1 to 4 scale. Suggest that students choose a second passage if they need more practice reading aloud, or give them an opportunity to continue practicing and then reread the passage to you.

See *Oral Reading Fluency Assessment* for monitoring progress.

LESSON 19

"Red Writing Hood"

BEFORE

Building
Background
and Vocabulary

Review Phonics: Vowel Variants /ô/aw, au(gh)

Identify the sound. Ask students to repeat the following sentence aloud three times: *Saul caught the prawns at dawn.* Have students identify the words that have the /ô/ sound. (*Saul, caught, prawns, dawn*)

Associate letters to sound. Write the above sentence on the board. Underline the letters *au, aw,* or *augh* in each word in which they appear. Point out that the letters *au, aw,* and *augh* stand for the /ô/ sound.

Word blending. Write *caught* on the board and tell students that the letters *gh* are silent in this word. Model how to blend and read the word *caught*. Point to *c* and say /k/. Slide your hand under the rest of the word as you say the sounds /kôôt/. Then say the word naturally—*caught*.

INTERVENTION
PRACTICE
BOOK

page 76

Apply the skill. *Letter Substitution* Write the following words, and have students read them aloud. Make the changes necessary to form the words in parentheses. Have a volunteer read each new word.

clap (claw)	**say** (saw)	**lunch** (launch)	**pal** (paw)
cat (caught)	**hail** (haul)	**fan** (fawn)	**fall** (fault)

Introduce Vocabulary

PRETEACH lesson vocabulary. Tell students they are going to learn eight new words that they will see again when they read a story called "Red Writing Hood." Teach each Vocabulary Word using the following process.

Use the following suggestions or similar ideas to give the meaning or context.

> Write the word.
> Say the word.
> Track the word and have students repeat it.
> Give the meaning or context.

script	Review the parts of a script: characters, setting, dialogue, stage directions, acts, scenes.
desperately	Break the word into syllables: *des/per/ate/ly.*
acceptable	Discuss the root word *accept*, which means "to meet approval." Discuss the suffix *-able*, which means "capable." Combine the meanings to understand *acceptable.*
injustice	Relate to times when students have had to deal with unfair actions.
circumstances	Explain that *circum-* refers to *round* things. Here it means "the facts surrounding something."
repentant	Discuss times when people are sorry for their actions.

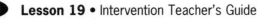

| discards | Make a list of items people get rid of, such as junk mail and broken things. |
| triumphantly | Demonstrate running a race and winning triumphantly. |

For vocabulary activities, see Vocabulary Games on pages 2–7.

For vocabulary activities, see Vocabulary Games on pages 2–7.

Apply Vocabulary Strategies

Use reference sources. Write on the board *He smiled triumphantly after winning the race.* Tell students that using a thesaurus to find synonyms can help them understand meanings. Model using the strategy.

> **MODEL** When I look up *triumphantly* in a thesaurus, I find that another word for *triumphantly* is *joyfully*. When I substitute *joyfully* in the sentence, it makes sense.

Guide students to use a thesaurus to find synonyms for other words.

RETEACH lesson vocabulary. Write a continuum on the board with the words *justice* and *injustice* at either end. Ask volunteers to show on the line whether they think these situations are characterized by justice, injustice, or something in between. Discuss differences in opinion.

1. When the girl stole my pencil and did not seem *repentant*, I grabbed it back from her.
2. Tim *desperately* wanted to win a medal, so he swam daily for years.
3. He *triumphantly* won the 100-meter foot race.
4. Mr. Moody *discards* any idea he disagrees with.
5. It is *acceptable* to give flowers at the end of a performance.
6. The *circumstances* surrounding the accident suggested that the driver was not paying attention. He was given a ticket.
7. The *script* was impossible to understand, so the teacher asked the student to rewrite it before actors learned the lines.

Vocabulary Words

script the written text of a play

desperately in a way that is full of anxiety

acceptable capable of meeting approval or being accepted

injustice unfairness

circumstances the events that affect or surround a situation

repentant regretful or sorry for one's actions

discards gets rid of

triumphantly in a way that is joyful

FLUENCY BUILDER Read the first word on *Intervention Practice Book* page 75. Ask students to listen to the pronunciation, look at the spelling, and ask any questions they have about the sounds of certain letter combinations. Then reread the word and have students repeat it. Continue with other words. Finally, have pairs of students read the words to each other, underlining words that give them difficulty. Help students by pronouncing these words.

INTERVENTION PRACTICE BOOK

page 75

USE SKILL CARD 19A

★ (Focus Skill) Sequence

PRETEACH **the skill.** Explain that stories make sense when they have a believable order of events, or **sequence**. Tell students that each event serves a purpose and affects the other events and that if one event is changed, the story will not make sense or it will have another outcome. Give an example such as changing the day of a test.

Have students look at **side A of Skill Card 19: Sequence.** Read aloud the explanation and "The Sneezy Wolf and the Three Little Pigs." Note how the sequence of events for both the traditional story and the new story are recorded in the sequence charts. Have students compare the paragraph they just read with the traditional story of the "Three Little Pigs." Ask:

- **Which event is the first difference from the traditional "Three Little Pigs" story?** (*Possible response: The wolf is invited in for tea.*)

- **Why is the outcome in this story different from the traditional "Three Little Pigs" story?** (*Possible response: The events are different.*)

Explain that when one event is changed in a story, those that follow will be different as well.

Prepare to Read: "Red Writing Hood"

Preview. Tell students that they are going to read "Red Writing Hood." Explain that it is a play based on the tale "Little Red Riding Hood." Explain that the sequence of events changes. Then preview the selection.

LEAD
THE WAY

pages
456–466

- **Pages 456–457:** I don't remember all these people from the story. The Cast of Characters includes Prince Charming, Bo Peep, and the Three Bears! This must have more than one fairy tale in it.

- **Pages 458–459:** Uh-oh. I wonder how the wolf got into a tutu! This looks like it will be a funny story.

- **Pages 460–461:** This must be Prince Charming and Little Miss Muffet. I wonder why they are together in this story.

- **Pages 462–463:** Cinderella is with two princes. She looks upset!

- **Pages 464–465:** Everyone in this picture looks bothered now. Are the men in black glasses there to straighten everything out?

Set purpose. Model setting a purpose for reading the story.

MODEL From my preview I can tell that the story is a different version of "Little Red Riding Hood." I will read for enjoyment and to find out what funny things happen.

Reread and Summarize

Have students reread and summarize "Red Writing Hood" in sections, as described in the chart below.

Pages 456–457

Let's reread page 457 to recall the Cast of Characters.

Summary: Characters from many fairy tales are listed here, including Red Riding Hood, the Wolf, Little Miss Muffet, two Princes, the Three Bears, Cinderella; two authors of fairy tales: (the Brothers) Grimm and (Hans Christian) Andersen; and one illustrator of classic fairy tales, (Arthur) Rackham.

Pages 458–459

As we reread pages 458–459, let's find out why the wolf ends up wearing a tutu.

Summary: Red Writing Hood changes her story by turning the wolf into a ballet dancer.

Pages 460–461

Let's reread pages 460–461 to remember how Prince Charming gets into Little Miss Muffet's story.

Summary: Red Writing Hood told Miss Muffet that she could write the spider out of her story and write Prince Charming into it.

Pages 462–463

As we reread pages 462–463, let's find out why Cinderella is upset.

Summary: Cinderella is upset because there is more than one Prince Charming. All the other characters start to get upset, too.

Pages 464–465

Let's reread pages 464–465 to see how the story ends.

Summary: The men in glasses, named after two famous fairy tale authors and one famous illustrator, tell everyone that the stories must return to their original forms.

FLUENCY BUILDER Use the bottom of *Intervention Practice Book* page 75. Read each sentence and ask students to repeat it after you. Have them underline any sentence parts they are having trouble reading. Then have pairs work together by first reading and then giving feedback on the parts they underlined. Finally, have them read each of the sentences to one another.

INTERVENTION
PRACTICE
BOOK

page 75

 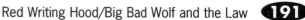

Directed Reading: "Big Bad Wolf and the Law," pp. 150–157

MOVING
AHEAD
pp. 150–157

Pages 150–151

Ask students to explain what they know about the Big Bad Wolf from such fairy tales as "Little Red Riding Hood." Then read aloud the title and the cast of characters on page 150. Explain that a bailiff is an officer of the court. Explain that the words in slanted type after a character's name give stage directions. Read aloud page 151. Then ask volunteers to take parts and reread it aloud. Ask: **What events led up to Wolf appearing in court?** (*He was found chasing a grandma and her granddaughter.*) (Focus Skill) **SEQUENCE**

Ask: **Does Judge Peep feel sympathy toward Wolf? Why or why not?** (*No; she thinks it's awful that Wolf was chasing the grandma and her granddaughter.*) **DETERMINE CHARACTERS' EMOTIONS**

Page 152

Ask: **How can you tell that Wolf wants Judge Peep to like him?** (*Possible response: He tells the judge she is beautiful.*) **DRAW CONCLUSIONS**

Ask: **Do you think Wolf's flattery is having an effect on the judge?** (*Possible response: Yes; because Judge Peep says that his words show he is truthful.*) **ANALYZE CHARACTERS**

Page 153

Have students identify the new character in the picture. Point out that in this play, Red Riding Hood is called Red Riding Cap. Read aloud page 153, with feeling. Ask: **Why is Red Riding Cap upset?** (*She says that Wolf said her grandma would be delicious.*) **DETERMINE CHARACTERS' EMOTIONS**

Page 154

Have students read silently. Ask: **Why doesn't Wolf think he should be put in jail?** (*He says that the author is to blame for how he acts.*) **IMPORTANT DETAILS**

Page 155

Have volunteers read dialogue aloud. Ask: **How does Wolf compare himself to Bo Peep and Red Riding Cap?** (*He says that they are all story characters that don't have any choice in what they do.*) **MAKE COMPARISONS**

Page 156

Tell students that creating a mental image of a scene can help them understand it better. For example, to understand how the wolf reacts when the three little pigs come into the courtroom, you might create a mental image of their entrance. Model using the create mental images strategy:

> **MODEL** I can just see the look on the wolf's face when the three little pigs come into the courtroom! He is probably frowning and looking scared because now he knows he will be found guilty. The pigs are probably looking quite smug since they have important facts to prove the wolf's guilt. (Focus Strategy) **CREATE MENTAL IMAGES**

Discuss whether students agree with your thinking.

Summarize the selection. Have students discuss the outcome of "Big Bad Wolf and the Law." Then have them complete *Intervention Practice Book* page 77 to help them summarize the story.

INTERVENTION
PRACTICE
BOOK

page 77

Answers to *Think About It* Questions

1. The wolf chases Red Riding Cap and her grandmother and says that the girl's grandma would be delicious. He tries to defend himself by flattering the judge and saying he was only following the script. **SUMMARY**

2. Possible response: The wolf knows the three little pigs will tell that he blew their houses down, and then no one will believe he's innocent. **INTERPRETATION**

3. Scenes should be written in play format and should show characters issuing and responding to a judgment in the trial. **WRITE A SCENE**

AFTER

Skill Review
pages 470–471

USE SKILL CARD 19B

(Focus Skill) **Sequence**

RETEACH **the skill.** Have students look at **side B of Skill Card 19: Sequence.** Read the skill reminder with students, and select a volunteer to read the sequence of events from "Little Red Riding Hood" included in the sequence chart.

Invite a volunteer to read aloud the next set of directions. Explain to students that they will now change one of the events in the "Little Red Riding Hood" sequence chart. Explain that by changing one event, the events that follow will need to be changed as well. After students have completed their sequence charts, encourage them to share their charts with the group. Discuss how changing the sequence of events changed the outcome of the original story.

FLUENCY BUILDER Return to the bottom of *Intervention Practice Book* page 75. Read aloud the sentences together with students. Have each student choose one sentence to practice and read aloud to a partner. After each student has read, have him or her choose another sentence to read to the entire group. Continue until each student has read at least one of the sentences to the entire group. Encourage students to give feedback on the pacing, expression, and pronunciation of each sentence.

INTERVENTION PRACTICE BOOK

page 75

Expository Writing: Compare and Contrast Statement

Build on prior knowledge. Tell students that they are going to plan and write compare and contrast statements together. Display the following chart.

Compare and Contrast: Wolves and Pet Dogs	
Compare	**Contrast**
strong teeth	Dogs bark, wolves howl.
good sense of smell	Dogs can be friendly to people, wolves are wild.

Invite students to brainstorm ways that wolves and pet dogs are similar and ways in which they are different. Add their ideas to the chart.

Construct the text. "Share the pen" with students in a collaborative group writing effort. Guide students to create sentences that compare and contrast.

- Write *Wolves and pet dogs are similar because they both . . .* and have students finish the sentence with a fact from the chart, such as *have strong teeth.*

- Repeat the process to write a sentence that contrasts wolves and pet dogs.

Revisit the text. Go back and read the statement with students. Have them add adjectives and other details to enhance their sentences, such as *Wolves and pet dogs both have sharp, strong teeth that help them chew their food.* Then have them read aloud their completed statement.

On Your Own

Have students choose two animals they want to compare and contrast. Tell them to list how the animals are the same under the heading *Compare* and how they are different under the heading *Contrast.* Then have them write a sentence to compare and a sentence to contrast the animals.

Connect Spelling and Phonics

RETEACH **vowel variants /ô/ aw, au(gh).** Write the word *jaw* on the board. Explain that you will say four words in which the /ô/ sound is spelled *aw*. Have students write the words. Then provide the correct spelling for students to check their work. Write the word *taught* on the board. Explain that you will say four words in which the /ô/ sound is spelled *au*. Repeat the process.

1. raw	2. dawn*	3. awful*	4. paw*
5. launch*	6. caused*	7. naughty	8. caught*

*Word appears in "Big Bad Wolf and the Law."

Dictate the following sentence and have students write it: *Paul taught us how to draw a fawn.*

Build and Read Longer Words

INTERVENTION
ASSESSMENT
BOOK

Write these words on the board: *yawning, naughty, unlawful, astronaut.* Tell students that the letter combinations *au* and *aw* usually stay together when a word is broken into syllables. Point to *yawning* and ask: **Which part of the word sounds like /yôn/? Which part sounds like /ing/?** Then point to *naughty*, and tell students that the letters *augh* stay together when this word is divided. Have students read *naughty* aloud. Ask volunteers to read the remaining words and explain how they would break each one into parts.

FLUENCY BUILDER Students can practice reading aloud passages from "Big Bad Wolf and the Law" in small groups. Each member of a group can choose a character's part to read. Remind students not to read the characters' names or the stage directions in parentheses. Suggest:

- Four children can read together pages 126–127.
  (Total: 121 words)

- Five children can read together pages 128–129.
  (Total: 100 words)

- Four children can read together pages 130–131.
  (Total: 122 words)

Encourage students to use the stage directions to direct how they read their lines. After practicing, a small group could read their pages aloud to another small group, which could provide comments on their reading as well as rate the reading on a scale of 1 to 4.

Review Vocabulary

Write the Vocabulary Words on index cards: *script, desperately, acceptable, injustice, circumstances, repentant, discards,* and *triumphantly.* Have a volunteer choose one card and use the word on it in a sentence. Then have the next volunteer choose another word card and create a sentence using the word. Challenge students to link their sentences to the content of the preceding sentence in some way.

You may want to display the Vocabulary Words and definitions on page 189 and have students copy them to use when they study for the vocabulary test.

INTERVENTION
PRACTICE
BOOK

page 78

(Focus Skill) Review Sequence

Distribute *Intervention Practice Book* page 78 to help students review sequence. Remind students that each event in a story affects later events. If one event is changed, the outcome of the story changes. Guide them to change the order of events in "Little Red Riding Hood" to create a new outcome.

Review Test Prep

Refer students to page 471 of the *Pupil Edition.* Explain that the tips given at the bottom of the page will help them answer these questions as well as similar questions they may see on other tests.

LEAD
THE WAY

page 471

INTERVENTION
ASSESSMENT
BOOK

Read aloud each test question and the tip that goes with it. Discuss whether all stories use sequence words. Tell them that they must think very carefully about the order when there are no sequence words. You can encourage them to add sequence words in their heads, such as *first, second, next,* and *last,* as they read to help them determine the sequence of a story.

Self-Selected Reading

Encourage students to select their own books to read independently. They can choose their own from the classroom library shelf, or you may wish to offer a group of appropriate books from which students can choose.

- *An Interview with the Brothers Grimm.* (see page 471K of the *Teacher's Edition* for a lesson plan.)
- *Wolf!* by Becky Bloom. Orchard, 1999
- *Dinosaur Dream* by Dennis Nolan. Macmillan, 1990

You may also wish to recommend other twisted fairy tales or books that are in the same genre that students would find amusing.

Provide a copy of My Reading Log, which can be found on page R38 in the back of the *Teacher's Edition*, for each student. Have students complete the information at the top of the form. Encourage them to record their reading and responses to literature on the log.

Conduct student-teacher conferences. Arrange time for each student to confer with you individually about his or her self-selected reading. Provide time to discuss the story and ask questions as well as review each student's Reading Log. If students read a story variation, you might ask questions such as: How does this story remind you of another story you have read? What events are different? What is the changed outcome?

FLUENCY PERFORMANCE Have students recall the passages from "Red Writing Hood" that they practiced in small groups. Have them read aloud to you. Ask the student to rate his or her own reading on a scale of 1 to 4. If students are not happy with their oral reading, give them an opportunity to continue practicing and then to read the passage to you again.

See *Oral Reading Fluency Assessment* for monitoring progress.

LESSON 20

BEFORE

Building Background and Vocabulary

INTERVENTION PRACTICE BOOK

page 80

Use with

"One Grain of Rice"

Review Phonics: Vowel Variants /o͝o/ *oo, ou*

Identify the sound. Ask students to repeat the tongue twister *How much wood would a woodchuck chuck if a woodchuck could chuck wood? He'd chuck all the wood that a woodchuck could if a woodchuck could chuck wood.* Have students identify words that have the vowel sound heard in *good.* (*wood, would, woodchuck, could*)

Associate letters to sound. Write the first sentence of the tongue twister on the board. Underline the vowels *oo* or *ou* in each word in which they appear. Tell students that in these words, the letters *oo* or *ou* stand for the /o͝o/ sound in *wood* and *could.*

Word blending. Model how to blend and read the word *would.* Point to *w* and say /w/. Point to *ou* and say /o͝o/. Point to *d* and say /d/. Slide your hand under the whole word as you elongate the sounds: /wwo͝od/. Then say the word naturally—*would.* Point out that the *l* is silent.

Apply the skill. *Letter Substitution* Write the following words on the board, and have students read them aloud. Make the changes necessary to form the words in parentheses. Have volunteers read the new words.

boat (book)   **coal** (could)   **shake** (shook)

shone (should)   **wade** (would)   **broke** (brook)

Introduce Vocabulary

PRETEACH lesson vocabulary. Tell students they are going to learn five new words that they will see again when they read a story called "One Grain of Rice." Teach each Vocabulary Word using the following process.

Use the following suggestions or similar ideas to give the meaning or context.

> Write the word.
> Say the word.
> Track the word and have students repeat it.
> Give the meaning or context.

trickle	Demonstrate a trickle of water by pouring some from a glass.
plentifully	Ask students to describe situations in which there was "plenty of" something.
implored	Ask students if they've ever wanted something so badly that they begged for it.
famine	Discuss causes of famines such as drought, floods, earthquakes. Then discuss its effects on a country.

 198 Lesson 20 • Intervention Teacher's Guide

decreed   Point out the root word *decree* meaning "to command someone to do something."

For vocabulary activities, see Vocabulary Games on pages 2–7.

Vocabulary Words

trickle a thin stream

plentifully in great quantity

implored begged

famine widespread lack of food, causing many to starve

decreed ordered formally; commanded

AFTER

Building Background and Vocabulary

Apply Vocabulary Strategies

Use sentence and word context. Write these sentences on the board: *"Please, can I stay up tonight?" implored Jason. "I promise I'll still get up early!"* Remind students that they can use the context of a sentence to understand the meaning of an unfamiliar word. Model using the strategy.

> **MODEL** *When I read the sentences, I am unsure what* implored *means. The context of the sentences tells me that Jason seems to really want to do something. He seems to be begging, or pleading. I think* implored *must mean "begged".*

Guide students to use this strategy to figure out other unfamiliar words.

RETEACH lesson vocabulary. Provide these sentence frames and ask students to complete each with words that will make sense in the context of the rest of the sentence.

1. The **famine** in Africa caused _____. (*Possible responses: people to go hungry* or *people to move to more fertile areas.*)

2. The _____ grew **plentifully** in the oasis. (*Possible responses: trees, fruit, plants, foliage*)

3. Even a **trickle** of _____ in the desert is valued. (*Possible responses: water, rain*)

4. People **implored** the camels to _____. (*Possible responses: carry them, walk, continue*)

5. The king **decreed** that _____. (*Possible response: all who grow rice must give it to him.*)

FLUENCY BUILDER Point out the lists of words at the top of *Intervention Practice Book* page 79. Tell students that these are words from the stories in this lesson. Explain that you will say each word as students listen to hear the correct pronunciation. Read each word and have the group repeat it. Then have each student in the group repeat the word. Continue this process with each of the words.

INTERVENTION PRACTICE BOOK

page 79

★
(Focus Skill) **Compare and Contrast**

PRETEACH **the skill.** Tell students that folktales are stories that often have a lesson about life in them. You can compare and contrast tales from different cultures by paying attention to the similarities and differences.

Have students look at **side A of Skill Card 20: Compare and Contrast.** Read aloud the definitions. Point out the characters, settings, plots, and lessons for the stories on the compare-and-contrast chart. If necessary, summarize the two stories. Ask:

- **How do the settings compare? How do they contrast?** (*Possible response: Compare—Both are outside and include a meadow. Contrast—Only one setting focuses on a bridge.*)

- **How do the lessons compare? How do they contrast?** (*Possible response: Compare—Both stories show that mental ability can overcome physical ability. Contrast—One story focuses on perseverance while the other story focuses on wit.*)

Tell students that comparing and contrasting stories will help them better appreciate the features of each one and the lessons common to cultures.

Prepare to Read: "One Grain of Rice"

Preview. Tell students that they are going to read a folktale called "One Grain of Rice." Encourage students to think how this folktale might be like others they have read. Then preview the selection.

LEAD THE WAY
pages 474–492

- **Pages 474–475:** "One Grain of Rice" looks as if it is set in Asia because of the type of clothing I see.

- **Pages 476–477:** I see people farming and people on elephants. Elephants must be used for transportation.

- **Pages 478–479:** The girl is catching something in her dress— perhaps rice. I wonder where she will take it.

- **Pages 480–483:** This must be a very important man, perhaps a raja. On pages 482–483 the girl looks very happy. Some goats and some deer appear to be carrying something. Maybe it's rice.

- **Pages 484–487:** More and more bags of something are being delivered to the girl. I think it must be rice.

- **Pages 488–49 I:** The people must be happy about the contents of the baskets.

Set purpose. Model setting a purpose for reading "One Grain of Rice."

MODEL From my preview I know this is a folktale. I'll read to find out what lesson the raja is learning and how it will affect his behavior as a leader.

Reread and Summarize

Have students reread and summarize "One Grain of Rice" in sections, as described in the chart below.

Pages 475–477

Let's reread pages 475–477 to recall why the people need more rice.

Summary: The raja forces the people to give him rice in exchange for protection. During a famine, they ask for rice, but he refuses.

Pages 478–479

As we reread pages 478–479, let's find out how the raja acted during the famine and how Rani's plan began.

Summary: The raja plans a private celebration and Rani catches the rice spilling from one of the raja's elephant's baskets.

Pages 480–481

Let's reread page 480 to find out how Rani presented her plan.

Summary: Rani returned the rice she gathered and pretended to need no reward. When the raja insisted, she asked to start with a single grain of rice and to double the amount each day for thirty days.

Pages 482–487

Let's reread pages 482–487 to recall how much rice the raja gave to Rani and how he reacted to the great loss of rice.

Summary: The raja was upset, but he kept his word and doubled the rice until Rani had received his last four storehouses of rice.

Pages 488–491

Let's reread pages 488–491 to recall how the story ended.

Summary: The raja and the people shared the rice so there was always enough for everyone.

FLUENCY BUILDER Ask students to refer to the bottom of *Intervention Practice Book* page 79. Read each sentence and ask students to repeat it after you. Have them underline any sentence parts they are having trouble reading. Then have pairs work together by first reading and then giving feedback on the parts they underlined. Finally, have them read each of the sentences to one another.

INTERVENTION PRACTICE BOOK

page 79

Directed Reading: "A Clever Plan," pp. 158–165

MOVING
AHEAD
pp. 158–165

Pages 158–159

Read aloud the title of the story. Make sure students know what a kingdom is. Read aloud the first paragraph. Ask: **What is life like in the kingdom of Woodlandia.** (*Life is good with plenty of food and firewood. King Roger is the only problem.*) **SUMMARIZE**

Have students read the rest of page 159. Tell them that they already know enough about King Roger to make some predictions about what might happen later in the story. Ask students to think about what kinds of problems King Roger might cause. Model the strategy:

> **MODEL** I know that King Roger is kind, but that he makes mistakes because he thinks everyone in the kingdom is just like himself. He will probably order the Woodlandians to do things they do not want to do. I will need to read on to find out whether my predictions are correct. **MAKE AND CONFIRM PREDICTIONS**

Page 160

Have students read page 160 to find out what happens when King Roger returns from a royal journey. Model confirming predictions:

> **MODEL** Already my prediction has come true. King Roger has asked the Woodlandians to get tigers as pets, which many of them won't want to do. **MAKE AND CONFIRM PREDICTIONS**

Page 161

Read aloud page 161. Then ask: **How does King Roger compare and contrast with his subjects?** (*They are all people living in Woodlandia, but the king is wealthy and can have whatever he wants and his subjects are poor and cannot live luxuriously.*) **COMPARE AND CONTRAST**

Page 162

Ask students to read page 162 to find out how the Woodlandians respond to the clothing decree. (*The ministers from the provinces gather for a meeting to search for a solution.*) **SUMMARIZE**

Ask: **What do you think the oldest minister's solution will be?** (Answers will vary.) **MAKE AND CONFIRM PREDICTIONS**

Page 163

Ask volunteers to read aloud page 163, while the other students listen to confirm their predictions. Ask: **What is the minister's solution?** (*Everyone makes clothing out of fruits and plants.*) **SUMMARIZE**

Page 164

Have students read page 164 to find out how King Roger responds to what the Woodlandians have done. (*He realizes his mistake and proclaims that from now on he will meet with his ministers before making a royal decree.*) **SUMMARIZE**

INTERVENTION PRACTICE BOOK

page 81

Ask: **Do you think the solution is a good one? Why or why not?** (Responses will vary.) **EXPRESS PERSONAL OPINIONS**

Summarize the selection. Have students discuss the problem and solution in the story. Then have them complete *Intervention Practice Book* page 81 and summarize the story.

Answers to *Think About It* Questions

1. The problem is that the king wants to help the Woodlandians but his ideas don't always work well. **SUMMARY**

2. Possible response: I think he learns that he has to think about what other people need, too. That is why he plans to meet with his ministers before making decisions. **INTERPRETATION**

3. Posters should be inviting and show important details such as time and place. **MAKE A POSTER**

AFTER

Skill Review
pages 498–499

USE SKILL CARD 20B

(Focus Skill) **Compare and Contrast**

RETEACH the skill. Point out **side B of Skill Card 20: Compare and Contrast** to students. Read the skill reminder with them and have a volunteer read the directions.

Have students use the chart to record the characters, setting, plot, and lessons for the story they chose. After they have completed their compare-and-contrast charts, encourage them to share their charts with the group.

Remind students that by looking at how these and other tales compare and contrast, they will better understand how stories can teach similar lessons yet tell about a particular culture.

FLUENCY BUILDER Look at *Intervention Practice Book* page 79 with students. Have them point out a sentence that they found particularly challenging to read aloud. Review the meanings of any unfamiliar words in the sentence and try to have students create a mental picture of the sentence as you read it aloud. Then ask them to repeat the sentence using intonation and pacing that might help listeners create a picture in their mind's eye of the meaning of the sentence.

INTERVENTION PRACTICE BOOK

page 79

BEFORE

Tested or Timed Writing
pages 499C–499D

Expository Writing: Compare and Contrast Sentences

Build on prior knowledge. Tell students that they are going to plan and write compare and contrast sentences together. Explain that sometimes during a test, they may be given a specific amount of time to complete a writing assignment. Encourage them to use their time wisely. Display the following chart.

Tic-Tac-Toe and Hangman	
Comparisons	**Contrasts**
Both are written games.	Tic-Tac-Toe allows two players only.
	Hangman allows multiple players.

Ask students to brainstorm ways that Tic-Tac-Toe and Hangman are similar and ways in which they are different. Add their ideas to the chart.

Construct the text. "Share the pen" with students in a collaborative group writing effort. Guide them to use the chart in writing their sentences.

- Write *Tic-Tac-Toe and Hangman are similar because they both . . .* and have students finish the sentence with a fact from the chart, such as *are written games.*

- Repeat the process to help students write a sentence that contrasts the two games.

- Have students add adjectives and other details to enhance their sentences.

Revisit the Text. Go back and read the sentences. Ask: **Are similarities grouped in one sentence? Are differences grouped in one sentence?**

- Have students make sure the similarities and differences are clear.

- Have them reread their sentences aloud.

On Your Own

Have students think of two places that they would like to visit in their community. Have them use a compare-and-contrast chart to record the similarities and differences of the places. Tell them to write two sentences that compare the places and two sentences that contrast them.

Connect Spelling and Phonics

RETEACH **vowel variants /o͝o/oo, ou.** Write *could* on the board. Tell students that this word has the /o͝o/ sound. Explain that you will dictate two words for them to write that have this sound spelled *ou*. After you dictate the first two words on the list below, provide time for students to proofread their own work. Write *good* on the board. Tell students that this word also has the /o͝o/ sound. Tell them that the rest of the words you will dictate have this sound spelled *oo*.

1. would*	2. should*	3. took*	4. books*
5. look*	6. wooden*	7. hood*	8. stood*

*Word appears in "A Clever Plan."

Dictate the following sentence for students to write: *I would like a book or a football.*

Build and Read Longer Words

INTERVENTION ASSESSMENT BOOK

Write these words on the board: *woolly, goodness, funny.* Point to *woolly* and read it aloud. Ask: **Which part of the word sounds like /wo͝ol/? Which part sounds like /lē/?** Draw a vertical line between the double consonants and remind students that when two consonants come together between two vowels, the word is usually divided into syllables between the two consonants. Follow a similar process with *goodness* and *funny.*

FLUENCY BUILDER Assign a passage from "A Clever Plan" for students to read aloud to a partner, or allow them to choose their own passages. Some options include:

- Read the last paragraph of page 159 and all of page 160. (Total: 114 words)

- Read all of page 164 to the end of the story. (Total: 98 words)

Students can record the selected passages on audiotape. As they listen to the tape, they can rate themselves on the 1 to 4 scale.

Review Vocabulary

Write these two Vocabulary Words on the board: *trickle* and *plentifully*. Ask students to sketch a picture that contrasts these two words. Ask them which picture relates to *famine*: the one showing *trickle* or the one showing *plentifully*. Then write these words on the board: *decreed* and *implored*. Have them draw two cartoon characters with speech balloons: one giving a decree and the other one imploring. Have them label all illustrations with the word each depicts.

INTERVENTION PRACTICE BOOK

page 82

(Focus Skill) Compare and Contrast

Provide *Intervention Practice Book* page 82 for students to review their ability to compare and contrast. Tell students that the graphic organizer will help them organize their ideas. Remind them to include at least two similarities and two differences for "One Grain of Rice" and "A Clever Plan."

Review Test Prep

Have students turn to page 499 of the *Pupil Edition*. Point out the tips for answering the test questions. Remind students that these tips provide valuable information that will help them answer these questions as well as other test questions that require them to compare or contrast.

LEAD THE WAY
page 499

Have students follow along as you read aloud each test question and the tip that goes with it. Discuss how contrast questions often include the word *not*.

INTERVENTION ASSESSMENT BOOK

✔

Self-Selected Reading

Have students select their own books to read independently. They might choose books from the classroom library shelf, or you may wish to offer a group of appropriate books from which students can choose.

- *The Raja's Elephant* (See page 499K of the *Teacher's Edition* for a lesson plan.)

- *The Empty Pot* by Demi. Henry Holt, 1991

- *In the Eyes of the Cat* by Demi. Henry Holt, 1994

- *Mission: Addition* by Loreen Leedy. Holiday House, 1997

After students have chosen their books, give each student a copy of My Reading Log, which can be found on page R38 in the back of the *Teacher's Edition*. Have students fill in the information at the top of the form. Then have them use the log to keep track of their reading and to record their responses to the literature.

Conduct student-teacher conferences. After students have chosen and read a self-selected reading choice, have them schedule an individual conference time with you. Begin the conference by asking them how this story compared and contrasted with "One Grain of Rice." Then ask questions about the text they read and provide an opportunity for students to read aloud to you from their book. Review students' Reading Log to make sure they are reading a variety of selections.

FLUENCY PERFORMANCE Tell students that reading aloud can help with their pronunciation and pacing. Point out that the correct pronunciation of a word can often lead to its meaning. Have students read the passage from "A Clever Plan" that they have practiced with a partner. Have students rate their own performance on a scale of 1 to 4.

See *Oral Reading Fluency Assessment* for monitoring progress.

LESSON 21

BEFORE

Building Background and Vocabulary

Use with

"Fire!"

Review Phonics: /ōō/ *oo, ue, ew, ui*

Identify the sound. Tell students to listen for /ōō/ as you say these words: *moon, true, stew, juice.* Then say this sentence and have students repeat it twice: *Sue put the new tools in her suitcase.* Ask students to name the words with the /ōō/ sound they hear in *moon.* (*Sue, new, tools, suitcase*)

Associate letters to sound. Write the above sentence on the board. Underline the letters *ue* in *Sue, ew* in *new, oo* in *tools,* and *ui* in *suitcase.* Explain that these letter combinations can stand for the /ōō/ sound.

Word blending. Model how to blend and read the word *fruit.* Point to *f* and say /f/. Point to *r* and say /r/. Run your hand under *ui* and say /ōō/. Touch *t* and say /t/. Slide your hand under the whole word as you elongate the sounds to say /ffrrōōt/. Then say the word naturally—*fruit.* Follow a similar procedure for *chew, boot,* and *blue.*

INTERVENTION PRACTICE BOOK

page 84

Apply the skill. *Letter Substitution* Write the following words on the board. Have students read each word aloud. Make the changes necessary to form the words in parentheses. Ask volunteers to read the new words.

drop (droop)	**nest** (news)	**dug** (due)	**sit** (suit)
romp (room)	**fled** (flew)	**sun** (sue)	**brush** (bruise)

Introduce Vocabulary

PRETEACH **lesson vocabulary.** Tell students that they will learn six new words that they will see again when they read a story called "Fire!" Use the following process to teach the Vocabulary Words.

Use the following suggestions or similar ideas to give the meaning or context.

> Write the word.
> Say the word.
> Track the word and have students repeat it.
> Give the meaning or context.

dedication	Relate to being so focused on a goal that nothing can get in the way of fulfilling the goal.
billowing	Use paper fans to make a piece of tissue move. Point out how it makes wavelike movements.
brigade	Relate to a police brigade or a fire brigade.
ventilate	Compare ventilating to opening the car vent to let in fresh air.
flammable	Relate to safety. Name objects such as clothes or tables and ask whether each is flammable.

curfew   Relate curfew to a time when they must be home.

For vocabulary activities, see Vocabulary Games on pages 2–7.

Apply Vocabulary Strategies

Use syllabication. Write *dedication* on a strip of paper, leaving spaces between the letters. Show the word and tell students that they will be able to read long words more easily when they divide them into smaller parts called syllables. Model using the strategy.

> **MODEL** The word *dedication* is difficult to read. When I break it into syllables, I find I can read the word—*ded•i•ca•tion.*

Guide students to repeat the strategy with *flammable* and *ventilate.*

RETEACH **lesson vocabulary.** Divide the class into teams. Give one clue at a time, alternating between the teams. Award fifteen points if the word is guessed after the first clue and ten points if the word is guessed after the second clue. As a bonus, award ten points if the team can spell the word correctly.

Word	Clue 1	Clue 2
curfew	One syllable is *few.*	It means "a rule that something cannot happen after a certain time."
ventilate	One syllable is *late.*	It means "to create an opening to let air in and out."
billowing	One syllable is *low.*	It means "rising in big waves."
brigade	One syllable is *gade.*	It means "a group of people organized to do something."
flammable	One syllable is *ma.*	It means "easily set on fire."
dedication	One syllable is *tion.*	It means "the will to keep working hard."

Vocabulary Words

dedication the will to keep working hard on a task

billowing rising in big waves

brigade a group of people organized to do something

ventilate to create a vent, or an opening, for letting air in and out

flammable easily set on fire

curfew law or rule that says something cannot happen after a certain time

FLUENCY BUILDER Tell students to follow along as you read the words at the top of *Intervention Practice Book* page 83. Have the class repeat the entire list. Indicate row or column numbers and call on volunteers to read the words in the row or column you named. Allow time for students to practice all of the words.

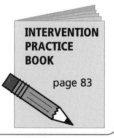
INTERVENTION PRACTICE BOOK

page 83

USE SKILL CARD 21A

(Focus Skill) Elements of Nonfiction: Text Structure

PRETEACH **the skill.** Explain that nonfiction writers communicate information by organizing their ideas into one of four main structures: main idea and details, cause and effect, comparison and contrast, or sequence of events.

Have students look at **side A of Skill Card 21: Text Structure.** Call on volunteers to read aloud the selection and the chart. Ask:

- **Which text structure did the writer use to organize the text?** (*sequence*)

- **How do you know?** (Possible response: *The author relates a series of events in the order in which they happened.*)

Explain that making an outline or a chart of the main points of a nonfiction selection can help students determine the text structure.

Prepare to Read: "Fire!"

Preview. Tell students they will be reading a nonfiction selection called "Fire!" Tell them they can get a good idea of what the text is about by reading headings and by looking at the pictures and their captions. Then preview the selection.

LEAD THE WAY
pages 504–516

- **Pages 504–505:** From the title and photos, I can tell that the selection is about fighting fires. After reading the introduction, I think I'll learn how firefighters work and how they feel about their job.

- **Page 506:** From the title, "Different. . . Yet the Same," I think this page will compare and contrast firefighters in big cities and firefighters in small towns.

- **Pages 507–511:** There are several subheadings that tell about different parts of a firefighter's day. I think that the author wants me to imagine that I am a firefighter. The photos will help me visualize what fighting a fire is like.

- **Pages 512–515:** The title and the pictures show that this section is about the history of firefighting.

- **Pages 516–517:** The information on these pages includes a diagram that shows all the gear a firefighter has to wear and carry. The "Meet the Author" section lets me know why Joy Masoff is qualified to write about firefighters.

Set purpose. Model setting a purpose for reading "Fire."

MODEL From my preview, I know this selection will tell me about how fires are fought in cities and small towns, how it feels to be a firefighter, and the history of fire departments. I will read to learn more about what firefighters do.

Reread and Summarize

Have students reread and summarize "Fire!" in sections, as described in the chart below.

Page 505

Let's reread the introduction on page 505 to find out what the author wants us to learn from this selection.

Summary: This selection will show the importance of firefighting to the community and to the firefighters themselves.

Page 506

Reread page 506 to find out how small-town and big-city firefighters are alike and how they are different.

Summary: All firefighters feel the same way when they hear a fire alarm, but big-city firefighters are professionals who live at the firehouse when they are on duty. Small-town firefighters are often volunteers.

Pages 507–511

By rereading pages 507–511 and looking at the photos, we can get an idea about how it would feel to be a firefighter.

Summary: On a typical workday, firefighters go to the firehouse where they perform regular duties and live when they are on duty. They must always be ready to go fight a fire whenever a call comes in.

Pages 512–515

On pages 512–515, we learn the history of firefighting.

Summary: Early settlements did not have fire departments, so the whole town had to pitch in to try to fight fires. Later, laws were passed to establish fire departments and to make people build homes that were less flammable.

FLUENCY BUILDER Have students look at the bottom of *Intervention Practice Book* page 83. As you read each sentence aloud, ask students to repeat after you. If they are having difficulty, read each phrase before students repeat it. Have them echo the appropriate pace, expression, and phrasing that you model. Then have students practice reading each sentence with a partner.

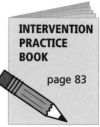

INTERVENTION
PRACTICE
BOOK

page 83

Directed Reading: "Fire in the Forest" pp. 166–172

**MOVING
AHEAD**
pp. 166–172

Page 166

Read the title. Ask volunteers to tell what they know about Smokey Bear. Then have students read page 166. Ask: **How have people's ideas about forest fires changed?** (*Rangers no longer feel that forest fires are all bad.*) **MAIN IDEA**

Ask: **How might a fire help a forest?** (Possible response: *Fires clear out dead and weak trees.*) **MAKE PREDICTIONS**

Page 167

Have students read page 167 to confirm or disprove their predictions. Ask: **How is fire good for a forest?** (*It burns old branches, underbrush, and sick trees. It enriches the soil and helps strong new trees grow.*) **IMPORTANT DETAILS/SUMMARIZE**

Page 168

Have students read about choices rangers must make about fighting fires. Ask: **Why do planes drop chemicals?** (*to make forests less flammable; to slow the flames*) **CAUSE-EFFECT**

Page 169

Ask: **What can make forest fires get out of control?** (*wind; hot, dry days that dry out the brush and trees*) **CAUSE-EFFECT**

Page 170

Have students read about fires that blazed in Yellowstone National Park. Model using the summarize strategy:

> **MODEL** Page 170 is all about one special fire. I can summarize this page by saying: A fire in Yellowstone National Park seemed likely to destroy huge areas of forest. After the fire went out, plants and animals came back and the cycle of life began once again. (Focus Strategy) **SUMMARIZE**

Ask: **Why do you think the rangers decided it was safe to let the Yellowstone fires burn?** (Possible response: *because the fires were deep in the forest.*) **DRAW CONCLUSIONS**

Ask: **How could you tell that the forest was not destroyed?** (*By the next summer wildflowers and grass had begun to grow.*) **INTERPRET STORY EVENTS**

Remind students that this selection is nonfiction because it tells facts rather than a story. Ask: **How did the author organize this piece of writing?** (*using main ideas and supporting details*) (Focus Skill) **TEXT STRUCTURE**

**INTERVENTION
PRACTICE
BOOK**

page 85

Summarize the selection. Ask students to think about how they would decide whether to put out a forest fire if they were rangers. Then have them complete *Intervention Practice Book* page 85 and summarize the story.

Answers to *Think About It* Questions

1. Possible response: Rangers think that fires are part of a forest's life cycle. Some fires start deep in a forest, away from people and homes. **SUMMARY**

2. Possible response: Fires started by people are likely to put other people in danger. **INTERPRETATION**

3. Letters should be written in correct friendly letter format, should describe firefighting activities, and might express an opinion about how or when the fire will be extinguished. **WRITE A LETTER**

AFTER

Skill Review
pages 520–521

USE SKILL CARD 21B

(Focus Skill) Elements of Nonfiction: Text Structure

RETEACH **the skill.** Have students look at **side B of Skill Card 21: Text Structure.** Read aloud the skill reminder and invite students to read along. Have a volunteer read aloud the paragraph. Encourage the rest of the group to think about which text structure the author uses.

Have a volunteer read aloud the next set of directions. Explain that students can now work with a partner to fill in their own graphic organizers. Remind students to write the main idea of the paragraph in the center of the web and only one detail in each of the boxes.

FLUENCY BUILDER Be sure students have copies of *Intervention Practice Book* page 83. Have students practice reading one of the sentences individually. Then have them read the sentence to a small group of listeners. Have the group give feedback about the expression and pacing each reader uses.

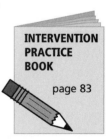

INTERVENTION
PRACTICE
BOOK

page 83

Expository Writing: Research Paragraph

Build on prior knowledge. Tell students that they are going to work together to write a research-based paragraph on firefighter gear and equipment. Display the following information:

Tell students to look at page 168 of "Fire in the Forest" to find information on firefighter gear and equipment. Help students locate examples of gear and equipment and add the items to your group notes in bulleted form. (*gear: fireproof coats, gloves; equipment: axes, hoes*) Point out that you did not copy complete sentences for your notes, but just jotted down important ideas.

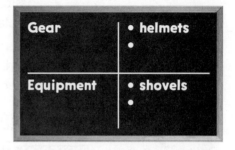

Gear	• helmets
	•
Equipment	• shovels
	•

Construct the text. "Share the pen" with students in a collaborative group writing effort. Guide them in writing a research-based paragraph about firefighter gear and equipment.

- Write a sentence that introduces the subject of firefighter gear and equipment.

- Write one or two sentences that summarize the research notes from the chart.

- Cite the source used in the group research: "Fire in the Forest," page 168.

- Write a concluding statement summarizing the main idea.

Revisit the text. Go back and reread the paragraph. Make sure students have paraphrased the information and that the paragraph is organized in one of the four text structures. Have students read their completed paragraph aloud.

On Your Own

Have students use a reference source to take at least two notes about a community worker of their choice. Remind students to jot down only the essential words and to write the sources of information they used.

Connect Spelling and Phonics

RETEACH /oo/oo, ue, ew, ui. Remind students that /oo/ can be spelled several ways. Tell them that you will dictate /oo/ words for them to write. Write *spoon* on the board, and tell students that in the first two words /oo/ is spelled *oo* as in *spoon*. Dictate words 1 and 2, and have students write them. After each word, display the correct spelling so students can proofread their work. Tell students to draw a line through any incorrectly spelled word and write the correct spelling beside it. Continue by writing *flew*, *clue*, and *suit* on the board before dictating words 3 and 4, words 5 and 6, and words 7 and 8.

| 1. broom | 2. sloop | 3. renews* | 4. blew |
| 5. glue | 6. true* | 7. cruise | 8. bruise |

*Word appears in "Fire in the Forest."

Dictate the following sentence for students to write: *Andrew is due back from the cruise at noon.*

Build and Read Longer Words

Remind students that they have learned to read words in which /oo/ is spelled *oo*, *ue*, *ew*, and *ui*. Tell them that they can use what they learned to read longer words. Write *newborn* on the board. Remind students that long words are sometimes made up of two shorter words. Cover *born* and call on a volunteer to read the remaining word. Cover *new* and have another student read the remaining word. Slide your hand under *newborn* as students read it aloud. Follow the same procedure with *bluebell*, *fruitcake*, and *dewdrop*.

INTERVENTION
ASSESSMENT
BOOK

FLUENCY BUILDER Have students choose a passage from "Fire in the Forest" to read aloud to a partner. Tell students they may choose the passage they found most interesting or give them the following options:

- Read page 166 and the first paragraph of page 167. (Total: 89 words)

- Read the first two paragraphs on page 169. (Total: 102 words)

Tell students to read the selected passage aloud to their partner three times. Have the reader rate each reading on a scale from 1 to 4. Encourage students to note their progress from previous oral readings.

Review Vocabulary

Review the Vocabulary Words before the weekly assessment. Give each student six index cards. Have students write a Vocabulary Word on one side and the definition on the other. Then read the following groups of sentences and have students hold up the card with the word that completes the last sentence in each grouping.

1. The pioneers worked together to pass the water buckets back and forth. They had formed a _____ to put out all the fires on the main street. (*brigade*)

2. The smoke from the fireplace made everyone's eyes water. Dad raced to open a window to _____ the smoky room. (*ventilate*)

3. We had forgotten to close the windows when we left. A storm came up while we were gone. We came home to find that the _____ curtains had knocked over a vase. (*billowing*)

4. Dan's watch stopped while he was at his friend's house. He was an hour late getting home. Mom grounded Dan for breaking his _____. (*curfew*)

5. Jessica went to soccer practice every day. When she wasn't on the field, she was cheering for her teammates. At the end of the season, everyone agreed that she had proved her _____. (*dedication*)

6. Caleb forgot to turn off the stove after he made his dinner. It's a good thing the cast iron pot is not _____. (*flammable*)

(Focus Skill) Review Elements of Nonfiction: Text Structure

To review text structure before the weekly assessment, have students complete *Intervention Practice Book* page 86. Call on a volunteer to read aloud the paragraph. Review the different types of text structure. Guide students in understanding that the paragraph uses a sequence of events structure. Have students complete the chart by filling in the correct order of events.

INTERVENTION PRACTICE BOOK
page 86

Review Test Prep

Ask students to turn to page 521 of the *Pupil Edition*. Have volunteers read the tips for answering test questions. Tell students to look for clues about text structure in the opening sentence of each paragraph. Remind students that understanding text structure can help them organize and remember facts from a nonfiction selection.

INTERVENTION ASSESSMENT BOOK
✔

LEAD THE WAY
page 521

Self-Selected Reading

Have students select their own books to read independently. They might choose books from the classroom library shelf, or you may wish to offer a group of appropriate books from which the student can choose.

- *Where There's Smoke, There's Fire* (See page 52 IM of the *Teacher's Edition* for a lesson plan)

- *A Log's Life*, by Wendy Pfeffer. Simon & Schuster, 1997

- *Fire! Fire!* by Gail Gibbons. HarperCollins, 1987

After students have chosen their books, give each student a copy of My Reading Log, which can be found on page R38 in the back of the *Teacher's Edition*. Have students fill in the information at the top of the form. Then have them use the log to keep track of their reading and to record their responses to the literature.

Conduct student-teacher conferences. Arrange time for each student to conference with you individually about his or her self-selected reading. Tell students to bring their books and Reading Log to the conference. Ask them to prepare for the conference by rehearsing a favorite passage to read aloud. Ask students to describe the text structure of the selection. Have them tell what they learned from their book.

FLUENCY PERFORMANCE Have students read aloud the passage from "Fire in the Forest" that they rehearsed with their partner. Use students' reading errors to assess their application of phonics skills. Have students rate their own performance on a scale of 1 to 4. Allow students to reread the passage if they are not satisfied with their performance.

See *Oral Reading Fluency Assessment* for monitoring progress.

LESSON 22

"A Very Important Day"

BEFORE

Building
Background
and Vocabulary

Review Phonics: Digraphs /n/kn, gn; /r/wr

Identify the sound. Say the following words and have students listen for the /n/ sound: *knee, gnome*. Say this sentence and have students repeat it twice: *She wrung her gnarled hands and then knocked on the door.* Ask students to name the words that begin with the /n/ sound. Then have them listen for the /r/ sound in *wreath*. Have them repeat the sentence and name the word that begins with the /r/ sound.

Associate letters to sounds. Write the above sentence on the board. Underline *kn* in *knocked* and *gn* in *gnarled*. Tell students that the letters *kn* and *gn* stand for the /n/ sound. The *k* and *g* are *silent*. Next, underline *wr* in *wrung* and explain that the letters *wr* stand for /r/. The *w* is silent.

Word blending. Model how to blend and read *knit*. Slide your hand under the whole word and blend the sounds: /nniit/. Then say the word naturally—*knit*. Repeat the process for *gnat* and *wrist*.

INTERVENTION
PRACTICE
BOOK

page 88

Apply the skill. *Consonant Substitution* Write the following words on the board. Have students read them aloud. Make the changes necessary to form the words in parentheses. Have volunteers read the words aloud.

felt (knelt)   **white** (write)   **plot** (knot)   **straw** (gnaw)
bench (wrench)   **snob** (knob)   **check** (wreck)   **hat** (gnat)

Introduce Vocabulary

PRETEACH **lesson vocabulary.** Tell students that they will learn new words that will help them understand an informational story called "A Very Important Day." Use the following process to teach the Vocabulary Words.

Use the following suggestions or similar ideas to give the meaning or context.

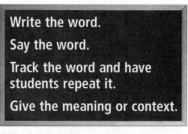

Write the word.
Say the word.
Track the word and have students repeat it.
Give the meaning or context.

apologized	Discuss reasons people might say they are sorry.
enrich	Point out the prefix *en-*, "to make," and the root word *rich*. Explain that *rich* can refer to anything valued, such as a friendship.
obliged	Related word: We all have *obligations* toward our families. We are obliged to help at home.
petitioners	Relate to signing a petition for longer lunch periods.
examiner	Discuss places where people are questioned in detail during

examinations, such as doctors' offices and schools. Explain that the suffix -er means "one who does something."

certificate — Make a word web of official papers like birth certificates and award certificates.

resounded — Circle the word *sound*. Explain that something that resounded was filled with sounds.

For vocabulary activities, see Vocabulary Games on pages 2–7.

For vocabulary activities, see Vocabulary Games on pages 2–7.

Vocabulary Words

apologized said he or she was sorry

enrich make better by adding something

obliged cooperated; did a favor

petitioners people officially requesting something

examiner one who asks questions to test people's knowledge

certificate document that states that something is a fact

resounded echoed; filled a place with sound

AFTER

Building Background and Vocabulary

Apply Vocabulary Strategies

Use prefixes and suffixes. Write the suffix -er on the board. Explain that recognizing suffixes and their meanings can help readers understand unfamiliar words. Model using the strategy.

> **MODEL** I am unsure what *examiner* means and how to pronounce it correctly. I know the suffix -er is pronounced /ər/ and that -er means "one who." When I sound out the word, *ex•am•in•er*, that is familiar to me. *Examiner* must mean "someone who examines."

Guide students to use prefixes and suffixes to decode other words.

RETEACH lesson vocabulary. Have students write *True* on one side of an index card and *False* on the other. Read the sentences. Tell students to hold up *True* if the statement is true and *False* if the statement is false.

1. You usually ask an **examiner** questions. (*False*)
2. A birth **certificate** tells when a person was born. (*True*)
3. You **apologize** if you knock something over. (*True*)
4. The gym **resounded** with noise. (*True*)
5. Friends **enrich** your life. (*True*)
6. School-age children are not **obliged** to attend school. (*False*)
7. A **petitioner** always gives you what you ask for. (*False*)

FLUENCY BUILDER Have students look at the words at the top of *Intervention Practice Book* page 87. Tell them to point to the words as you read down the columns. Then tell students to read along with you as you reread the words. Read the list of words several times with students. Increase the pace with each rereading. Allow time for students to practice the words on their own.

INTERVENTION PRACTICE BOOK

page 87

(Focus Skill) Author's Purpose

PRETEACH the skill. Ask students to think about a story they have read and to tell why it might have been written. Explain that the reason an author writes is called the author's purpose.

Have students look at **side A of Skill Card 22: Author's Purpose.** Review the three main purposes. Have a volunteer read aloud the passage. Ask:

- **Where might you read a passage of this kind?** (Possible responses: *in a biography, a textbook, or an encyclopedia*)

- **How can you tell the author's purpose for writing is to inform?** (*There is lots of information about Benjamin Franklin.*)

Tell students that determining the genre of a selection can give clues about the author's purpose.

Prepare to Read: "A Very Important Day"

Preview. Tell students they will be reading a story that is realistic fiction. Explain that realistic fiction is made up, but that the characters and situations are things that could really happen. Then preview the selection.

LEAD THE WAY
pages 524–537

- **Pages 524–525:** The title is "A Very Important Day." I wonder what makes it an important day. I see the Statue of Liberty and a girl wearing a party hat.

- **Pages 526–527:** I see a family who has just gotten up from the table. It must be very early, because it's still dark outside. And it's snowing. In the text there are pronunciation guides beside the names. The people all seem to be of different nationalities.

- **Pages 528–531:** It is later in the morning because it's lighter now. Two families are walking in two different neighborhoods. Since they're in the same story, there must be a connection.

- **Pages 532–533:** Here's a new family and they look dressed up. Maybe that's because it is an important day.

- **Pages 534–535:** I see a man wearing robes. He looks like a judge. He's speaking to a large group of people. I think all the families we saw earlier are probably in that big crowd.

- **Pages 536–537:** Now the crowd is leaving a big, official looking building with a flag. The ones in front look happy. The children are running and cheering. One is carrying a little flag.

Set purpose. Model setting a purpose for reading "A Very Important Day."

MODEL From the preview, I can guess that the story might be about people from different countries who are doing something important together in the United States. I'll read to find out why the author wrote the story and what her message is.

Reread and Summarize

Have students reread and summarize "A Very Important Day" in sections, as described below.

Pages 526–527

Let's reread these pages to find out where some of the people in the story came from.

Summary: The people on these pages come from the Philippines, Mexico, India, and Russia.

Pages 528–533

Reread pages 528–533 to find out how all the different families describe the day as they talk to friends, neighbors, and each other.

Summary: All the families indicate that the day is special. They say things like "big day," "very important day," "day of all days," "the most important day," and "such an important day."

Pages 534–536

Reread pages 534–536 to explain what happened to all the families in the story.

Summary: The families received their citizenship certificates, took the oath of citizenship, were congratulated by the judge, and said the Pledge of Allegiance. Then they celebrated their very important day.

FLUENCY BUILDER Have students look at the bottom of *Intervention Practice Book* page 87. Model reading the sentences aloud. Have students repeat each sentence after you. Tell them to imitate your expression, phrasing, and pace. Then have students practice reading each sentence to a partner.

INTERVENTION
PRACTICE
BOOK

page 87

Directed Reading: "A Place of New Beginnings" pp. 174–181

Read the title. Help students identify the Statue of Liberty and Ellis Island in the illustration. Invite them to tell what they know about these places. Ask: **Why do Dad and Karen have a special interest in visiting Ellis Island?** (*Their ancestor entered the United States there.*) **DRAW CONCLUSIONS**

MOVING AHEAD
pp. 174–181

Have students read page 175. Point out the word *gnawed*. Model using the use decoding/phonics strategy.

> **MODEL** I see a word in the last sentence of the first paragraph that is not spelled the way it sounds. If I didn't know the word, I might say /g/-/nôd/. I know that's wrong, because it doesn't sound like any word I've ever heard. But I remember that the letters *gn* are a digraph that stands for this sound: /n/. I should have said /nôd/. That makes sense. (Focus Strategy) **USE DECODING/PHONICS**

Pages 176–177

Have volunteers read aloud the dialogue between Dad and Karen. Ask: **What were the two main purposes of the Registry Room?** (*checking papers; checking health*) **MAIN IDEA**

Why was it important to check people's health? (*Preventing sick people from entering the country protected U.S. residents from certain diseases.*) **IMPORTANT DETAILS**

Pages 178–179

Have students read page 179. Ask: **What does Karen think about while in the Registry Room?** (*She imagines all the noise and the excitement and nervousness people felt in the hall.*) **IMPORTANT DETAILS**

Ask: **Why can it be difficult to find out whether a female ancestor entered the United States at Ellis Island?** (*Most women took their husband's last name when they married, so if they were already married when they entered the country, there may not be a record of their original name.*) **CAUSE/EFFECT**

What does Karen want to help Dad do? (*She wants to help him research to find out whether her grandfather's grandmother entered the U.S. at Ellis Island, too.*) **MAIN IDEA**

Page 180

Ask: **How do Dad and Karen plan to honor their ancestor?** (*They want to have his name added to the Wall of Honor.*) **NOTE DETAILS**

INTERVENTION PRACTICE BOOK

page 93

What do you think was the author's purpose for writing? (*He wanted readers to understand what immigrants went through to become U.S. citizens. His purpose was to inform.*) (Focus Skill) **AUTHOR'S PURPOSE**

Summarize the selection. Ask students to tell what used to happen at Ellis Island and what happens there now. Then have them complete *Intervention Practice Book* page 93.

Answers to *Think About It* Questions

1. They want to see where Karen's great-great-grandfather, Poppa Joe, started life in the U.S. They also want to find out what immigrants did when they came to Ellis Island. **SUMMARY**

2. Possible response: He may have been excited about starting life in a new country, and he was probably a little nervous, too. **INTERPRETATION**

3. Postcards should describe some of the sights and express personal reactions to Ellis Island. **WRITE A POSTCARD**

AFTER

Skill Review
pages 542–543

USE SKILL CARD 22B

(Focus Skill) Author's Purpose

RETEACH the skill. Have students look at **side B of Skill Card 22: Author's Purpose.** Call on a volunteer to read aloud the skill reminder. Have students define *genre*. Then have a volunteer read the paragraph. Tell pairs of students to copy the organizer and complete the chart.

After students have identified the author's purpose, have them share with the group details from the passage that helped them know that the purpose of this passage is to entertain.

FLUENCY BUILDER Be sure students have copies of *Intervention Practice Book* page 87. Organize the class into groups of four. Make each student responsible for modeling how to read two sentences. Tell the leaders to read one of their sentences and then lead the rest of the group in a choral reading of the same sentence. Have the group continue until they have read all the sentences. Remind students to offer feedback on expression, pacing, and tone.

INTERVENTION
PRACTICE
BOOK

page 87

Expository Writing: Outline

Build on prior knowledge. Explain that the whole group will work together to make an outline for a report. The report will explain how to research to find out more about a family's past. Write the information below on the board.

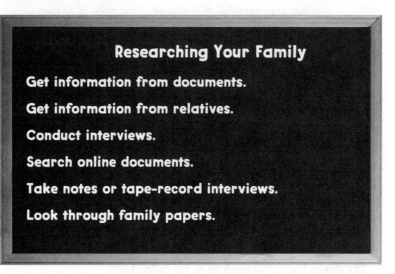

Researching Your Family

Get information from documents.

Get information from relatives.

Conduct interviews.

Search online documents.

Take notes or tape-record interviews.

Look through family papers.

Construct the text. "Share the pen" with students by working with them to help complete an outline. You may wish to use the steps below as you guide students through the writing process.

- Make an incomplete outline on the board. Guide students to write the title, the Roman numerals, and the section heads.

- Have students read aloud the remaining details and tell you where to write them to complete the outline.

Revisit the text. With students, reread the outline. Help students see that the two Roman numeral topics support the main idea in the title. Have them make sure that the details identified with letters support the topic under which they appear. Help students rearrange the details if necessary. Remind them to check for any mistakes in spelling and grammar. Point out that details may not be in complete sentences, so they might not include end punctuation.

On Your Own

Invite students to write details for stories or reports about family traditions or something they know about their families' histories. They should write the details on cards, one detail per card. Then they can arrange the details to make outlines. Encourage them to use the cards to create written outlines.

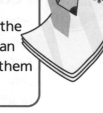

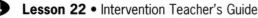

Connect Spelling and Phonics

RETEACH digraphs: /n/*kn, gn;* /r/*wr.* Remind students that sometimes two consonants together can stand for one sound. Tell them that *kn* and *gn* can stand for /n/, and *wr* stands for /r/. Tell students that you will dictate words for them to spell. In the first three words you will say, /n/ is spelled *kn.* Dictate words 1–3 and have students write them. After students write each one, display the correct spelling so they can proofread their work. Then tell students that in the next two words, /n/ is spelled *gn.* Dictate words 4–5 and have students proofread as before. Follow a similar procedure for /r/ in words 6–8.

1. know*	2. knuckle	3. knapsack	4. gnat
5. gnawed*	6. wrong	7. written*	8. unwrap

*Word appears in "A Place of New Beginnings."

Dictate the following sentences for students to write: *Pam knocked until her knuckles hurt. She had gone to the wrong door.*

Build and Read Longer Words

INTERVENTION
ASSESSMENT
BOOK

Write these words on the board: *knitted, wrapping, written.* Remind students that when two or more consonants appear between two vowels, the word in which they appear is often divided into syllables between the consonants. Point to *knitted.* Cover *ted* and have a volunteer read *knit.* Then cover *knit* and ask a volunteer to read *ted.* Slide your hand under the whole word as students read it aloud. Call on volunteers to read the remaining words and tell how they sounded them out.

FLUENCY BUILDER Have students choose a passage from "A Place of New Beginnings" to read aloud to a partner. Tell students they may choose a passage with interesting information, or have them read one of the following passages:

- Read page 175 and the first paragraph of page 176. (From *We started our tour. . .* through *. . . just the starting place.* Total: 113 words)

- Read page 180. (From *The tour guide . . .* through *. . . looking forward to it!* Total: 98 words)

Tell students to read the selected passage aloud to their partner three times. Have the reader rate each reading on a scale from 1 to 4. Encourage students to assess their progress from previous readings.

Review Vocabulary

Review the Vocabulary Words before the weekly assessment. Divide the class into teams and have the teams sit together with a list of Vocabulary Words in front of them. Read the definitions from page 219, one at a time. Have the group decide together which word fits the definition and send one team member to the board to write the word. Tell students that each team member must write at least one word. Award points to the team that is the first to write the word correctly.

**INTERVENTION
PRACTICE
BOOK**

page 90

(Focus Skill) Review Author's Purpose

To review author's purpose before the weekly assessment, have students complete *Intervention Practice Book* page 90. Call on students to name the purposes for writing. (*to entertain, to inform, to persuade*) Then have students read the passage and complete the chart.

Review Test Prep

Have students turn to page 543 of the *Pupil Edition*. Call attention to the tips for answering the test questions. Tell students that paying attention to these tips can help them answer not only the test questions on this page but also other test questions like these.

**INTERVENTION
ASSESSMENT
BOOK**

**LEAD
THE WAY**

page 543

Have students follow along as you read aloud each test question and the tip that goes with it. Have students name genres that are often used with each of the three purposes for writing.

Self-Selected Reading

Have students choose books to read on their own. Tell students they may select books from the classroom library shelf, or you may wish to offer a group of appropriate books from which students can choose.

- *Today I Am an American*. (See page 543M of the *Teacher's Edition* for a lesson plan.)

- *The Butterfly Seeds*, by Mary Watson. William Morrow, 1995

- *Lights for Gita*, by Rachna Gilmore. Tilbury House, 1994

After students have chosen their books, give each student a copy of My Reading Log, which can be found on page R38 in the back of the *Teacher's Edition*. Have students fill in the information at the top of the form. Then have them use the log to keep track of their reading and to record their responses to the literature.

Conduct student-teacher conferences. Schedule time for individual reading conferences for each student to discuss his or her self-selected reading. Tell students to bring their book and Reading Log to the conference and to prepare by practicing a favorite passage to read aloud. Ask students what they think the author's purpose is for writing.

FLUENCY PERFORMANCE Have students read aloud the passage from "A Place of New Beginnings" that they practiced with a partner. Use the reading to assess students' pace and expression. Have the student use the 1 to 4 scale to rate his or her own performance. If students are not satisfied with their oral reading, allow time for extra oral reading practice and then let students try again.

See *Oral Reading Fluency Assessment* for monitoring progress.

LESSON 23

Use with

"Saguaro Cactus"

BEFORE

**Building
Background
and Vocabulary**

Review Phonics: Digraphs /f/ph, gh

Identify the sound. Tell students to listen for the /f/ sound in the words *graph* and *enough*. Then have students listen to this sentence and repeat it twice: *The photos made Ralph laugh.* Have students identify words with the /f/ sound. (*photos, Ralph, laugh*)

Associate letters to sound. Write the above sentence on the board. Underline the letters *ph* in *photos* and *Ralph*. Explain that the letters *ph* stand for the /f/ sound. Then underline *gh* in *laugh*, and tell students that the letters *gh* can also stand for the /f/ sound. Write *cough* and underline the letters *ough*. Tell students that the letters *gh* usually stand for the /f/ sound in words with the letter pattern *ough*.

Word blending. Model how to blend *laugh*. Slide your hand under the word as you elongate the sounds: /lllaaff/. Say the word naturally: *laugh*. Follow a similar procedure with *photos* and *Ralph*.

Apply the skill. *Letter Substitution* Write the following words on the board, and have students read them aloud. Make the changes necessary to form the words in parentheses. Have volunteers read the new words.

**INTERVENTION
PRACTICE
BOOK**

page 92

rug (rough)	**pony** (phony)	**prone** (phone)
grab (graph)	**touch** (tough)	**telegram** (telegraph)

Introduce Vocabulary

PRETEACH **lesson vocabulary.** Explain that students will learn eight new words that will help them read a nonfiction selection called "Saguaro Cactus." Use the following process to teach the Vocabulary Words.

Use the following suggestions or similiar ideas to give the meaning or context.

> Write the word.
> Say the word.
> Track the word and have students repeat it.
> Give the meaning or context.

spiny	Compare spines to thorns and needles.
decomposes	Explain that when something is composed, it is made. Point out the prefix *de-*, meaning "the opposite of." Explain that *decomposes* means "falls apart."
topple	Demonstrate by stacking books and knocking them over.
brush	Relate to a weedy field, with short trees.
habitat	Related word: You live in, or inhabit, your home. Some animals live in a forest habitat.

teeming	Explain that *teeming* means "full of." Help students make up phrases such as *a school teeming with students*.
perch	Have students look for places where birds or other animals might perch.
nectar	Explain that nectar is a sweet-tasting juice that attracts birds, butterflies, and insects to flowers.

AFTER

Building Background and Vocabulary

Apply Vocabulary Strategies

Use sentence and context. Write this sentence on the board: *Strong winds made the plant topple to the ground.* Explain that readers can often figure out the meaning of an unfamiliar word by reading the words around that word. Model the strategy.

> **MODEL** When I read this sentence, I am unsure what topple means. I reread it and notice the words "strong winds" and "to the ground." I know strong winds can make trees and plants fall over. So topple must mean "to fall over."

Guide students to use this strategy with other unfamiliar words.

RETEACH lesson vocabulary. Have each student make a set of word cards for the Vocabulary Words. Say the sentences and tell students to hold up the word that completes each rhyme. Reread each sentence.

1. The flower inspector tasted the __(nectar)__ .
2. The anteater is dreaming of an anthill that's __(teeming)__ .
3. A little cat shares my __(habitat)__ .
4. A mouse in a rush ran to hide in the __(brush)__ .
5. Some leaves are shiny, but some are __(spiny)__ .
6. Observation discloses that a dead plant __(decomposes)__ .
7. Little birds search for a good place to __(perch)__ .
8. A quick move or hop will make the block tower __(topple)__ .

FLUENCY BUILDER Have students look at *Intervention Practice Book* page 91. Read each word in the first column aloud and have students repeat it. Then have pairs of students read the words in the first column aloud to each other. Tell students to follow the same procedure to read the remaining columns. After partners have practiced reading the columns of words, have them read aloud the entire list.

INTERVENTION PRACTICE BOOK

page 91

(Focus Skill) Elements of Nonfiction: Text Structure

PRETEACH the skill. Tell students that nonfiction writers might use one of these text structures to organize information: main idea and details, cause and effect, comparison and contrast, and sequence of events.

Have students look at **side A of Skill Card 23: Text Structure**. Read the introductory copy. Ask students to name other signal words that show order. Then ask a student to read the paragraph aloud. Ask:

- **Which text structure did the writer use to organize the text?** (*sequence*)

- **How do you know?** (Possible response: *The writer provided actual times of the day.*)

Have students use the time line to retell the events in sequence.

Prepare to Read: "Saguaro Cactus"

Preview. Tell students they will be reading a nonfiction selection called "Saguaro Cactus." Explain that nonfiction gives information about a particular topic. It often includes photos with captions. Tell students that "Saguaro Cactus" gives information about a desert habitat. Then preview the selection.

**LEAD
THE WAY**
pages
546–560

- **Pages 546–547:** I see the title and the names of the authors. Those large plants in the photo must be saguaro cactuses.

- **Pages 548–549:** On these pages, I see pictures of different kinds of animals. There is also a picture of a cactus. This selection must have information about animals that live in the desert where the cactus lives.

- **Pages 550–551:** The plant in the picture on page 550 looks like a young cactus. It is much shorter than the tree, and it doesn't have any limbs. The diagrams on the next page show how a little cactus grows. It looks like a cactus can have flowers, too.

- **Pages 552–555:** The photos on these pages show birds on and around cactuses. I can guess that the selection will tell about birds that live in cactuses.

- **Pages 556–559:** Here I see other kinds of animals around cactuses. These animals must live in the same habitat.

Set purpose. Model setting a purpose for reading "Saguaro Cactus."

MODEL From my preview, I think I will learn how saguaro cactuses grow. I also expect to learn about different birds and animals that live near the saguaro cactus. I will read to find out how a cactus is able to survive and grow in the harsh desert.

Reread and Summarize

Have students reread and summarize "Saguaro Cactus" in sections, described below.

Pages 548–549

Let's reread pages 548 and 549 to recall where the saguaro cactus grows and why the cactus is so important in the desert.

Summary: The saguaro cactus grows in the desert. It is important because it is the center of life for many creatures.

....

Pages 550–551

Now let's reread pages 550–551 to find out how the saguaro cactus grows and survives in the desert.

Summary: The saguaro grows very slowly. It can survive in the desert because it holds a lot of water.

....

Pages 552–557

As we reread pages 552–557, let's find out why the saguaro cactus is important to birds and animals.

Summary: Birds make nests in the cactus because it is a safe, cool place. Animals live, eat, and hunt on or around the cactus.

....

Page 558

Let's reread page 558 to recall what happens to the saguaro when it dies.

Summary: After the saguaro dies, it still gives many creatures food and shelter as it slowly decomposes and returns to the earth.

FLUENCY BUILDER Be sure students have copies of *Intervention Practice Book* page 91. Call attention to the sentences on the bottom half of the page. Model reading aloud the sentences. Have students repeat after you, imitating your expression, phrasing, and pace. Then have students practice reading each sentence aloud three times to a partner.

INTERVENTION
PRACTICE
BOOK

page 91

Directed Reading: "Desert Animals," pp. 182–188

Pages 182–183

Have a volunteer read the title aloud. Help students identify the setting in the illustration as a desert. Read pages 182–183 while students listen to find out what the desert is like. Ask: **What words do the authors use to help you see and feel what the desert is like in daytime?** (*brightly, clear, hot, dry, baking, burning*) **LITERARY ANALYSIS**

MOVING
AHEAD
pp. 182–188

Ask: **What is happening to the old cactus now? What do the authors say happened earlier?** (*Now the cactus is lying on the desert floor, decomposing. Before this, it died of a disease and toppled over.*) (Focus Skill) **TEXT STRUCTURE**

Pages 184–185

Read aloud page 184 quickly. Model using the adjust reading rate strategy:

> **MODEL** I'm not sure I can remember everything I read on this page. I think I read too quickly. The first two pages were an introduction. The information I read was more general. But on this page the authors give information about many different insects that I want to remember. If I read more slowly, I'll have time to understand the facts on the page. (Focus Skill) **ADJUST READING RATE**

Reread page 184 slowly.

Ask: **How do ants, beetles, and bees survive in the desert?** (*They dig burrows and stay underground.*) **MAIN IDEA**

Pages 186–187

Have students read page 186 to find out about other animals in the desert. Ask: **How do rattlesnakes, jackrabbits, and hummingbirds survive in the desert?** (*Rattlesnakes avoid the heat by resting by day and hunting at night. Jackrabbits let out body heat through their big ears. Hummingbirds drink nectar.*) **DRAW CONCLUSIONS**

INTERVENTION
PRACTICE
BOOK

page 93

Ask: **Which sentence tells the main idea of page 187?** (*The main idea is in the last sentence: Day and night, the desert is alive with animals.*) **MAIN IDEA**

Summarize the selection. Ask students to summarize the selection by naming different ways animals survive in the harsh desert. Then have them complete *Intervention Practice Book* page 93.

Answers to *Think About It* Questions

1. The main problem for desert animals is protecting themselves from the heat. **SUMMARY**

2. Many desert animals hide by day to protect themselves from the sun. **INTERPRETATION**

3. Accept reasonable responses. **FORMULATE QUESTIONS**

Skill Review
pages 566–567

USE SKILL CARD 23B

 Elements of Nonfiction: Text Structure

RETEACH the skill. Have students look at **side B of Skill Card 23: Text Structure**. Read aloud the skill reminder and the directions. Ask a volunteer to read the paragraph aloud.

Have students tell ways in which a writer can show sequence of events. Then have students copy the time line, write the events in the paragraph on the time line, and retell the sequence of events.

After students have completed their time lines, have them display and explain their work. Point out that the selection "Saguaro Cactus" is organized according to sequence. It tells the time order about the events in the life of a saguaro cactus.

 FLUENCY BUILDER Be sure students have copies of *Intervention Practice Book* page 91. Explain that they will practice the sentences at the bottom of the page by recording them on tape. Have students choose new partners. Tell the partners to take turns reading the sentences aloud to each other and then recording them. Have students listen to the tape and tell how they think their reading has improved. Then have them record the sentences one more time.

INTERVENTION PRACTICE BOOK

page 91

Expository Writing: Drafting

Build on prior knowledge. Tell students that they are going to work together to draft two paragraphs about the desert habitat. Remind students that a research report includes facts, or true pieces of information. Display the following information on chart paper:

Desert Animals	elf owl
Desert Surroundings	50-foot cactus

Tell students to look back at the selection "Saguaro Cactus" to find other facts about desert animals and desert surroundings. As they locate examples of animals and surroundings, add the items to the chart. Let students know that they will use these lists to help them draft sentences for a report.

Construct the text. "Share the pen" with students in a collaborative group writing effort. Use the steps that follow to guide students through the process.

- Help students craft an opening sentence for the report. The sentence should give a preview about animals and surroundings in a desert habitat.

- Have students use the items on the chart paper to dictate detail sentences for each paragraph. Then help students draft the report in an order that makes sense. Students, for example, may put sentences about desert animals together in one paragraph and sentences about desert plants and other surroundings together in another paragraph.

- Students should add a concluding sentence at the end of the report.

Revisit the text. Guide students to work together to revise their draft. Remind them to focus on whether the sentences are details that support the topic sentence of each paragraph. Ask them to evaluate their sentences to see if they are presented in an order that makes sense. Have students read the completed report aloud.

On Your Own

Have students choose other habitats to write about, such as the ocean, rain forest, and so on. Provide simple references for them to use. Remind them that, in the drafting part of writing, they should be most interested in writing down complete and interesting details.

Correct Spelling and Phonics

RETEACH digraphs /f/*ph, gh*. Remind students that the /f/ sound can be spelled with the letters *ph* or *gh*. Tell students they will write words you dictate. Write *tough* on the board and explain that in the first two words you say, the letters *gh* have the /f/ sound. Dictate words 1–2, and have students write them. After each word, display the correct spelling so students can proofread their work. Write *graph* on the board and explain that in the next six words, the /f/ sound is spelled with the letters *ph*, as in *graph*. Dictate the remaining words and have students write and proofread them.

1. laugh	2. rough*	3. telephone	4. photograph*
5. telegraph	6. asphalt	7. elephants	8. graphic

*Word appears in "Desert Animals."

Dictate the following sentence and have students write it: *The elephants in the photos were walking on rough ground.*

Build and Read Longer Words

Tell students that they can use what they have learned about *gh* and *ph* to read longer words in which the /f/ sound is spelled with the letters *gh* or *ph*. Write *elephant* on the board. Remind students that when two or more consonants appear between two vowels, the word is usually divided into syllables between the consonants if they stand for different sounds. Point out that when *gh* and *ph* stand for one sound, /f/, the two letters always stay together. Point to each syllable as you say *elephant* (el-e-phant). Have students repeat the syllables and then read the word. Write *alphabet* (al-pha-bet) and *atmosphere* (at-mos-phere) on the board. Have students read the syllables and then the complete words.

INTERVENTION
ASSESSMENT
BOOK

FLUENCY BUILDER Have students choose a passage from "Desert Animals" to read aloud to a partner. Tell students they may select an interesting passage, or give them the following choices:

- Read the second paragraph on page 182 and all of page 183. (From *The desert looks empty . . .* through *. . . could not survive*. Total: 108 words)

- Read page 187. (From *The roadrunner . . .* through *. . . alive with animals*. Total: 100 words)

Tell students to read the selected passage aloud to their partner three times. Have the reader rate each reading on a scale from 1 to 4. Encourage students to rate their own progress from readings they have previously completed.

Review Vocabulary

Before the weekly assessment, review the Vocabulary Words. Have students answer the following questions and then discuss their answers with a partner.

1. What kinds of **spiny** plants might you find in the **brush**? (Possible responses: *any plants with thorns, such as nettles or berry bushes*)

2. Why might a garden of **nectar**-filled flowers be **teeming** with bees? (Possible response: *Lots of bees would come to get nectar to make honey.*)

3. What might happen if you **toppled** from your **perch** on a tree branch? (Possible response: *You might be hurt. You might break a leg or an arm.*)

4. What might a **decomposed** log be a **habitat** for? (Possible responses: *insects, mushrooms, other fungi*)

⭐ (Focus Skill) Review Elements of Nonfiction: Text Structure

Review text structure before the weekly assessment by having students name different ways in which writers use text structure. Then have them complete *Intervention Practice Book* page 94. Students should read the passage, identify its text structure, and use information from the passage to complete the time line.

Review Test Prep

Have students turn to page 567 of the *Pupil Edition*. Call attention to the tips for answering test questions. Tell students that these tips will help them answer not only the questions on this page but also other test questions.

LEAD THE WAY
page 567

Have students follow along as you read aloud each test question and its tip. For the first item, help students understand why the phrase is a heading and cannot be any of the other options in the test question. For the second item, point out the word *not* in the test question. Tell students that it is important to read each and every question slowly and carefully. The insertion of the word *not* in this kind of question changes the answer students might choose.

INTERVENTION PRACTICE BOOK
page 94

INTERVENTION ASSESSMENT BOOK

Self-Selected Reading

Have students select their own books to read independently. They might choose books from the classroom library shelf, or you may wish to offer a group of appropriate books from which students can choose. Titles might include the following:

- *The Land of Little Water* (See page 567K of the *Teacher's Edition* for a lesson plan.)

- *Desert Giant* by Barbara Bash. Little, Brown, 1990

- *The Desert Is Theirs* by Byrd Baylor. Aladdin, 1987

After students have chosen their books, give each student a copy of My Reading Log, which can be found on page R38 in the back of the Teacher's Edition. Have students fill in the information at the top of the form. Then have them use the log to keep track of their reading and to record their responses to the literature.

Conduct student-teacher conferences. Arrange time for each student to confer with you individually about his or her self-selected reading. Tell students to bring their book and Reading Log to the conference and to prepare for the conference by rehearsing a favorite passage to read aloud. Have students tell why they selected the book and whether the book was what they expected.

FLUENCY PERFORMANCE Have students read aloud the passage from "Desert Animals" that they practiced. Observe students' pronunciation, intonation, and phrasing. Have students use the 1 to 4 scale to rate their performance. Give students a second chance to read if they are not satisfied with their performance.

See *Oral Reading Fluency Assessment* for monitoring progress.

LESSON 24

"Blue Willow"

BEFORE

Building Background and Vocabulary

Review Phonics: Short Vowel /e/ea

Identify the sound. Tell students to listen for the /e/ or short *e* vowel sound as you say these words: *head, breath*. Then have students repeat this sentence twice: *Bread can be part of a healthful breakfast.* Ask students to identify the words with the vowel sound they hear in *head*. (*bread, healthful, breakfast*)

Associate letters to sound. Write the above sentence on the board. Underline *ea* in *bread, healthful*, and *breakfast*. Remind students that two vowels together often stand for a long vowel sound. Explain that *ea* can also stand for /e/, the short *e* vowel sound.

Word blending. Model how to blend and read *thread*. Slide your hand under the whole word as you elongate the sounds to say /thrreed/. Then say the word naturally—*thread*. Follow a similar procedure for *head* and *tread*.

Apply the skill. *Vowel Substitution* Write the words below on the board. Have students read them aloud. Make the changes necessary to form the words in parentheses. Call on volunteers to read the new words.

INTERVENTION PRACTICE BOOK

page 96

Brad (bread)	**sweet** (sweat)	**throat** (threat)
broth (breath)	**deed** (dead)	**heed** (head)

⭐ (Focus Skill) Introduce Vocabulary

PRETEACH lesson vocabulary. Explain that students will learn new words that will help them read a story called "Blue Willow." Use the following process to teach the Vocabulary Words.

Use ideas such as these to give the meaning or context of the new words.

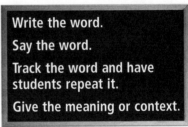

Write the word.
Say the word.
Track the word and have students repeat it.
Give the meaning or context.

undoubtedly Point out the negative prefix *un-*, meaning "not." Relate to the opposite of *doubt*.

loathe Have students use the sentences "I love..." and "I loathe..." to name TV shows they like and shows they dislike.

certainty Point out the root word *certain*. Ask questions and have students tell whether they are unsure or certain about the answer.

protruded Point to things that protrude, such as a book on a bookshelf.

indifferent	Tell students that *indifferent* has nothing to do with being unlike something else. The word describes the feeling people have when they don't care about something.
sulkily	Demonstrate by pouting and acting as if you are in a bad mood.
heartily	Relate *heartily* to the heart as a symbol of strong emotion.

For vocabulary activities, see Vocabulary Games on pages 2–7.

For vocabulary activities, see Vocabulary Games on pages 2–7.

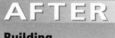

AFTER

Building Background and Vocabulary

Apply Vocabulary Strategies

Use suffixes and root words. Write the word *sulkily* on chart paper and underline the suffix *-ly*. Explain that students can use root words and suffixes to figure out the meaning of an unfamiliar word. Model using the strategy.

> **MODEL** This is a word I do not recognize. I see a smaller word, *sulk*, and the suffix *-ly*. I know when people *sulk* they pout and are unhappy. The suffix *-ly* means "like" or "characteristic of." Maybe *sulkily* means "in a way that shows unhappiness."

Guide students to use this strategy to figure out the meanings of other words.

RETEACH **lesson vocabulary.** Explain that synonyms are words with the same or almost the same meaning, while antonyms are words with opposite meanings. Give a synonym and an antonym for each Vocabulary Word. Have students name the word and use it in a sentence.

Word	Synonym	Antonym
1. *undoubtedly*	surely	maybe
2. *loathe*	detest	love
3. *certainty*	confidence	doubt
4. *protruded*	jutted	sank
5. *indifferent*	disinterested	excited
6. *sulkily*	glumly	cheerfully
7. *heartily*	enthusiastically	dully

Vocabulary Words

undoubtedly without a doubt

loathe to dislike immensely

certainty the feeling or belief that something is for sure

protruded stuck out; pushed out

indifferent not caring; unconcerned

sulkily in a way that shows unhappiness

heartily with enthusiasm

FLUENCY BUILDER Have students turn to *Intervention Practice Book* page 95. Read each word and have students echo it. Have partners take turns reading each column of words aloud. After partners have practiced reading aloud the words in each of the columns, allow time for them to practice all of the words.

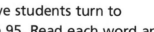

INTERVENTION PRACTICE BOOK

page 95

⭐(Focus Skill) Author's Purpose

PRETEACH **the skill.** Explain that authors write for a purpose, which may be to entertain, to inform, or to persuade readers. Authors also have their own perspective, which comes from their own ideas about a topic.

Have students look at **side A of Skill Card 24: Author's Purpose.** Read the definitions and the information for figuring out the author's perspective.

Call on a volunteer to read the paragraph aloud. Ask:

- **How can you tell the author's purpose is to entertain?** (*The details don't provide information about a topic and they don't try to persuade.*)

- **Do you think the author likes flying? Why?** (*Possible response: The author must enjoy flying. The details in the paragraph make flying sound like fun.*)

Explain that looking at the details will help students decide the author's purpose. They should look for clues to tell them how the author feels about the topic — these clues will lead them to the author's perspective.

Prepare to Read: "Blue Willow"

Preview. Tell students they will read a story called "Blue Willow." Remind students that fiction authors often write to entertain. Then do a preview of the selection.

LEAD THE WAY
pages 570–582

- **Pages 570–571:** The title of this story is "Blue Willow." After reading the introduction, I know what the title relates to— a plate that is a family heirloom.

- **Pages 572–573:** The car must belong to Janey's family. It looks old, which fits since the story took place in the 1940s.

- **Pages 574–577:** Janey seems to be headed for the building. I wonder if the building is a one-room school. She is alone. But, she's staring at a toad. And the toad is staring back.

- **Pages 578–579:** Janey caught the toad. She's showing it to someone. Maybe it's the teacher.

- **Pages 580–581:** This must be the inside of the school. I don't see Janey, so I can't tell whether she is happy, but the pink petunias are a clue that the story must end happily.

- **Pages 582–583:** There's the plate. So that's what a blue-willow plate looks like. And I see a picture of the author. I want to know how she knows so much about migrant workers.

Set purpose. Model setting a purpose for reading "Blue Willow."

> **MODEL** From the preview, I know that Janey's family moves around a lot. I think the story must be about Janey's first day at a new school. I will read to find out why the author wrote this story and how she feels about what life is like for migrant workers.

Reread and Summarize

Use the chart below as a guide for helping students reread and summarize each section of "Blue Willow."

Page 571

Let's reread page 571 to find out what Janey wants.

Summary: Janey hopes that her family will stop moving around and stay in the community where they live now.

- -

Pages 572–575

Reread pages 572 and 573 to find out how Janey feels about going to a new school.

Summary: Janey feels sad because she doesn't want to go to the school.

- -

Pages 577–578

On pages 577–578, we can find out how Janey plans to use the toad.

Summary: Janey will observe her new teacher's reaction to the toad to judge whether or not she will like the teacher.

- -

Pages 579–582

Reread to the end of the story to find out how Janey's attitude toward school has changed.

Summary: In the beginning, Janey felt nervous and angry about going to her new school, but now she likes school because she likes her new teacher.

FLUENCY BUILDER Have students look at the sentences at the bottom of *Intervention Practice Book* page 95. Tell students to read the sentences silently and look up or ask about any words they do not know how to pronounce. Model how to say Heather's words in sentence 8 heartily. Then have students take turns reading and rereading the sentences to each other until they can read them smoothly and conversationally.

INTERVENTION PRACTICE BOOK

page 95

Directed Reading: "School Days" pp. 190–197

MOVING AHEAD pp. 190–197

Page 190

Have a volunteer read the story title. Explain that it is Heather's first day in a new school. Ask how students might feel if they were Heather. Have students listen to find out how Heather feels as you read page 190 aloud. Ask: **How does Heather feel about going to school?** (*She dreads it.*) **DETERMINE CHARACTERS' EMOTIONS**

Page 191

Have students read page 191 to understand Heather's mood. Ask: **What does Heather's response to her mother's greeting tell about her mood?** (Possible response: *Because Heather feels grumpy, she thinks her mother is too cheerful*). **INTERPRET STORY EVENTS**

Pages 192–193

Have students read page 193. Ask: **What idea does Heather have for getting out of school?** (*She thinks she could pretend to be sick.*) **IMPORTANT DETAILS**

Ask: **Why does Heather give up her plan?** (*She prides herself on being trustworthy.*) **DETERMINE CHARACTERS' TRAITS**

Pages 194–195

Call on volunteers to take the parts of Heather, Dad, and Mom and read page 195 aloud. Ask: **How is Heather feeling now? How do you know?** (Possible response: *She's joking and smiling a little, so we can tell she feels more cheerful.*) **DETERMINE CHARACTERS' EMOTIONS**

Page 196

Have students read page 196. Model using the summarize strategy:

> **MODEL** If I wanted to tell a friend what this story is about in just one sentence, here is what I would say: Heather is nervous and unhappy about going to a new school, but she feels better when she meets her new teacher. (Focus Strategy) **SUMMARIZE**

Ask: **What purpose did the author have for writing this story? How do you think the author feels about the topic of the story?** (*To entertain readers; to tell a good story. The author seems to think that going to a new school can be a little scary, but it can also be exciting.*) (Focus Skill) **AUTHOR'S PURPOSE**

INTERVENTION PRACTICE BOOK

page 97

Summarize the selection. Ask how Heather's attitude changed during the story. Then have students write a one-sentence summary about the selection and complete *Intervention Practice Book* page 97.

Answers to *Think About It* Questions

1. She is going to a new school and will miss her old teacher. **SUMMARY**

2. Possible response: Heather's parents may be asking the woman to help Heather adjust to her new school. **INTERPRETATION**

3. The entry should be written in first person. It should describe logical events and Heather's feelings about them. **WRITE A JOURNAL ENTRY**

AFTER

Skill Review
pages 588–589

USE SKILL CARD 24B

(Focus Skill) Author's Purpose

RETEACH the skill. Call attention to **side B of Skill Card 24: Author's Purpose.** Read aloud the skill reminder. Review that readers can determine an author's perspective by noting which details the author has chosen to include.

Call on a volunteer to read aloud the paragraph. Explain that students can now work with a partner to create their own charts. Remind students to look for clues in the paragraph to tell them why the author wrote the paragraph and how he or she feels about the topic of the paragraph. After students have completed their chart, have them explain their work. Point out that the author's purpose in writing "Blue Willow" is to entertain readers.

FLUENCY BUILDER Have students look at their copies of *Intervention Practice Book* page 95. Remind them that they have already read the sentences once before. Have them reread the sentences silently. Call out a number between 1 and 8. Then say a student's name and have that student read the corresponding sentence aloud to the class. Remind students to focus on pacing, expression, and tone. Consider allowing students to read the sentence multiple times to give them confidence in the reading.

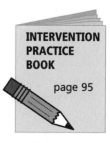

INTERVENTION PRACTICE BOOK

page 95

Expository Writing: Edit a Report

Build on prior knowledge. Tell students that they are going to work together to edit a research report that someone wrote about his new town. Remind students that editing has two steps:

■ Revise: Check facts and add details. Make sure the report says what it needs to say.

■ Proofread: Check for punctuation, capitalization, grammar, and spelling errors.

In advance, write the following draft of a student's research report on chart paper for display.

Draft

Our town was founded by James Peterson. At first, our town was called Peter's Town. My family livs on Stone Street in a brown house. When the town finally got a post office, Pleasant town was the name it used.

Construct the text. "Share the pen" with students in a collaborative group effort. Read aloud the draft of the student's research report. Then use the steps that follow to guide students through the editing process.

■ Start by focusing on revising. Ask leading questions such as *Is the main idea of the paragraph stated clearly? Do all the sentences make sense? How would you change it so that it is easier to understand?*

■ Have students take turns making up details that support the main idea.

■ Tell them to cut the sentence that does not belong in this report and explain why it doesn't belong.

■ Finally, have students add a title to the report and then reread all the sentences to see if they make sense and are in a logical order.

Revisit the text. Ask students to proofread the revised version of the report. Have them identify errors in spelling, grammar, and punctuation. Guide them to add proofreading marks to show how to change the report.

On Your Own

Have students write paragraphs about their own town. Once students have written a draft, they can revise and proofread it. You might have them work with a partner to edit each other's work.

Connecting Spelling and Phonics

RETEACH short vowel /e/ea. Write *head* on the board. Tell students you will dictate words in which the /e/ sound is spelled *ea*, as in *head*. Have students write each word on paper. After you dictate each word, write the word on the board so students can proofread their spelling. Tell students to draw a line through any incorrect word and write the correct spelling beside it.

I. dread*	2. spread	3. thread*	4. meadow
5. breath*	6. health	7. weather*	8. pleasant*

*Word appears in "School Days."

Dictate the following sentence and have students write it: *I dread the spread of bad weather.*

Build and Read Longer Words

Write the following words on the board: *dreadful, unread, threadbare.* Remind students that when two consonants appear between two vowels, the word is usually broken into syllables between the consonants. Point out the two consonants in the middle of the word *dreadful. (d, f)* Then cover the ending *ful* and have a volunteer read the word *dread.* Cover *dread* and have a volunteer read *ful.* Uncover both parts and draw your hand under the entire word as students read it aloud. Follow a similar procedure with the two remaining words. Write *healthy* on the board. Remind students that the letters *th* in *healthy* stand for one sound, /th/, and that this letter combination stays together when words are broken into syllables. Have students read *healthy* as you frame each part of the word. (*heal-thy*) Repeat with *wealthy* (*weal-thy*) and *breathless* (*breath-less*).

INTERVENTION
ASSESSMENT
BOOK

FLUENCY BUILDER Have students choose a passage from "School Days" to read aloud to a partner. Tell students to choose a passage they found especially interesting or have them choose one of the following options:

- Read page 190. (From *Heather woke. . .* through *. . . warmth of her comforter.* Total: 98 words)

- Read the second and third paragraphs on page 194 and the first four paragraphs on page 195. (From *"Ready for breakfast?". . .* through *. . . from Heather's skirt.* Total: 110 words)

Tell students to read the selected passage aloud to their partner three times. Have the student rate each of his or her own readings on a scale from I to 4. Encourage readers to note their improvement from previous readings.

Review Vocabulary

Have students print *yes* in large letters on the front of a file card and *no* on the back. Then use the Vocabulary Words in questions like the ones that follow. Have students answer by showing the appropriate side of the card.

1. Does your ear **protrude** from your head? (*yes*)
2. Do you know your name with **certainty**? (*yes*)
3. Would you cheer **heartily** for a sports team you feel indifferent about? (*no*)
4. Will summer **undoubtedly** come? (*yes*)
5. Would you smile **sulkily** when you meet a friend unexpectedly? (*no*)
6. Do you enjoy eating a food that you **loathe**? (*no*)
7. Would you always be **indifferent** toward your best friend? (*no*)

⭐ Focus Skill Review Author's Purpose

To review author's purpose before the weekly assessment, have students complete *Intervention Practice Book* page 98. Have students read the paragraph independently and ask themselves *Why did the author write this?* Have students complete the chart, encouraging them to use details in the selection to fill in the boxes.

**INTERVENTION
PRACTICE
BOOK**

page 98

Review Test Prep

Have students turn to page 589 of the *Pupil Edition*. Call attention to the tips for answering test questions. Tell students that paying attention to these tips will help them answer the test questions.

**LEAD
THE WAY**

page 589

**INTERVENTION
ASSESSMENT
BOOK**

Read aloud each test question and the tip that goes with it. Explain that fiction is often written to entertain and nonfiction is often written to inform or persuade. Remind students to look for words and ideas that show feelings to determine the author's perspective.

Self-Selected Reading

Have students select their own books to read independently. They might choose books from the classroom library shelf, or you may wish to offer a group of appropriate books from which the student can choose.

- *The Little School in the Valley.* (See page 589M of the *Teacher's Edition* for a lesson plan.)

- *Ramona and Her Father* by Beverly Cleary. Camelot, 1999

- *Hey, New Kid!* by Betsy Duffey. Puffin, 1998

After students have chosen their books, give each student a copy of My Reading Log, which can be found on page R38 in the back of the *Teacher's Edition*. Have students fill in the information at the top of the form. Then have them use the log to keep track of their reading and to record their responses to the literature.

Conduct student-teacher conferences. Arrange time for each student to confer with you individually about his or her self-selected reading. Tell students to bring the book they read and their Reading Logs to the conference. Have students tell why they liked or did not like the book. Students might also like to choose a favorite passage to read aloud to you. Ask questions to stimulate discussion.

FLUENCY PERFORMANCE Have students read aloud to you the passage from "School Days" that they practiced with their partners. Take note of words the student misreads to assess areas of difficulty. Have the student rate his or her own reading performance on the 1–4 scale. Give students who are not satisfied with their reading time to practice. They can then reread the passage at a later time.

See *Oral Reading Fluency Assessment* for monitoring progress.

LESSON 25

"In My Family"

BEFORE

Building
Background
and Vocabulary

Review Phonics: Long Vowel /ā/ *ea, ei, eigh*

Identify the sound. Tell students to listen for the /ā/ sound in these words as you read them aloud: *steak, beige, neigh*. Have them listen to this sentence and repeat it twice: *Do not break the reins on the sleigh*. Ask students to name the words that have the long *a* vowel sound. (*break, reins, sleigh*)

Associate letters to sound. Write the above sentence on the board and underline *ea* in *break*. Point out that in *break* the letters *ea* stand for the /ā/ sound. Then underline *ei* in *reins* and *eigh* in *sleigh*, and tell students that these letter combinations can also stand for the /ā/ sound. Point out that in words with the *eigh* pattern, the *gh* is silent.

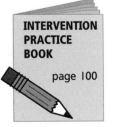

INTERVENTION
PRACTICE
BOOK

page 100

Word blending. Model how to blend and read *weight*. Slide your hand under the whole word as you elongate the sound: /wwāāt/. Then say the word naturally—*weight*. Repeat the procedure with *great*.

Apply the skill. *Letter Substitution* Write the following words on the board, and have students read them aloud. Make the changes necessary to form the words in parentheses. Have volunteers read the new words.

stack (steak)   **wet** (weight)   **grant** (great)   **van** (vein)   **fret** (freight)

Introduce Vocabulary

PRETEACH **lesson vocabulary.** Tell students that they are going to learn six new words that they will see again when they read "In My Family." Use the following process to teach the Vocabulary Words.

Use the following suggestions or similar ideas to give the meaning or context.

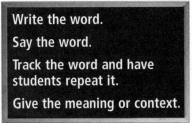

Write the word.

Say the word.

Track the word and have students repeat it.

Give the meaning or context.

culture	Relate to traditions that are part of the culture of a particular group of people.
chile	Explain that peppers called chiles are often used to make spicy Mexican dishes.
mesquite	Explain that many people use a wood called mesquite to build a fire because the smoke gives the food a special flavor.
barbecue	Cover *barbe* and have students read *cue*. Then have them read the whole word. Point out that there is no *q* in *barbecue*.

accordion	Show pictures of an accordion. Explain how the instrument is played.
confetti	Demonstrate what confetti is by tearing paper into tiny pieces and tossing it.

For vocabulary activities, see Vocabulary Games on pages 2–7.

For vocabulary activities, see Vocabulary Games on pages 2–7.

AFTER
Building Background and Vocabulary

Apply Vocabulary Strategies

Use word origins. Write the word *culture* on the board. Tell students that most English words come from other languages. Students can use a dictionary to find out where words came from. Model the strategy.

> **MODEL** I know I can use a dictionary to find out the origin of the word *culture*. I find the word and directly after it, I see the word *Latin*. That tells me *culture* originated from Latin.

Guide students to use a dictionary to find the origins of the other Vocabulary Words.

RETEACH lesson vocabulary. Have students listen to each sentence. Tell them to hold up the word card that completes each one. Reread the sentence with the correct word and discuss its meaning.

1. The singer also played the (accordion).
2. The wood from the (mesquite) bush is used for charcoal.
3. After the party they cleaned up the (confetti).
4. Her family's meals were always cooked on the (barbecue).
5. There are many traditions in the Mexican American (culture).
6. Many people eat foods flavored with (chile).

Vocabulary Words
culture the customs, beliefs, and arts of a group of people

chile the fruit of a pepper plant, which is often used to make hot seasonings

mesquite a shrub or small tree found in the southwestern United States and Mexico; its wood is used to make charcoal

barbecue a special kind of grill or pit used for cooking outdoors

accordion a musical instrument with keys and hand-operated bellows

confetti tiny pieces of paper, often thrown during celebrations

FLUENCY BUILDER Have students look at the word lists on *Intervention Practice Book* page 99. Read the first column of words from top to bottom, and have students repeat each word after you. Then repeat the exercise, reading the same column from bottom to top. Repeat the procedure with the remaining two columns. Allow time for students to practice words they find problematic.

INTERVENTION PRACTICE BOOK

page 99

USE SKILL CARD 25A

⭐Focus Skill Sequence

PRETEACH the skill. Tell students that when writers relate events, they sometimes organize the writing according to sequence, or the order in which the events actually occurred.

Have students look at **side A of Skill Card 25: Sequence**. Read the skill definition. Ask a volunteer to read the paragraph aloud. Then, direct students' attention to the chart. Have students match events from the chart with events in the paragraph. Ask: **What makes it easy to follow the sequence of events in the story?** (*Possible response: The events happen in a logical order and time order words are used*.)

Discuss how time order words, such as *before, next,* and *finally*, can clarify the sequence of events within a passage.

Prepare to Read: "In My Family"

Preview. Tell students they will be reading an autobiography called "In My Family." Explain that an auto-biography is a story that someone writes about his or her own life. Tell students that "In My Family" describes the author's own childhood memories. Then preview the selection.

LEAD
THE WAY

pages
592–601

- **Pages 592–593:** The title of this selection is "In My Family," and the author/illustrator is Carmen Lomas Garza. Since the selection is an autobiography, the stories must be about her family.

- **Pages 594–595:** These pages have their own separate title, "The Horned Toad." The animal on page 594 must be a horned toad. I wonder why the ant picture is there. The big picture shows two children looking at a horned toad. Maybe the girl in the picture is Carmen Lomas Garza.

- **Pages 596–598:** Each of these pages has its own title, too, so each page must tell a separate story. When I read the titles and look at the pictures, I can predict that all the stories will have something to do with food.

- **Page 599:** This page must show another tradition in the family—making Easter eggs.

- **Pages 600–601:** These pages don't have a title, but they have a big picture. It looks like a party. I see a band and grown-ups and children enjoying the music together.

Set purpose. Model setting a purpose for reading "In My Family."

> **MODEL** From the preview, I can guess that the author is telling about special memories of her childhood. I wonder if her family's traditions are anything like my family's customs. I will read to find out about the author's culture and what traditions her family enjoyed.

Reread and Summarize

Have students read and summarize "In My Family" in sections, as described below.

Pages 592–593

Let's reread page 593 to remember what purpose the author hopes her writing will serve.

Summary: She wrote to show her pride in her heritage.

Pages 594–595

We can reread these pages to find out what the author thinks about when she sees a horned toad.

Summary: The author thinks of what her mother and grandmother used to say—that she and her brother were like horned toads, playing without a care.

Pages 596–597

Reread pages 596 and 597 to recall what the author thinks of when she sees *nopalitos* and empanadas.

Summary: *Nopalitos* remind her of eating breakfast in late winter and early spring. Empanadas bring memories of family gatherings.

Pages 598–599

On these pages, we can read to remember what family celebrations happened at the author's own house.

Summary: Often the extended family came over to celebrate, but Carmen and her brothers enjoyed special times by themselves.

Pages 600–601

Let's reread these pages to find out why the author thinks her hometown is special.

Summary: Friends and family members gathered at a local restaurant to dance and enjoy the music together.

FLUENCY BUILDER Be sure students have copies of *Intervention Practice Book* page 99. Call attention to the sentences on the bottom half of the page. Model reading the sentences aloud, focusing on intonation, expression, and pacing. Have students follow your lead by reading each sentence aloud after you model. Allow time for students to practice reading the sentences to a partner.

INTERVENTION
PRACTICE
BOOK

page 99

Directed Reading: "When I Was Eight" pp. 198–205

Page 198

Read aloud the selection title and point out the photograph on page 198. Explain that the photograph shows the person who told the story. Ask: **Why do you think honoring their Mexican culture is important to Junior's family?** (*Possible response: They don't want to forget their traditions.*) **SYNTHESIZE**

MOVING
AHEAD
pp. 198–205

Page 199

Ask: **Do you think Junior has a large or a small family? Why?** (*Possible response: I think his family is large because he has some relatives in Mexico and many other relatives in California.*) **DRAW CONCLUSIONS**

Pages 200–201

Ask: **What are the steps in making tortillas?** (*First, the ingredients are mixed together. Next, little balls are made and flattened. Finally, the tortillas are cooked.*) (Focus Skill) **SEQUENCE**

Page 202

Have students read the first paragraph on page 202. Point out the word *chile*. Model using the use context to confirm meaning strategy:

> **MODEL** If I didn't know what *chile* is, I could use clues on this page to figure out the word's meaning. First I would read the rest of the page to see if there is any more information about chile. There is! In the next paragraph, I learn that a chile is a pepper and that Junior's father eats an extra pepper to make his food hotter. I can get help from the picture, too. The picture shows chile peppers. (Focus Skill) **USE CONTEXT TO CONFIRM MEANING**

Pages 203–204

Ask: **What memories do family members share during dinner?** (*They tell what happened during celebrations they attended as children in Mexico.*) **MAIN IDEA**

Ask: **Now that Junior's grandmother has made tortillas with him, how has Junior's attitude toward tortillas changed?** (*He's always liked tortillas, but now they remind them of happy memories, too.*) **COMPARE AND CONTRAST**

INTERVENTION
PRACTICE
BOOK

page 101

Summarize the selection. Ask students to discuss how Junior feels about his family traditions. Then have them complete *Intervention Practice Book* page 101 to summarize the story.

Answers to *Think About It* Questions

1. Junior has good memories about the visit because he learned from his grandmother how to make tortillas and he learned about family traditions. **SUMMARY**

2. Junior is proud of his Mexican culture. He likes to hear stories of his parents' childhood in Mexico and is glad that his family speaks Spanish at home. **INTERPRETATION**

3. Paragraphs should include descriptive language and be written in a first-person point of view. **WRITE A DESCRIPTION**

AFTER

Skill Review
pages 608–609

USE SKILL CARD 25B

(Focus Skill) Sequence

RETEACH the skill. Have students look at **side B of Skill Card 25: Sequence**. Call on volunteers to read the skill reminder and the paragraph. Then have students name all the events in the Fourth of July celebration schedule.

Invite a volunteer to read aloud the next set of directions. Explain that students can now create their own sequence charts like the one on the card.

After students complete their charts, have them form small groups. Encourage them to take turns reading the information in their sequence boxes. Discuss any differences in students' charts.

FLUENCY BUILDER Have students look at their copies of *Intervention Practice Book* page 99. Tell students to slide their finger under each phrase as they read the sentences to a partner. Encourage students to continue practicing the sentences until they can read them naturally, as if they were holding a conversation. Encourage partners to give feedback on the pacing, expression, and pronunciation of each sentence.

INTERVENTION PRACTICE BOOK

page 99

Expository Writing: Publish Sentences

Build on prior knowledge. Tell students that they will work together to publish a few sentences about their own favorite family memories. Explain that publishing always means sharing writing with others, but that publishing can take many forms. Write the following list on the board.

> **Ways to Publish**
> - Have a partner read the writing.
> - Give an oral report.
> - Make a class book.

Construct the text. "Share the pen" with students to help them publish family memories by creating a class book. Follow these steps:

- Ask students to think about their favorite family memory, such as a special vacation they took with their family, a certain birthday celebration, and so on.

- Help students write two sentences about their memory.

- Invite students to draw pictures that show what they wrote about.

- Compile students' work into a class book. Each student will have a page with two sentences and an accompanying picture.

Revisit the text. Encourage students to reflect on their work in the class book. To spark students' thinking, ask the following questions: **How does your picture add to your writing? What could you do to make your writing even better?** Remind students that their memory should be in sequence. Have students share the book with other classes or family members.

> **On Your Own**
>
> Encourage students to write a few sentences about a book they have enjoyed. After they have written their sentences, invite them to "publish" their work by reading what they wrote to the class or in small groups.

Connect Spelling and Phonics

RETEACH **long vowel /ā/ea, ei, eigh.** Remind students that the letter combinations *ea*, *ei*, and *eigh* can spell the long *a* vowel sound. Write *steak* on the board and explain that in the first two words you will say, the letters *ea* stand for the /ā/ sound. Dictate words 1–2, and have students write them. After each word, display the correct spelling so students can proofread their work. Follow a similar procedure with the remaining words, using *veil* and *weigh* as examples.

1. great*	2. break*	3. vein	4. reins
5. neighbors*	6. eight*	7. sleigh	8. weightless

*Word appears in "When I Was Eight."

Dictate the following sentence and have students write it: *This store has eight great kinds of chow mein.*

Build and Read Longer Words

Write *reindeer* on the board and have students identify the two consonants that come together in the middle of the word. (*n, d*) Remind students that words with two consonants between vowels are usually divided between the consonants. Then write *weighing* on the board. Ask students which letters stand for the /ā/ sound. (*eigh*) Explain that when a longer word with the *eigh* spelling pattern is divided into syllables, the letters *g* and *h* must stay together. Divide *weighing* by drawing a line between *weigh* and *ing*. Point to each syllable and have students read it. Then slide your hand under the entire word and have students read *weighing*. Repeat the procedure for *neighing* and *eighteen*.

INTERVENTION
ASSESSMENT
BOOK

FLUENCY BUILDER Have students choose a passage from "When I Was Eight" to read aloud to a partner. Tell students they may select a passage they especially enjoyed, or give them the following choices:

- Read the second paragraph on page 200 and all of page 201. (Total: 121 words)

- Read page 203 and the first paragraph of page 204. (Total: 115 words)

Tell students to read the selected passage aloud to their partner three times. Have the reader rate each of his or her own readings on a scale from 1 to 4. Encourage students to assess how they have progressed from previous readings.

Review Vocabulary

Review the Vocabulary Words prior to the weekly assessment. Have students put up one finger for *yes* answers and two fingers for *no* answers. Call on volunteers to explain their answers.

1. Is an **accordion** a musical instrument? (*yes*)
2. Do some people throw **confetti** on New Year's Eve? (*yes*)
3. Could a little **mesquite** bite you? (*no*)
4. Is a **barbecue** a kind of a toy? (*no*)
5. Does a **chile** taste sour? (*no*)
6. Are family traditions a part of your **culture**? (*yes*)

INTERVENTION PRACTICE BOOK

page 102

(Focus Skill) Review Sequence

To review sequence, have students complete *Intervention Practice Book* page 102. Remind students that sequence is the order of events in a story. Have students read the passage, circle words and phrases that signal the sequence, and use information from the passage to complete the sequence chart.

Review Test Prep

Have students turn to page 609 of the *Pupil Edition*. Remind students that the tips will help them answer these questions as well as similar questions they may see on other tests. Call on a volunteer to read the tips for answering test questions. Discuss whether all stories use sequence words. Tell students that they must think very carefully about the order when there are no sequence words. You can encourage them to add sequence words in their heads, such as *first*, *second*, *next*, and *last*, to help them determine the sequence of a story.

LEAD THE WAY

page 609

INTERVENTION ASSESSMENT BOOK

Self-Selected Reading

Have students select their own books to read independently. They might choose books from the classroom library shelf, or you may wish to offer a group of appropriate books from which students can choose.

- *North of the Río Grande.* (See page 609K of the *Teacher's Edition* for the lesson plan.)
- *Arctic Son*, by Jean Craighead George. Hyperion. 1997
- *What You Know First*, by Patricia MacLachlan. HarperCollins, 1998

After students have chosen their books, give each student a copy of My Reading Log, which can be found on page R38 in the back of the *Teacher's Edition*. Have students fill in the information at the top of the form. Then have them use the log to keep track of their reading and to record their responses to the books they selected.

Conduct student-teacher conferences. Arrange time for each student to confer with you individually about his or her self-selected reading. Have students bring the books and their Reading Logs to the conference. Suggest that they prepare a favorite passage to read aloud to you. Have students tell why they enjoyed the book and what they learned from reading it. Ask students to relate main events from the book in sequence.

FLUENCY PERFORMANCE Have students read aloud to you the passage from "When I Was Eight" that they read to their partner. Ask students to comment on their pronunciation, intonation, and phrasing. Have students use the 1 to 4 scale to rate their own performance. Give students a second chance if they are not satisfied with their performance.

See *Oral Reading Fluency Assessment* for monitoring progress.

Use with

"The Gold Rush"

Review Phonics: Suffixes *-ly, -ful, -able, -less*

Identify the meanings. Have students repeat the following sentence aloud twice: *Julia slowly carried the stackable boxes upstairs.* Ask: **What does *slowly* mean?** (*in a way that is slow*) **Which word describes something that can be stacked?** (*stackable*) Then have students repeat aloud twice: *I was careful not to harm the helpless slug.* Ask: **Which word means "full of care"?** (*careful*) **Which word describes a creature that cannot help itself?** (*helpless*)

Associate suffixes to meanings. Write the sentences from above on the board. Explain that a suffix is a word part added to the end of a word to change the meaning. Cover up the suffix *-ly* in the word *slowly*, and ask a volunteer to identify the word that remains. (*slow*) Then do the same for *slow*. Slide your hand under the entire word as students read it aloud. Then explain that the suffix *-ly* means "in a way that is" and that *slowly* means "in a way that is slow." Follow a similar procedure for the suffix *-able* (*able to be*), *-ful* (*full of, with*), and *-less* (*without*).

INTERVENTION
PRACTICE
BOOK

page 104

Apply the skill. *Suffix Addition* Write the following words on the board, and have students read each aloud. Make the changes necessary to form the words in parentheses. Have volunteers read each new word aloud and explain its meaning.

quick (quickly)	**respect** (respectful)	**afford** (affordable)	**care** (careless)
weak (weakly)	**pain** (painful)	**wash** (washable)	**worth** (worthless)

Introduce Vocabulary

PRETEACH **lesson vocabulary.** Tell students that they are going to learn six new words that they will see again when they read a selection called "The Gold Rush." Teach each Vocabulary Word using the following process.

Use the following suggestions or similar ideas to give the meaning or context.

> Write the word.
> Say the word.
> Track the word and have students repeat it.
> Give the meaning or context.

abandoned	Relate to an abandoned lot.
profitable	Point out the suffix *-able* and the root word *profit.* Explain that *profitable* means "able to make a profit."
beckons	Pretend to hold up a dog bone, and role-play luring a dog.
fares	Explain that this word is a homonym (*fairs/fares*). Role-play paying a fare when boarding a bus.

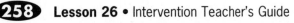

| rugged | Relate to a rugged path or road near your school. |
| multicultural | Point out the prefix *multi-*, which means "many." Explain that a multicultural community includes people from many cultures. |

For vocabulary activities, see Vocabulary Games on pages 2–7.

AFTER
Building Background and Vocabulary

Apply Vocabulary Strategies

Use affixes and root words. Write this sentence on the board: *My company became profitable in the first year.* Tell students that sometimes they can figure out the meaning of a word by using prefixes and suffixes. Model using the strategy.

> **MODEL** I am unsure what the word *profitable* means. I know the word *profit* has to do with money that is made. The suffix *-able* means "able to" so *profitable* must mean "able to make money."

Guide students to use this strategy to figure out the meanings of other words.

RETEACH lesson vocabulary. Have students listen to these sentences. Tell them to give "thumbs up" if the sentence is true, and "thumbs down" if it is false. Ask a student to change each false sentence to make it true.

1. An **abandoned** lot has a house on it. (*false*)
2. A **profitable** business loses money each year. (*false*)
3. If I **beckon** to someone, I'm calling that person over. (*true*)
4. An airline's **fares** are its ticket prices. (*true*)
5. A **rugged** road is smooth. (*false*)
6. A **multicultural** community welcomes people of all cultures. (*true*)

Vocabulary Words

abandoned deserted or left behind

profitable bringing advantage or monetary gain

beckons attracts or lures by tempting with something desirable

fares money paid for rides in a ship, bus, train, or airplane

rugged having a rough, or broken surface

multicultural showing the varied customs, religions, or beliefs of different people

FLUENCY BUILDER Using *Intervention Practice Book* page 103, read the first word. Ask students to listen to the pronunciation, look at the spelling, and ask questions they have about the sounds of letter combinations. Then reread the word and have students repeat it. Continue the process with other words. Finally, have students read the words in pairs underlining words that give them difficulty. Help students by pronouncing troublesome words.

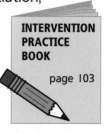

INTERVENTION PRACTICE BOOK

page 103

(Focus Skill) Fact and Opinion

PRETEACH the skill. Explain to students that some things they read contain both facts, statements that can be proven, and opinions, statements that tell how someone feels. Give an example of each, such as *James Marshall found gold in California* and *I believe James Marshall was brave*. Discuss the differences between them.

Have students look at **side A of Skill Card 26: Fact and Opinion**. Read the definitions. Then ask a volunteer to read the paragraph aloud. Read aloud the characteristics of a fact and an opinion. Then select a volunteer to read aloud the examples of each from the paragraph. Ask: **What is the difference between a fact and an opinion?** (*fact—can be proved; opinion—a belief that cannot be proved.*) **In which kinds of books might you find facts?** (*nonfiction*) **In which kinds of writing might there be more opinions?** (*editorials*)

Explain that knowing the difference between fact and opinion helps readers decide what is true and what is someone's belief.

Prepare to Read: "The Gold Rush"

Preview. Tell students they are going to read a nonfiction selection called "The Gold Rush" that has both facts and opinions. Then preview the selection.

LEAD THE WAY
pages 614–632

- **Pages 614–615:** I see the title, the author's name, and a man holding a pan. He might have gold.

- **Pages 616–621:** The text is divided into sections, each with a heading. The article is about the California gold rush. The headings tell me that the author is describing the dangers that gold miners faced. I wonder what "staking a claim" means.

- **Pages 622–625:** On page 623 I see a man digging for gold at the bottom of a hole. The pictures and headings on these pages let me know that they are about the tools miners used.

- **Pages 626–629:** These first two pages are like a photo gallery of old pictures. On the next pages, I see the word *Boomtown*, which tells me that I'll be learning about the towns that sprang up as a result of the gold rush.

- **Pages 630–632:** The picture and caption on page 631 catch my attention. What exactly is "fool's gold"?

Set purpose. Model setting a purpose for reading "The Gold Rush."

MODEL From my preview, I think I will learn about a time when people were excited about finding gold. I will read to find out what the gold rush was and why it was important.

Reread and Summarize

Have students reread and summarize "The Gold Rush" in sections, as described in the chart below.

Pages 616–619

Let's reread pages 616–619 to find out how the gold rush began and what other gold rushes took place during that time.

Summary: The California gold rush began in 1848. There were also gold rushes in Nevada, Colorado, and the Yukon territory.

Pages 620–621

We'll reread these pages aloud. Think about some of the hardships miners faced in their search for gold.

Summary: The journey to California was long and dangerous. Once the miners arrived, it was important to stake a good claim.

Pages 622–625

Let's reread to find how miners found gold and the tools they used.

Summary: The author describes panning and digging for gold. The miners used basic tools—shovels, picks, and pans.

Pages 626–627

Let's look at the photos and captions to find out about life at the mines.

Summary: Men, women, and children searched for gold hoping they would get rich. Others made money selling food and goods to miners.

Pages 628–632

We'll reread these pages to find out more about boomtowns and to find out how often miners actually struck it rich.

Summary: Some miners made millions. Others made a fortune by selling services to the miners. The gold rushes ended when the supply of gold began to run out.

FLUENCY BUILDER Redirect students to *Intervention Practice Book* page 103. Point out the sentences at the bottom of the page. Do a choral reading of each sentence. Explain that you'd like the group to read aloud with you. When you've finished, ask volunteers to read sentences aloud. Monitor for difficulties with pace and pronunciation. Allow time for practice with partners.

INTERVENTION PRACTICE BOOK

page 103

Directed Reading: "The West Beckons," pp. 206–212

Before reading the selection, ask students to skim it and notice how it is organized. Model using the text structure and format strategy:

MOVING AHEAD
pp. 206–212

Pages 206–207

MODEL As I skim through the selection, I notice that the first sentence of each paragraph gives me a preview of what I will learn in the rest of the paragraph. This is called a topic sentence. I see that the other sentences give details to support this topic sentence. I think the author organized the story this way to help me remember and understand what I am learning.
(Focus Skill) **USE TEXT STRUCTURE AND FORMAT**

Then have students read page 206 to find whom the article is about. (*James Marshall*) **IMPORTANT DETAILS**

Ask: **Why did Marshall travel to California and where did he find work?** (*He wanted to make his fortune. He and John Sutter started a sawmill business.*) **UNDERSTAND CHARACTER'S MOTIVATION**

Pages 208–209

Have students read pages 208–209. Ask: **What did Marshall discover in the ditch?** (*gold*) **IMPORTANT DETAILS**

Ask: **How was Sutter's response different from Marshall's?** (*Sutter was not nearly as excited as Marshall. He wanted Marshall to forget about the gold and continue working in the sawmill.*) **MAKE COMPARISONS**

Pages 210–211

Direct students to read page 210 to find out more about the "gold-seekers" who flocked to California. Ask: **How do you think the miners' discovery of gold made Marshall feel?** (Possible response: *It probably made him feel frustrated and disappointed. He would have liked to have had that gold for himself.*) **UNDERSTAND CHARACTERS' EMOTIONS**

Next have students read page 211. Ask: **How did the gold rush change California?** (*The gold rush helped settle much of California and made it a multicultural state with inhabitants who had come from all over the world.*) **DRAW CONCLUSIONS**

Have students reread the last line of the article. Ask: **How do you think the author feels about James Marshall?** (Possible response: *He admires him. He says his find "led to an important event in American history."*)
(Focus Skill) **FACT AND OPINION**

INTERVENTION PRACTICE BOOK
page 105

Summarize the selection. Help students create a sequence chart that shows the series of events Ben Farrell describes in "The West Beckons." Then have them complete *Intervention Practice Book* page 105 to summarize the selection in one sentence.

Answers to *Think About It* Questions

1. His discovery of gold changed his life. **SUMMARY**
2. Possible response: It helped California. The discovery of gold led to the settlement of the state and made it the multicultural state it is today. **INTERPRETATION**
3. Posters should show items miners used, including a shovel, pick, and pan. **MAKE A POSTER**

AFTER

Skill Review
pages 636–637

USE SKILL CARD 26B

(Focus Skill) Fact and Opinion

RETEACH the skill. Have students look at **side B of Skill Card 26: Fact and Opinion**. Read the skill reminder aloud and invite students to read along. Ask a volunteer to explain the difference between fact and opinion. (*A fact can be proved true or false; an opinion is what someone thinks or believes.*)

Tell students to listen as you read the paragraph aloud. Then, direct them to create a chart like the one on the card and complete it. Explain that a chart like this one can help a reader sort facts from opinions. You may want to work together to complete the characteristics section and have students work independently to list facts and opinions. Consider reading each of the sentences, one at a time, and having students classify them as facts and opinions before noting them in the chart.

FLUENCY BUILDER Be sure students have copies of *Intervention Practice Book* page 103. Tell them that they will practice reading sentences aloud to partners. Model how each sentence should be read. Then have partners read each sentence aloud three times. Ask them to strive to improve the rate and expression of their reading.

INTERVENTION PRACTICE BOOK

page 103

Informative Writing: Descriptive Sentences

Build on prior knowledge. Tell students that they are going to work as a group to write descriptive sentences about a day at the beach. The sentences will help readers get a clear picture of what it is like on the beach.

See	Hear	Smell	Touch	Taste
■ *blue* water ■ *bright* sun	■ *crashing* waves ■ *laughter* of little children	■ the *sweet smell* of coconut lotion ■ the *stench* of dying fish	■ *rough* sand ■ *soft* wave foam	■ *sand-coated* snacks ■ *creamy* ice cream

Read the descriptive phrases aloud. Remind students that these sensory words and phrases can help the reader "see," "hear," "smell," "taste," and "touch" what the writer describes. Invite students to suggest descriptive details that you can add to the chart.

Construct the text. "Share the pen" with students in a collaborative group writing effort. Guide them to create sentences that incorporate the descriptive words and phrases from the chart.

- Write a topic sentence that introduces the subject of a day at the beach.

- Add one sentence that describes what is seen and heard.

- Write a sentence that describes what they smell, taste, and touch.

- Write a concluding statement that tells how they feel about their day at the beach.

Revisit the text. Go back and read the sentences together. Ask: **What details could be added to make the sentences more descriptive?**

- Guide students to add details that tell what they saw, heard, smelled, touched, or tasted.

- Have students include their opinion in their description.

- Have students read aloud their sentences.

On Your Own

Ask students to write four descriptive sentences about their favorite places. To guide their writing, have students brainstorm words and phrases on a sensory chart similar to the one you wrote on the board. Students can share their finished sentences with small groups.

Connect Spelling and Phonics

RETEACH **suffixes -ly, -ful, -able, -less.** Have a volunteer write *sadly* and *fruitless* on the board. Check that each word is spelled correctly. Underline the suffixes and ask volunteers to explain how the suffixes change the meanings of the root words. Then explain that you will dictate more words with the suffixes -*ly*, -*ful*, -*able*, and -*less*. Dictate the following words, and have students write them. After they write each one, display the correct spelling so that students can proofread their work. Model drawing a line through the incorrectly spelled word and writing the word correctly.

I. excitedly*	2. promptly*	3. playful	4. hopeful*
5. workable*	6. washable	7. senseless	8. pointless

*Word appears in "The West Beckons."

Dictate the following sentence for students to write: *The playful and adorable kitten ran quickly across the windowless room.*

Build and Read Longer Words

Write these words on the board: *skillful, restless.* Explain to students that the letters of the suffix stay together when the word is broken into syllables. Point to *skillful,* and ask students which part of the word sounds like /skill/ and which part sounds like /fəl/. Follow a similar procedure with *restless.* Then remind students that the letters that make up a prefix also stay together when a word is broken into syllables. Write these words on the board: *reusable, unequally, distasteful, untruthful.* Have volunteers read the words aloud and explain how each is broken into syllables.

INTERVENTION
ASSESSMENT
BOOK

✓

FLUENCY BUILDER Have students select a passage from "The West Beckons" to read aloud to a partner. Ask them to choose a passage that they thought was particularly interesting. If they have trouble selecting a passage, suggest one of these options:

- Read all of the text on page 208. (Total: 82 words)
- Read all of the text on page 211. (Total: 82 words)

Have students read the selected passage aloud to their partner three times. Ask the student to rate each of his or her own readings on a scale from I to 4. Encourage students to think about and rate the progress they have made from previous readings.

Review Vocabulary

Review the Vocabulary Words before the weekly assessment. Divide the class into six teams. Assign a word to each team to define and spell properly. Do this "secretly" so that groups do not know which word was assigned to each team. Team members should work together to write a sentence showing they know the meaning of the word. One member should read the sentence aloud, leaving out the Vocabulary Word. Other teams can determine which Vocabulary Word would best fit in the context of the sentence. Then have the team that correctly identifies the missing word use the word in another sentence.

INTERVENTION PRACTICE BOOK

page 106

★ Focus Skill Review Fact and Opinion

Distribute *Intervention Practice Book* page 106 to review fact and opinion before the weekly assessment. Choose a volunteer to read the paragraph aloud. As a class, work together to decide which statements in the paragraph are facts and which are opinions. Have students make notes on the chart.

Review Test Prep

Invite students to turn to page 637 of the *Pupil Edition*. Explain that the tips given at the bottom of the page will help them answer these questions as well as similar questions they may see on other tests.

LEAD THE WAY

page 637

INTERVENTION ASSESSMENT BOOK

Read aloud each test question and the tip that goes with it. Remind students of the differences between a fact and an opinion. Explain how important it is to search for signal words or phrases when deciding if a statement is fact or opinion.

Self-Selected Reading

Have students select their own book to read independently. They might choose a book from the classroom library shelf, or you may wish to offer a group of appropriate books from which students can choose.

- *Gold Rush News* (See page 637M of the *Teacher's Edition* for a lesson plan.)

- *Going West* by Jean Van Leeuwen. Puffin, 1997

- *Coyote Steals the Blanket* by Janet Stevens. Holiday House, 1993

After students have chosen their books, give each student a copy of My Reading Log, which can be found on page R38 in the back of the *Teacher's Edition*. Have students fill in the information at the top of the form. Then have them use the log to keep track of their reading and to record their responses to the literature.

Conduct student-teacher conferences. Arrange time to conference with each student individually about his or her self-selected reading. Have students bring their Reading Log to share with you at the conference. Students might also like to choose a favorite passage to read aloud to you. Ask questions about the book to stimulate discussion. Use a portion of your time to reinforce students' understanding of fact and opinion.

FLUENCY PERFORMANCE Invite students to read aloud to you the passage they practiced from "The West Beckons." Keep track of the number of words students read correctly and incorrectly. Ask them to tell what rating they would give themselves on the 1 to 4 scale. Offer students the opportunity to reread the passage until they are happy with their oral reading.

See *Oral Reading Fluency Assessment* for monitoring progress.

BEFORE

Building
Background
and Vocabulary

Use with

"I Have Heard of a Land"

Review Phonics: Letter Pattern *ough*

Identify the sound. Have students repeat the following sentence aloud two times: *By the time they were through, their hands were rough from kneading the dough Jill had brought.* Ask them to identify the word that has the /uf/ sound they hear in *enough.* (*rough*) Then have students identify which word has the same /ô/ sound as in *fought* (*brought*), the /ō/ sound as in *though* (*dough*), and the same /ōō/ sound as in *true.* (*through*)

Associate letters to sounds. Write on the board the above sentence. Underline the letters *ough* in *rough.* Explain to students that the letters *ough* can stand for several different sounds and that in *rough,* the *ough* stands for the /uf/ sound they hear in *enough.* Then write *brought, through, dough,* and *thoroughly* on the board, underlining the *ough* in each word. Point out the sound the letters stand for in each word. Consider saying each word slowly, isolating the sound made by *ough* and having students repeat the word and then the sound.

Word blending. Write *brought, cough, though,* and *through* on the board. Then model how to blend and read the word *brought.* Slide your finger under *ough* and say /ô/. Use your whole hand to blend the phonemes of this word: /brrôôt/. Then say the word naturally—*brought.* Repeat with the remaining words.

INTERVENTION
PRACTICE
BOOK

page 108

Apply the skill. *Letter Substitution* Write the following words on the board, and have students read each aloud. Make the changes necessary to form the words in parentheses. Have volunteers read the words aloud.

tug (though)	**out** (ought)	**bright** (brought)	**throat** (through)
round (rough)	**that** (thought)	**dog** (dough)	**cost** (cough)

Introduce Vocabulary

PRETEACH **lesson vocabulary.** Tell students that they are going to learn five new words that will be in the narrative poem "I Have Heard of a Land." Teach each Vocabulary Word using the following process.

Use the following suggestions or similar ideas to give the meaning or context.

pioneer   Relate to stories of pioneers such as those by Laura Ingalls Wilder.

> Write the word.
> Say the word.
> Track the word and have students repeat it.
> Give the meaning or context.

harmony	Relate the word to music. Ask: **What is a song's harmony?**
possibilities	Point out the root word *possible*, which means "can occur." Discuss the meaning of *possibilities*.
fertile	Tell students that *fertile* is an antonym for *barren*, a word that means "unable to grow."
arbor	Draw a picture of a grape arbor or show a photograph of an arbor.

For vocabulary activities, see Vocabulary Games on pages 2–7.

Vocabulary Words

pioneer one of the first people to settle in a region

harmony an orderly and pleasing arrangement of sounds

possibilities things that are possible or that may occur

fertile able to support much plant growth

arbor a shelter of branches or vines

AFTER

Building Background and Vocabulary

Apply Vocabulary Strategies

Use context clues. Write this sentence on the board: *We can grow many kinds of fruits and vegetables in our fertile garden.* Tell students that sometimes they can figure out the meaning of an unfamiliar word by reading the rest of the sentence. Model using the strategy.

> **MODEL** When I read the sentence, I am unsure what *fertile* means. As I reread the sentence, I notice that many fruits and vegetables grow in the garden. Maybe *fertile* means "able to grow lots of fruits and vegetables."

Guide students in using a similar procedure to figure out the meaning of the other Vocabulary Words.

RETEACH lesson vocabulary. Write the five Vocabulary Words on the board. Then read aloud these sentences, one at a time, and ask students which word best completes each one.

1. We sat under the __(arbor)__ and picked grapes from the vines.
2. When you're young, life's __(possibilities)__ are endless.
3. The music's __(harmony)__ was pleasing to my ear.
4. A __(pioneer)__ family rode in a covered wagon across the plains.
5. The __(fertile)__ prairie was covered in wildflowers.

 FLUENCY BUILDER Show students *Intervention Practice Book* page 107. Read each word aloud. Have students echo after you and read each one. Then call on volunteers to read aloud sets of two or three words. Monitor for pronunciation problems.

INTERVENTION PRACTICE BOOK

page 107

BEFORE

(Focus Skill) Word Relationships

PRETEACH the skill. Tell students that when they're reading, they may come across words they do not know. Remind them to use other words in the sentence to figure out the meaning. Point out that context clues may show the relationship between words and that readers can use that relationship to figure out the meanings of unfamiliar words.

USE SKILL CARD 27A

Have students look at **side A of Skill Card 27: Word Relationships**. Ask a volunteer to read aloud the definitions in column 1 of the chart. Then draw students' attention to the examples in column 2. Ask:

- **What other examples of antonyms can you think of?** (Responses will vary. Direct students to brainstorm pairs of words that have opposite meanings.)

- **How can you tell which meaning and pronunciation of homograph to use?** (Read the entire sentence and use the context.)

Continue questioning students' understanding of the other word relationship terms on the chart. Remind students that understanding word relationships will help them understand what they read.

Prepare to Read: "I Have Heard of a Land"

Preview. Tell students that they are going to read a selection called "I Have Heard of a Land," which is historical fiction. Then preview the selection.

LEAD THE WAY
pages 640–660

- **Pages 640–643:** I see a picture of a family in a covered wagon, so this selection must have taken place a long time ago. I wonder where the family is going.

- **Pages 644–647:** The woman on page 645 looks as if she is hammering a stake into the ground. On the next page, I see a family in front of a house, but it looks different from houses of today.

- **Pages 648–651:** Now it's snowing, and it looks very cold. The family on page 649 looks snug in their house, but this must be a hard place to live. There is snow all over the prairie.

- **Pages 653–660:** The woman on page 655 looks like she's having a good dream, and pages 656–657 show people building a log cabin. Was the woman dreaming about this house? The same woman is writing in a book or journal on page 658. Maybe she's writing about her house. The whole group standing in front of the newly built house looks really happy!

Set purpose. Model setting a purpose for reading the poem.

MODEL From the preview, I have a good idea that this poem will tell what it was like to live on the prairie long ago. It looks like this was hard sometimes. I will read to find out what happens to the family in the poem.

Reread and Summarize

Have students reread and summarize "I Have Heard of a Land" in sections, as described on the chart below.

Pages 642–645

Let's reread to find out about the "land" of the title.

Summary: The land is filled with promises. It is fertile and goes on forever.

Pages 646–649

Let's reread to find out some things that make this land special.

Summary: Nothing in this land can block your imagination. Things here are "larger than life."

Pages 650–653

As we reread these pages, look for details about what winter was like and what life was like for the children.

Summary: The winters are so harsh that pioneers wonder if spring will ever come again. Childhood is filled with fun and laughter on this land.

Pages 654–657

Let's reread to find out about worship and houses in this land.

Summary: People worship in an outdoor church, since there is no church building. They make sod houses but dream of houses made of logs. Neighbors help one woman build her house.

Pages 658–661

Reread to find out what the woman writes in her journal. How does she feel about the land?

Summary: The woman shows the pride she has in herself and her ability to live on the land. She raises nearly everything she eats.

FLUENCY BUILDER Redirect students to the *Intervention Practice Book* page 107. Point out the sentences at the bottom of the page. Read each one with expression and appropriate pacing. After you've read them all, read one at a time and ask students to read chorally, repeating after you. Randomly call on students to read sentences aloud. Monitor for difficulties with pace and pronunciation.

INTERVENTION PRACTICE BOOK

page 107

Directed Reading: "Purple Mountain Majesty," pp. 214–220

Pages 214–215

Read the first paragraph and discuss the meanings of *plain*. Ask: **What is the meaning of *plains* in this sentence?** (Possible response: *Plain can mean "not fancy," but, in this sentence,* plains *refers to a land or a place.*) (Focus Skill) **WORD RELATIONSHIPS**

MOVING
AHEAD
pp. 214–220

Ask: **What role did the great mountain play in the lives of Native Americans?** (Possible response: *It provided them with water to drink and bathe in; they thought it brought harmony to their world.*) **DRAW CONCLUSIONS**

Pages 216–217

Have students read the first paragraph on page 216. Ask: **What happened next in the history of the mountain?** (*A man named Stephen Long climbed it.*)

Ask: **How do you think the discovery of gold affected the mountain?** (Possible response: *Miners probably dug and blasted into the mountain rock.*) **SPECULATE**

Have students read page 217. Ask: **Was the gold rush a dream come true for most people?** (*No, many people lost everything; very few got rich.*) **MAKE JUDGMENTS**

Pages 218–219

Have a student read these two pages aloud to find out what else happened to the mountain. Ask: **Why did people continue to come to Pikes Peak?** (*They came in search of health or to settle in a town.*) **SUMMARIZE**

Ask: **How did the mountain change? How did it stay the same?** (*Changes included more settlers, visitors, a cog railroad, and a road.*) **COMPARE AND CONTRAST**

Ask students to think about the title of the selection. Model using the self-question strategy:

> **MODEL** I have heard the selection, but I'm still not sure of the title. I know I've heard that phrase before, but why did the author call this selection "Purple Mountain Majesty"? When I look at the last page, I see that the author mentions that Bates wrote the song "America, the Beautiful" because of Pikes Peak. That phrase—the title—is in that song! The author must have thought that phrase tells how many people felt about Pikes Peak. When I look back through the selection, my idea makes sense. (Focus Skill) **SELF-QUESTION**

INTERVENTION
PRACTICE
BOOK

page 109

Summarize the selection. Ask students to think about the story of Pikes Peak. Have them summarize in two or three sentences what happened to the mountain before, during, and after Zebulon Pike's "discovery" of it. Then direct them to complete *Intervention Practice Book* page 109.

Answers to *Think About It* Questions

1. The mountain kept the world in harmony for the first Americans. It was a healthful place for sick people. It inspired Bates to write the words of "America the Beautiful." **SUMMARY**

2. Pike felt the mountain was beautiful and he wanted to climb it. **INTERPRETATION**

3. Poems should reflect the students' reactions to a place. **WRITE A POEM**

AFTER

Skill Review
pages 666–667

USE SKILL CARD 27B

(Focus Skill) Word Relationships

RETEACH **the skill.** Have students look at **side B of Skill Card 27: Word Relationships**. Read the skill reminder aloud and invite students to read along. Then ask a student to read aloud the paragraph.

Explain that students will work with partners to create a chart similar to the one shown. Ask them to think about the word relationships in the paragraph. Have them write examples of each relationship described in column 1.

After students have completed their charts, invite them to share their work with the group. Point out that using the other words in the sentences that appear in "I Have Heard of a Land" will help them figure out the meaning of unfamiliar words.

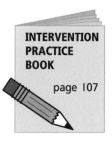

FLUENCY BUILDER Be sure students have copies of *Intervention Practice Book* page 107. Point out that students should read these sentences as if they are speaking, with natural phrasing and intonation. Model for students how to read naturally. Then pair up students and allow time for them to take turns reading the sentences aloud to each other.

INTERVENTION PRACTICE BOOK

page 107

Expressive Writing: Poem

Build on prior knowledge. Tell students that they are going to work as a group to write a four-line poem that describes a snowstorm. Display the following information.

Rhyming Words	
snowing / blowing	white / bright
fall / small	ground / found
cold / bold / hold	sky / my
flake / make	sled / bed
shiver / river	sweep / weep

Read the rhyming words aloud. Explain that in the poems, the last word of line one should rhyme with the last word of line two, and that the last word of line three should rhyme with the last word of line four. Remind students that the goal of a poem is to create a vivid image that will help readers "see" a place as they are reading or listening to the poem.

Construct the text. "Share the pen" with students in a collaborative group writing effort. Have them brainstorm other words that they might use in the poem. Write their ideas on the board. Then help them write four lines about a snowstorm. Use rhymes from the Rhyming Words box to create a rhymed poem.

- Think of what a snowstorm looks and feels like. Then write lines one and two.

- Think of what a snowstorm sounds and tastes like. Then write lines three and four.

- Check to be sure that the final words of lines one and two rhyme, and that the final words of lines three and four rhyme.

Revisit the text. Invite students to review the sentences. Have them look for problems with beginning and end punctuation, spelling, and grammar. Explain that most poetic lines begin with a capital letter. Be sure that the poem creates a clear picture of a snowstorm and uses rhyming words.

On Your Own

Ask students to write a four-line poem about another weather event. Have them begin by brainstorming a Rhyming Words box. Then they can brainstorm other words for the poem and write each line. Students may also choose to write poems with unrhymed lines.

Connecting Spelling and Phonics

RETEACH **letter pattern *ough*.** Write the words *tough* and *through* on the board. Ask students to pronounce the words as you point to each one. Tell them that in the first three words you will say, the letters *ough* stand for the /uf/ sound. Dictate words 1–3, and have students write them. After students write each one, display the correct spelling so that they can proofread. Repeat the procedure for the remaining words by pointing out the sound that *ough* stands for in each group of words.

I. enough	2. tough*	3. rough	4. thought*
5. sought	6. through*	7. dough	8. although*

*****Word appears in "Purple Mountain Majesty."**

Dictate the following sentence and have students write it: *Although last night had been rough for Lisa, she thought she could make it.*

Build and Read Longer Words

Write the following words on the board: *thorough, thoughtful*. Explain to students that in a word with the letter pattern *ough*, this combination of letters stays together when the word is broken into syllables. Point to *thorough* and ask students which part of the word sounds like /thər/ and which part sounds like /ō/. Follow a similar procedure with *thoughtful*. Then write the following words on the board: *doughnut, toughness, roughhouse*. Invite volunteers to pronounce the words and divide them into syllables.

INTERVENTION ASSESSMENT BOOK

FLUENCY BUILDER Have students select a page from "Purple Mountain Majesty" to read aloud to a partner. Ask them to choose a page that they thought was interesting or exciting, or suggest one of these choices:

- Read the paragraphs about Zebulon Pike on page 215. (Total: 99 words)

- Read about the miners who arrived at the mountain on page 217. (Total: 105 words)

Have students read the selected passage aloud to their partner three times. Ask the student to rate each of his or her own readings on a scale from 1 to 4. Encourage them to assess their progress from previous readings.

Review Vocabulary

Have students work in pairs to review the Vocabulary Words. Partners can write the words on slips of paper and put them in a bag. One student should draw a word and give the other student a clue. The "guesser" should determine the word based on the clue. Model if necessary: *The word I drew describes a farmer's field. The word is* (fertile).

INTERVENTION
PRACTICE
BOOK

page 110

(Focus Skill) Word Relationships

Distribute *Intervention Practice Book* page 110 to review Word Relationships before the weekly assessment. Choose a volunteer to read the paragraph aloud. As a class, work together to find synonyms, antonyms, homophones, homographs, and multiple-meaning words in the paragraph. Have students make notes on the chart.

Review Test Prep

Invite students to turn to page 667 of the *Pupil Edition*. Read aloud and review the tips for answering questions. Remind students that context clues can help them understand an unfamiliar word. In addition, it's important that they understand basic word relationships such as synonyms, antonyms, homophones, and so on. These word relationships can help them uncover context clues. Review the definitions of these word relationship clues as necessary.

LEAD
THE WAY

page 667

INTERVENTION
ASSESSMENT
BOOK

Self-Selected Reading

Have students select their own book to read independently. They might choose books from the classroom library shelf, or you may wish to offer a group of appropriate books from which students can choose.

- *Days of the Exodusters.* (See page 667M of the Teacher's Edition for a lesson plan.)

- *This Is Our House*, by Michael Rosen. Candlewick, 1998

- *The Zebra-Riding Cowboy*, by Angela Shelf Medearis, Henry Holt. 1997

After the group has chosen their books, give each student a copy of My Reading Log, which can be found on page R38 in the back of the *Teacher's Edition*. Have students fill in the information at the top of the form. Then have them use the log to keep track of their reading and to record their responses to the literature.

Conduct student-teacher conferences. Arrange time for each student to conference with you individually about his or her self-selected reading. Ask students to summarize the reading and explain why they did or did not like it. Have students bring their Reading Log to share with you at the conference. Students might also like to choose a favorite passage to read aloud to you. Ask students to find examples of interesting word relationships in the selection.

FLUENCY PERFORMANCE Invite students to read aloud to you the passage they practiced from "Purple Mountain Majesty." Keep track of the number of words the student reads correctly and incorrectly. Ask him or her to tell what rating he or she would give themselves on the 1 to 4 scale. Offer students the opportunity to reread the passage until they are happy with their oral reading.

See *Oral Reading Fluency Assessment* for monitoring progress.

LESSON 28

BEFORE

Building Background and Vocabulary

Use with

"Paul Bunyan and Babe the Blue Ox"

Review Phonics: Prefixes *un-, re-, dis-, im-, non-, pre-*

Identify the meanings. Have students repeat the following sentence aloud twice: *It's impossible to untie my brother's shoes.* Ask: **What does impossible mean?** (*not possible*) **Which word means "the opposite of tie"?** (*untie*) Follow a similar procedure to introduce the prefixes *dis-* (meaning "opposite of"), *re-* (meaning "again"), *non-* (meaning "not" or "without"), and *pre-* (meaning "before"), using the examples that follow. *That stain on your shirt will <u>disappear</u> if you wash it. The walls have to be <u>repainted</u>. A baby speaks <u>nonsense</u>. I saw a <u>preview</u> of the show.*

Associate prefixes to meanings. Write the sentences from above on the board. Explain to students that a prefix is a word part added to the beginning of a word that changes the meaning of the word. Underline the prefixes in the words in which they appear. Then use the word *untie* to explain how a prefix changes meaning. Cover up the prefix *un-*, and ask a volunteer to identify the word that remains. (*tie*) Then cover up the word *tie*, and have a volunteer identify the prefix. (*un-*) Explain that this prefix means "the opposite of" or "not" and that *untie* means "the opposite of tie." Repeat the procedure for the remaining prefixes.

INTERVENTION PRACTICE BOOK

page 112

Apply the skill. *Prefix Addition* Write the following words on the board. Have students read each aloud. Make the changes necessary to form the words in parentheses. Have volunteers read each new word aloud and explain its meaning.

fair (unfair)	**fat** (nonfat)	**polite** (impolite)	**obey** (disobey)
write (rewrite)	**build** (rebuild)	**pay** (prepay)	**heat** (preheat)

Introduce Vocabulary

PRETEACH **lesson vocabulary.** Tell students that they are going to learn six new words that they will see again when they read "Paul Bunyan and Babe the Blue Ox." Teach each Vocabulary Word using the following process.

Use the following suggestions or similar ideas to give the meaning or context.

fateful	Relate to things that are beyond a person's control. *On that fateful day, a storm destroyed the island.*
tragedy	Explain that *tragedy* is an antonym for *comedy*.

> Write the word.
> Say the word.
> Track the word and have students repeat it.
> Give the meaning or context.

gadgets	Show pictures of small machines or other mechanical tools.
bellowing	Bellow "hello."
softhearted	Tell students about a time when you felt softhearted.
ration	Explain that zoo animals receive a ration of food.

For vocabulary activities, see Vocabulary Games on pages 2–7.

AFTER

Building Background and Vocabulary

Apply Vocabulary Strategies

Use word structure to gain meaning. Write on the board: *The softhearted girl let her friend play with her new toy first.* Explain that you can sometimes figure out the meaning of an unfamiliar word by looking at the word parts. Model using the strategy.

> **MODEL** I don't know the meaning of *softhearted*. I see the words *soft* and *heart*. I know that the suffix *-ed* can make a word an adjective. I know that *soft* can mean "gentle." Maybe *softhearted* means "having a gentle heart."

Guide students in using a similar procedure to figure out the meanings of *fateful* and *bellowing*.

RETEACH **lesson vocabulary.** Have students listen to each sentence. Tell them to nod their heads if the sentence you say is true and to shake their heads "no" if it is false. Ask volunteers to correct "false" sentences.

1. A **fateful** battle can bring hardship to a country. (*true*)
2. A **tragedy** is very funny. (*false*)
3. All **gadgets** are larger than a house. (*false*)
4. You should be cautious of a **bellowing** lion. (*true*)
5. A **softhearted** teacher screams and yells all the time. (*false*)
6. If I get a **ration** of meat, it means I can have all I want. (*false*)

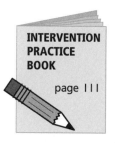

FLUENCY BUILDER Have students look at *Intervention Practice Book* page 111. Invite a volunteer to read aloud the words in column 1. Model pronunciations as necessary. Then have the class read all the words in the column in a choral reading. Follow the same procedure with each of the remaining columns.

INTERVENTION PRACTICE BOOK

page 111

USE SKILL CARD 28A

(Focus Skill) Fact and Opinion

PRETEACH the skill. Explain to students that in many stories they will find both facts and opinions. Review that a fact is a statement that can be proved and an opinion expresses someone's thoughts or feelings. Give an example of each such as, *Tall tales are stories that have exaggerated characters. I think tall tales are the funniest stories there are!* Discuss them.

Have students look at **side A of Skill Card 28: Fact and Opinion**. Ask a volunteer to read the story aloud with expression. Next, have students look at the chart. Ask:

- **What is the story about?** (*two people who build a house*)

- **Why is statement 1 a fact?** (*It can be proved that the characters were building a house.*)

- **Why is statement 2 an opinion?** (*It is someone's belief or idea.*)

Explain that distinguishing between fact and opinion can help readers understand how the characters feel.

Prepare to Read: "Paul Bunyan and Babe the Blue Ox"

Preview. Tell students that they are going to read "Paul Bunyan and Babe the Blue Ox." Explain that this is a tall tale. Tall tales have exaggerated characters and events, and they are often humorous. Preview the selection.

LEAD THE WAY
pages 670–681

- **Pages 670–671:** The picture on these two pages shows a huge man and an ox. I'm sure this must be Paul Bunyan and Babe. What an interesting name for an ox!

- **Pages 672–673:** Babe looks younger in this picture. These pages must explain what he was like when he was young.

- **Pages 674–675:** This page shows Babe licking Paul, who is laughing. I can tell that they are good friends.

- **Pages 676–677:** There is a giant illustration of Paul and Babe. He is pulling a lot of houses. He must be strong.

- **Pages 678–679:** Here are four men who look scared. Are they scared of the insects? What do Paul Bunyan and Babe have to do with this?

- **Pages 680–681:** After all these exciting things, I wonder if Paul and Babe ever settle down.

Set purpose. Model setting a purpose for reading the story.

MODEL From my preview, I expect to read some funny stories about Paul Bunyan and Babe. They look like amazing characters. I'll read to find out what adventures Paul and Babe have.

AFTER

Reading "Paul
Bunyan and Babe
the Blue Ox"
pages 670–681

Reread and Summarize

Have students reread and summarize "Paul Bunyan and Babe the Blue Ox,"
as described in the chart below.

Pages 672–673

**Let's read pages 672–673 to recall what we learned about Paul and
Babe.**

Summary: Paul finds Babe, who has fallen through the ice. Paul keeps
him, cares for him, and puts him to work when he gets older.

Pages 674–675

**Let's reread these two pages to find out what Paul and Babe do
together.**

Summary: Babe works for Paul. He hauls timber and can drain a river
with a single gulp. Sometimes he plays tricks on Paul's crew.

Pages 676–677

**Now let's read to find out what happens when Paul decides to move
to the next timber camp.**

Summary: Paul has Babe drag the camp buildings and cookhouse to
North Dakota. Paul meets the Seven Axemen at the new camp.

Pages 678–679

**As we reread these pages, let's watch for how Paul solves the prob-
lem of the giant mosquitoes.**

Summary: Giant mosquitoes drive Paul's crew crazy. Paul sends the cook
to Maine for some giant bees. The bees and mosquitoes have babies,
which results in more trouble.

Pages 680–681

Let's reread to find out how the tale ends.

Summary: Paul helps Babe by getting more oxen, but they die. Then
Paul and Babe move to the Arctic to work. Later, they retire to a cabin
in the woods.

FLUENCY BUILDER Redirect students to *Intervention
Practice Book* page 111. Point out the sentences at the
bottom of the page. Tell students that their goal is to
read each sentence smoothly and comfortably. Read the
sentences, one at a time, modeling expression, tone, and
pacing. Students should repeat each sentence after you.
Allow time for students to practice with a partner.

INTERVENTION
PRACTICE
BOOK

page 111

Directed Reading: "An American Legend," pp. 222–229

MOVING
AHEAD
pp. 222–229

Pages 222–223

Have a volunteer read the title of the selection aloud. Explain that this is a tall tale, in which larger-than-life characters accomplish impossible feats. Read page 222 aloud. Ask: **What legendary events have already happened to Pecos Bill by the time the story opens?** (Possible responses: *He was raised by coyotes. He invented the cowboy life.*) **DRAW CONCLUSIONS**

Next read aloud page 223. Ask: **Why does Bill want to leave Texas?** (Possible response: *Texas has become too tame for him.*) **CAUSE-EFFECT**

Pages 224–225

Have students read pages 224–225. Ask: **What does Bill reckon he needs for setting up a ranch?** (*cowboys*) **IMPORTANT DETAILS**

Do you think all real cowboys are "rough, tough, untamed, impolite, and disagreeable"? Why or why not? (Responses will vary.) (Focus Skill) **FACT AND OPINION**

After students read page 225, ask: **What happens when Pecos Bill meets the rattlesnake?** (*Bill gets into a fight with the rattlesnake and turns it into his new whip.*) **RETELL**

Pages 226–227

Ask: **What happens when Bill meets the wildcat?** (*At first the wildcat tries to bite off Bill's head, but then Bill rides the wildcat until it is tamed.*) **SEQUENCE/RETELL**

Next have students read page 227 to find out what happens when Bill finds the cowboys at their camp. Ask: **How does Bill help the cowboys?** (*He cracks his rattlesnake whip to get rid of the mosquitoes.*) **CAUSE-EFFECT**

Page 228

Have students read page 228. Ask them to create mental images of the scene. Model the create mental images strategy:

> **MODEL** As I read, I want to imagine what Pecos Bill's ranches look like. I know from the story that Pecos Bill is "larger than life," so I imagine a large ranch. I can see cows roaming the range and a huge campfire for the cowboys. When I read the last sentence, it helps me imagine how large the ranch is—the new ranch is an entire state! (Focus Skill) **CREATE MENTAL IMAGES**

INTERVENTION
PRACTICE
BOOK

page 113

Ask: **Are the things that Pecos Bill does believable, or are they impossible? Why?** (Possible response: *They're mostly impossible, because the strength needed to do them is more than any human has.*) **DISTINGUISHING BETWEEN FANTASY AND REALITY**

Summarize the selection. Ask students to discuss the events described in the story. Then have them summarize the legend in three sentences.

Answers to *Think About It* Questions

1. They feel they can't refuse to work for a man who rides a wildcat, uses a rattlesnake whip, and is so much tougher than they are. **SUMMARY**

2. Possible response: At first, the snake may feel that it can scare them off with its rattle. When Pecos Bill says he needs a new whip, the snake probably thinks it will be lucky to live through its meeting with Bill. **INTERPRETATION**

3. Stories should include the exaggeration and humor of a tall tale. **WRITE A TALL TALE**

AFTER

Skill Review
pages 688–689

USE SKILL CARD 28B

(Focus Skill) Fact and Opinion

RETEACH **the skill.** Have students look at **side B of Skill Card 28: Fact and Opinion.** Read the skill reminder aloud. Ask a volunteer to tell the difference between a fact (*a statement that can be proved*) and an opinion (*a statement that expresses someone's thoughts or feelings*).

Then have a volunteer read the story aloud. Direct students to create a chart similar to the one shown. Tell students to look for other facts and opinions in the story and have them add these to the chart. After students have finished their charts, have them share their work with the rest of the class.

FLUENCY BUILDER Turn students' attention to *Intervention Practice Book* page 111. Tell the group that they will practice reading the sentences at the bottom half of the page by echoing the sentences after you. Encourage them to copy your tone, inflection, and pace. Read aloud each sentence, phrase by phrase. Have students repeat (echo) the sentences, phrase by phrase. Students may want to follow up by practicing with a partner.

INTERVENTION
PRACTICE
BOOK

page 111

Persuasive Writing: Persuasive Paragraph

Build on prior knowledge. Tell students that together they are going to talk about and write a persuasive paragraph about recycling. Explain that a writer creates a persuasive essay to influence other people to feel a certain way about a topic. Draw the following chart on the board.

Recycling

My Opinion: We should recycle every day.		
Reason #1	**Reason #2**	**Reason #3**
easy to do	decreases garbage in landfills	less waste produced

Construct the text. "Share the pen" with students in a collaborative group writing effort. Guide them to create a paragraph that convinces readers to recycle. Use these steps to think through the process aloud:

- Open your paragraph with an opinion statement. The statement *In my opinion . . .* would be a good opening sentence.

- Write three sentences that support the opinion. Each of the reasons in the chart could be rewritten in the form of a sentence.

- End with a restatement of the opinion.

Revisit the text. Go back and read the paragraph together. Ask: **What could be added to the sentences to make them more persuasive?** (words such as *should, must*)

- Guide students to add persuasive words to express their opinions.

- Have them check that their opinion is clearly stated in a strong way.

- Have students read aloud their completed paragraph.

On Your Own

Ask students to think of a topic they feel strongly about. You might have them brainstorm topics, such as *Why we should have less (or more) homework* or *Why children should be allowed to vote*. Ask students to write their opinions and then create three sentences that support it. Students can share their work with a partner and discuss how well the reasons support the opinion.

Connecting Spelling and Phonics

RETEACH prefixes *un-, re-, dis-, im-, non-, pre-.* Write the prefixes *un-, re-, dis-, im-, non-,* and *pre-* on the board. Explain that you will say words that are spelled with one of these prefixes. Dictate the words below, and have students write them. After they write each one, display the correct spelling so students can proofread their work. Model how to cross out an incorrectly spelled word and rewrite the word.

1. unroll
2. untamed*
3. dishonest
4. displease
5. imperfect
6. impolite*
7. nonstop
8. nonsense*
9. precooked
10. rethink
11. preview
12. disagreeable*

*Word appears in "An American Legend."

Dictate the following sentences for students to write: *The unhappy painter did an imperfect job. Wanda was displeased and asked him to repaint the house.*

Build and Read Longer Words

Write these words on the board: *nonstandard, impractical.* Explain to students that in a word with a prefix, the letters of the prefix stay together when the word is broken into syllables. Frame each syllable of *nonstandard* as students read: /non-stan-dard/. Follow a similar procedure with *impractical.* Then ask students to read these words and explain how they would divide them into syllables: *nonresident, immature, discontinue, repayment, undeserved, prehistoric.* Discuss how the prefixes change the meanings of the root words.

INTERVENTION
ASSESSMENT
BOOK

FLUENCY BUILDER Have students select a passage from "An American Legend" to read aloud to a partner. Encourage them to choose the passage they think is funniest or most fun to read, or have them choose one of the following options:

- Read the three paragraphs on page 225. Use your voice to convey a humorous tone. (From *On the way . . .* through *. . . very pleased.* Total: 85 words)

- Read all four paragraphs on page 226. Imitate what you think Bill's voice sounds like. (From *Just then . . .* through *. . . I enjoyed that.* Total: 87 words)

Have students read the selected passage aloud to their partner three times. Ask the student to rate each of his or her own readings on a scale from 1 to 4. Encourage students to assess their progress from previous oral readings.

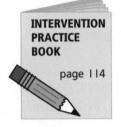
Review Vocabulary

Review the Vocabulary Words before the weekly assessment. Have students work with a partner to create a chart on a sheet of paper. Ask them to label column 1 "Words" and column 2 "Definitions." Then ask them to list the Vocabulary Words in column 1 and write brief (1- or 2-words) definitions in column 2. In the third column, partners can write sentences that show they know the meanings of the words.

INTERVENTION PRACTICE BOOK

page 114

 **Review Fact and Opinion**

Distribute *Intervention Practice Book* page 114 to review fact and opinion before the weekly assessment. Choose a volunteer to read the paragraph aloud. Students should then decide whether the statements in the chart are facts or opinions. You might first discuss with them clue words that would signal opinions.

INTERVENTION ASSESSMENT BOOK

Review Test Prep

Invite students to turn to page 689 of the *Pupil Edition*. Read aloud and review the tip for answering questions. Remind students how important it is to read the entire question before trying to answer it. Sometimes a test question will have two parts. To answer it correctly, you must understand both parts. Then point out the importance of reading each answer choice completely as well. Remind students that both parts have to be correct for the answer to be correct.

LEAD THE WAY
page 689

Self-Selected Reading

Have students select their own books to read independently. They might choose books from the classroom library shelf, or you may wish to offer a group of appropriate books from which students can choose.

- *Tall Tales, Big Numbers.* (See page 689K of the *Teacher's Edition* for a lesson plan.)

- *The Legend of Scarface: A Blackfeet Indian Tale* by Robert D. San Souci. Doubleday, 1996

- *The True Tale of Johnny Appleseed* by Margaret Hodges. Holiday House, 1997

After students have chosen their books, give each student a copy of My Reading Log, which can be found on page R38 in the back of the *Teacher's Edition*. Have students fill in the information at the top of the form. Then have them use the log to keep track of their reading and to record their responses to the literature.

Conduct student-teacher conferences. Arrange time for each student to conference with you individually about his or her self-selected reading. Have students bring their Reading Log to share with you at the conference. Students might also like to choose a favorite passage to read aloud to you. Ask questions to help students identify facts and opinions in their book. If you like, gather students who chose the same book and lead a small-group discussion about the selection. Use a part of this time to reinforce students' understanding of fact and opinion.

FLUENCY PERFORMANCE Invite students to read aloud to you the passage they practiced from "An American Legend." Keep track of the number of words each student reads correctly and incorrectly. Ask him or her to tell what rating he or she would give on the 1 to 4 scale. Offer students the opportunity to reread the passage until they are happy with their oral reading.

See *Oral Reading Fluency Assessment* for monitoring progress.

Use with

"Fly Traps!"

Review Phonics: Suffixes *-tion, -sion*

Identify the sounds. Have students repeat aloud three times: *Ivan took lots of possessions on his vacation.* Ask them to identify the words with the /shən/ sound they hear in *action.* (*possessions, vacation*)

Associate letters to sounds. Write the sentence from above on the board. Point out the *-sion* pattern in *possessions* and the *-tion* pattern in *vacation.* Tell students that these letter patterns often stand for the /shən/ sound. Explain that *-tion* and *-sion* are suffixes. Tell students that the suffixes *-tion* and *-sion* often change a verb into a noun.

Word blending. Write these words on the board: *collect, collection, tense, tension.* Read aloud the word *collect.* Model how to blend and read *collection.* Slide your hand under the word as you pronounce each syllable, and then blend the syllables together to read the entire word. Follow a similar procedure with *tense* and *tension.*

Apply the skill. *Suffix Addition* Write the following words on the board, and have students read each aloud. Make the changes necessary to form the words in parentheses. Students may notice spelling changes that had to be made before adding suffixes, such as the changing of *d* to *s* in the word *persuasion.* Volunteers can read the new words aloud.

INTERVENTION
PRACTICE
BOOK

page 116

act (action)	**perfect** (perfection)	**locate** (location)
collide (collision)	**intent** (intention)	**complete** (completion)
confess (confession)	**persuade** (persuasion)	

Introduce Vocabulary

PRETEACH **lesson vocabulary.** Tell students that they are going to learn seven new words that they will see again when they read the selection "Fly Traps!" Teach each Vocabulary Word using the following process.

Use the following suggestions or similar ideas to give the meaning or context.

boggiest	Show a picture of a swamp or other boggy area.
dissolve	Dissolve a spoonful of sugar in a glass of water.
chemicals	Show a picture of a chemist at work. Discuss materials a chemist uses.
carnivorous	Relate to carnivorous animals, such as lions.

> Write the word.
> Say the word.
> Track the word and have students repeat it.
> Give the meaning or context.

accidentally	Relate to something happening by mistake.
fertilizer	Show plant food. Explain that this is a type of fertilizer.
victim	Relate to people who live through a fire, attack, car accident or other tragedy.

For vocabulary activities, see Vocabulary Games on pages 2–7.

Apply Vocabulary Strategies

Use context to confirm meaning. Write these sentences on the board: *This ground is the boggiest I've ever seen. It's worse than a swamp.* Tell students that sometimes they can confirm the meaning of a word by checking for context clues in the same sentence or surrounding sentences. Model using the strategy.

MODEL I'm not sure of the meaning of *boggiest.* It might have to do with something wet and squishy. By reading other sentences, I see that the "boggiest" ground is compared to a swamp. I know that a swamp is wet and mushy, so *boggiest* must mean "wettest and mushiest."

Guide students to use this strategy for other unfamiliar words.

RETEACH lesson vocabulary. Write each Vocabulary Word on the board, have students copy it on a card, and then discuss its meaning. Then read aloud the sentences. Students should hold up the card that best fits the sentence.

1. We dropped the (chemicals) in the water and watched them (dissolve).
2. Our lawn is dying because we forgot to use (fertilizer).
3. I tripped and became a (victim) of my own clumsiness.
4. We (accidentally) walked through the (boggiest) part of the wet campground.
5. Wolves are (carnivorous) animals because they eat meat.

Vocabulary Words

boggiest very watery and spongy, like the ground in a bog or swamp

dissolve change from solid to liquid or to cause this to happen

chemicals substances with certain properties

carnivorous meat-eating

accidentally by mistake; without meaning to

fertilizer a substance put on or in the soil or water to feed plants

victim a person or animal that is mistreated or attacked by someone or something else

FLUENCY BUILDER Have students use *Intervention Practice Book* page 115. Do a choral reading of the twenty words with students, one column at a time. Then break the group into pairs and have students read the words to each other. Suggest they start at the bottoms of the columns and work up so that they don't simply memorize the lists. Monitor for pronunciation problems.

INTERVENTION PRACTICE BOOK

page 115

USE SKILL CARD 29A

(Focus Skill) Word Relationships

PRETEACH the skill. Remind students that as they read, they should pay attention to the way words are related. Explain that while reading, students may find synonyms, antonyms, homophones or multiple-meaning words that can help them figure out the meanings of other words.

Have students look at **side A of Skill Card 29: Word Relationships**. Read the paragraph aloud. Ask:

- **What are antonyms?** (*words that have opposite meanings*)

- **If a word has multiple meanings, how do you know which meaning is the correct one?** (*Use context clues in the rest of the sentence to determine the correct meaning.*)

Call on volunteers to read the example words in context within the paragraph. Then ask a student to explain how word relationships might help a reader figure out the meaning of a word.

Prepare to Read: "Fly Traps!"

Preview. Tell students that they are going to read a selection called "Fly Traps!," which is a nonfiction article. Explain that a nonfiction article contains facts and details about a real subject. Then preview the selection.

LEAD THE WAY

pages 692–706

- **Pages 692–693:** I see the title, "Fly Traps: Plants That Bite Back." Is one of these plants a fly trap? How does a fly trap "bite back"?

- **Pages 694–695:** Look at these great diagrams! The captions say this plant is called a *bladderwort*. I have never seen such a plant.

- **Pages 696–699:** The plants on page 696 look a little like cacti. I wonder what they are. The next pages show plants in pots, like those on a windowsill. Can a fly trap plant live in the house?

- **Pages 700–701:** Wow, page 700 is really funny-looking. I see the word *SNAP!* and a picture of a bug or fly being captured by a plant. I'm looking forward to reading this page.

- **Pages 702–703:** I recognize a cobra. I wonder why there's a picture of a cobra in an article about plants.

- **Pages 704–706:** These sure are odd-looking plants. They look like pitchers. I wonder if they are real or imaginary.

Set purpose. Model setting a purpose for reading "Fly Traps!"

MODEL From the preview, I can tell that this article will give me information about some interesting—and kind of strange—plants. I'll read to find out why the title says that fly traps bite back.

Reread and Summarize

Have students reread and summarize "Fly Traps!" in sections, as described in the chart below.

Pages 694–695

Let's reread these pages to find out details about bladderworts.

Summary: The bladderwort is a carnivorous plant. Bladderworts have "trap doors" that they use to catch water fleas and other bugs.

Pages 696–697

Let's reread to find out more about carnivorous plants.

Summary: The narrator is introduced to a kind of plant called the sundew. Sundews live in boggy places. A sundew has a sticky substance on its leaves. Flies and other insects become trapped in this substance.

Pages 698–699

The narrator makes a terrible mistake with his sundews. Do you recall what it is? Let's reread to find out.

Summary: The narrator sends away for sundew seeds and is pleased when they sprout into plants. By mistake, however, he uses fertilizer on the plants and they die. Later, he plants a Venus flytrap.

Pages 700–701

Let's reread to recall what the narrator describes.

Summary: Venus flytrap leaves trap flies and wasps. When the leaf is closed, the victim cannot get out. The bug slowly dissolves and nourishes the plant.

Pages 702–705

Let's reread to find out why the narrator goes to Malaysia.

Summary: The narrator goes to Malaysia to find even more fascinating plants. Pitcher plants eat spiders and even tree frogs!

FLUENCY BUILDER Redirect students to *Intervention Practice Book* page 115. Point out the sentences at the bottom of the page. Read each sentence aloud, modeling the correct pacing and expression. Call on individual students to repeat after you. Monitor for difficulties so that students can reread sentences that caused problems. Remind students to read as if they are speaking naturally. Oral readings should not sound stiff or unnatural.

INTERVENTION PRACTICE BOOK

page 115

Directed Reading: "Bug Catchers," pp. 230–237

MOVING
AHEAD
pp. 230–237

Pages 230–231

Explain that this selection is about animals that catch insects. Help students identify the brown bat pictured on pages 230 and 231. After students read page 231, ask: **Step-by-step, how does a bat catch a mosquito?** (*First, the bat screeches. It locates a mosquito by the way the sound bounces back. Next, it catches the mosquito in its wing and tosses it into its mouth.*) **SEQUENCE**

Pages 232–233

Ask students to study the pictures on pages 232 and 233 before reading. After students read, ask: **What makes bolas different from other spiders?** (*Instead of spinning webs to catch bugs, the bolas spider makes a bolas from a silky string with a sticky blob on the end, and then tosses the bolas at its prey.*) **COMPARE AND CONTRAST**

Ask: **How does a bolas spider prepare convenience foods?** (*It wraps a moth in silk and hangs it up; later, it injects a solution into the wrapping and sips up a meal.*) **SEQUENCE**

Pages 234–235

Ask: **How is a praying mantis's method of catching its prey different from that of the bat or spider?** (*The mantis doesn't go after bugs; it lets a bug come to it, and then it traps the bug between its strong legs and doesn't let go.*) **COMPARE AND CONTRAST**

Page 236

Have students read to find out what other carnivores eat bugs. Model using the strategy of rereading to clarify:

> **MODEL** As I finish the selection, I wonder if people eat bugs, too. I am going to reread to find out. Look what it says in the first paragraph. The girl mentions chocolate-covered ants. I guess that means that some people really do eat ants—and other insects! I wonder how they taste. ⭐(Focus Skill) **REREAD TO CLARIFY**

Ask: **The word *flies* has multiple meanings. What is the meaning of *flies* as it is used on this page?** (*a kind of insect*) ⭐(Focus Skill) **WORD RELATIONSHIPS**

INTERVENTION
PRACTICE
BOOK

page 117

Summarize the selection. Ask students to think about the ways some animals catch their prey. Then have them complete *Intervention Practice Book* page 117 and summarize the selection in one sentence.

Answers to *Think About It* Questions

I. A brown bat catches bugs in its wing and flips them into its mouth. A bolas spider tosses a sticky string around moths and pulls them in. A praying mantis waits quietly and pounces when its prey comes close. **SUMMARY**

2. Possible response: She is interested in the animal bug catchers and likes them. She knows a lot about them, and she says "thank you." **INTERPRETATION**

3. Stories should be written from the mosquito's point of view. They may express surprise or fear and describe actions the mosquito takes. **WRITE A PARAGRAPH**

AFTER

Skill Review
pages 712–713

USE SKILL CARD 29B

(Focus Skill) Word Relationships

RETEACH the skill. Have students look at **side B of Skill Card 29: Word Relationships**. Read the skill reminder and have a volunteer read the paragraph aloud. Review the word relationships if necessary: synonyms, antonyms, homophones, multiple-meaning words.

Then direct students to create a chart similar to the one shown on the skill card. Remind them to think about the word relationships in the paragraph and find examples of each kind of relationship.

After students have completed their charts, invite them to share their answers with the group.

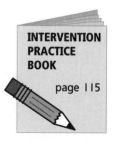

FLUENCY BUILDER Be sure students have copies of *Intervention Practice Book* page 115. Tell students you'd like them to work in groups of three. Each student in the group should choose a sentence to read aloud. After every group member has had a chance to read, they should switch sentences and begin again. Circulate and listen carefully for problems with pronunciation and pacing. Provide modeling as necessary.

INTERVENTION PRACTICE BOOK

page 115

Expressive Writing: Descriptive Sentence

Build on prior knowledge. Tell students that they are going to work as a group to write sentences that describe honeybees. Write the following chart on the board:

Descriptive Sentences: Honeybees

See	Hear	Smell	Touch
■ <u>yellow</u> <u>and</u> <u>black</u> fur ■ <u>plump</u> bodies	■ <u>buzz</u>, <u>buzz</u>, <u>buzz</u> ■ <u>cries</u> of children running away	■ <u>fragrance</u> of flowers ■ <u>sweet</u> honeycomb	■ <u>tickle</u> of a bee on your arm ■ <u>sharp</u>, sudden sting

Construct the text. "Share the pen" with students in a collaborative group writing effort. Guide them to create sentences that incorporate the descriptive words and phrases from the chart. Use these steps to think through the process aloud:

- Write one sentence that describes what honeybees look and sound like.

- Write another sentence that describes what you smell when a honeybee is near.

- Write a third sentence that tells what the touch of a honeybee is like.

- Write a fourth sentence that says how you feel about honeybees.

Revisit the text. Invite students to review the sentences. Ask: **What details could you add to make the sentences more interesting?** (*sensory details*)

- Guide students to add details that will help the reader create a mental image.

- Have students read the completed sentences aloud.

On Your Own

Ask students to write four descriptive sentences about a topic in nature. Suggest they write about an animal, an insect, a fish, or a flower. Have them brainstorm words and phrases on a sensory chart similar to the one above. When they have finished, ask students to share their work with the class.

Review Vocabulary

For a review of the Vocabulary Words before the weekly assessment, have students work in pairs. Have students write the words on slips of paper and place the slips in a bag. One student draws a word and reads it, and the other student uses the word in a sentence. Once students have reviewed the words, invite them to create a crossword or other type of puzzle that use the words. They can trade puzzles with another pair and complete them together.

INTERVENTION
PRACTICE
BOOK

page 118

★ Focus Skill Review Word Relationships

Distribute *Intervention Practice Book* page 118 to review word relationships before the weekly assessment. First, review the terms *synonym*, *antonym*, *homophone*, and *multiple-meaning word*. Define them as necessary, and offer examples to reinforce students' understanding. Then direct students to read the paragraph and complete the chart.

Review Test Prep

Invite students to turn to page 713 of the *Pupil Edition*. Read aloud and review the tips for answering questions. Remind students to read the answer choices carefully. In item 1, for example, students may confuse *antonym* and *synonym*. For item 2, encourage students to try out each of the answers in the sentence to see which makes the most sense.

LEAD
THE WAY

page 713

INTERVENTION
ASSESSMENT
BOOK

✔

Connect Spelling and Phonics

RETEACH suffixes *-tion, -sion.* Have a volunteer write *possession* and *vacation* on the board. Check that each word is spelled correctly. Then explain that you will dictate more words with the suffixes *-tion* and *-sion*. Tell the class that the first four words you will dictate have the suffix *-sion,* as in *possession.* Dictate words 1–4, and have students write them. After they write each word, display the correct spelling so students can proof-read their work. Then point to *vacation* on the board. Tell students that the next four words you will say have the suffix *-tion,* as in *vacation.* Dictate words 5–8, and have students proofread as before.

1. vision*	2. invasion	3. dimension	4. decision*
5. solution*	6. invention*	7. concentration*	8. population*

*Word appears in "Bug Catchers."

Dictate the following sentence for students to write: *Ella hopes her new invention will stop pollution.*

Build and Read Longer Words

INTERVENTION ASSESSMENT BOOK

Write these words on the board: *emotion, location.* Remind students that the letters of a suffix stay together when a word is broken into syllables. Frame each syllable in *emotion* (e•mo•tion) as students pronounce it. Repeat with the word *location.* Then write the following words on the board: *relaxation, invitation, construction, fraction.* Ask volunteers to read them aloud and explain how they would break each word into syllables.

FLUENCY BUILDER Have students select a page from "Bug Catchers" to read aloud to a partner. Ask them to choose a page that they thought was particularly informative. If they're not sure which passage to choose, offer one of these options:

- Read the information about brown bats on page 231. (From *I screech . . .* through *. . . bug catcher?* Total: 70 words)

- Turn to page 232. Read the text about bolas spiders. (From *Spiders are . . .* through *. . . in its direction.* Total: 108 words)

Have students read the selected passage aloud to a partner three times. Ask the student to rate each of his or her own readings on a scale from 1 to 4 and to note specific ways in which fluency has improved.

Self-Selected Reading

Have students select their own books to read independently. They might choose books from the classroom library shelf, or you may wish to offer a group of appropriate books from which students can choose.

- *The Mean, Green Carnivore* (See page 713K of the *Teacher's Edition* for a lesson plan.)

- *By a Blazing Sea* by S.T. Game. Mondo, 1994

- *Penguins!* by Gail Gibbons. Holiday House, 1998

After students have chosen their books, give each student a copy of My Reading Log, which can be found on page R38 in the back of the *Teacher's Edition*. Have students fill in the information at the top of the form. Then have them use the log to keep track of their reading and to record their responses to the literature.

Conduct student-teacher conferences. Budget time to conference with each student individually about his or her self-selected reading. Ask students to summarize their reading and explain why they did or did not like their choices. Have students bring their Reading Log to share with you at the conference. If you have time, ask students to find examples of interesting word relationships in the selections they chose.

FLUENCY PERFORMANCE Invite students to read aloud to you the passage they practiced from "Bug Catchers." Keep track of the number of words students read correctly and incorrectly. Ask them to tell what rating they would give themselves on the 1 to 4 scale. Offer students the opportunity to reread the passage until they are happy with their oral reading.

See *Oral Reading Fluency Assessment* for monitoring progress.

LESSON 30

"The Down and Up Fall"

BEFORE

Building
Background
and Vocabulary

Review Phonics: Syllable Patterns

Identify the syllables. Explain that a syllable is a word part that has one vowel sound and that can be said by itself. Say these words aloud, and have students hold up one, two, or three fingers to show how many syllables each word has: *market, photograph, prepay, pilot, found, snowing.*

Associate syllables to patterns. Write *market* on the board. Remind students that when two consonants come together in the middle of a two-syllable word, the word is usually broken between them. When *r* follows a vowel, as in *mar*, the *ar* stays together when the word is divided.

Follow a similar process with the words below. Guide students in identifying the pattern of syllables in each, focusing on the points in parentheses.

- **eighteen** (The letters *eigh* stay together.)

- **photograph** (The letters *ph* stay together.)

- **prepackage** (The prefix *pre-* forms a syllable.)

- **powerful** (The letters *ow* stay together. *-Ful* forms a syllable.)

- **pilot, open** (The words are divided after the first vowel.)

- **summer** (The word is divided between the double consonants.)

- **rice** (This word has the consonant-vowel-consonant-*e* [CVCe] pattern, which usually means a long vowel sound.)

- **snowman** (This word is made up of two smaller words, *snow* and *man*. These two words form the syllables in *snowman*.)

**INTERVENTION
PRACTICE
BOOK**

page 120

Apply the skill. Write the following words on the board, and have students read each aloud and identify its syllable pattern(s): *petting, pick, stage, baseball, acorn.*

Introduce Vocabulary

PRETEACH **lesson vocabulary.** Tell students that they are going to learn six new words that they will see again when they read "The Down and Up Fall." Teach each Vocabulary Word using the following process.

Use the following suggestions or similar ideas to give the meaning or context.

transformed	Point out the prefix *trans-* meaning "across, over, or beyond." *Transform* means to "make over" or "change."

> Write the word.
> Say the word.
> Track the word and have students repeat it.
> Give the meaning or context.

investigate	Relate the word to a detective who looks for clues.
enthusiastically	Demonstrate by saying something enthusiastically.
decor	Related words: They used a *decorator* to *decorate* their house. The *decor* is modern.
apparently	Explain that something that is *apparent* is obvious.
corridor	Explain that *corridor* is a synonym for *hallway*.

For vocabulary activities, see Vocabulary Games on pages 2–7.

For vocabulary activities, see Vocabulary Games on pages 2–7.

Vocabulary Words

transformed changed; made to look or be different

investigate look into thoroughly to find out something

enthusiastically eagerly; in a way that shows strong approval

decor the decorative style of a room

apparently seeming to be

corridor long, narrow hallway or passageway

AFTER

Building Background and Vocabulary

Apply Vocabulary Strategies

Use sentence and word context. Write on the board: *The scientist will investigate the problem and write a report about her findings.* Tell students that they can use other words in the sentence to help them figure out the meanings of unfamiliar words. Model using the strategy.

> **MODEL** I am unsure of the meaning of *investigate*. When I read the sentence, I see the words *problem*, *write a report*, and *findings*. All these words tell me that *investigate* must have to do with looking for something.

Guide students to use this strategy to figure out the meaning of other words.

RETEACH lesson vocabulary. Have students listen to each of the following sentences. Tell them to hold up the word card that completes each sentence. Ask a volunteer to say the sentence with the word in place.

1. My room needed a new look, so I chose a modern __(decor)__ .
2. At the big parade, we waved our flags __(enthusiastically)__ .
3. Which __(corridor)__ should I take to reach the gym?
4. Their new front porch __(transformed)__ the front of the house.
5. __(Apparently)__ , I am the last to know about this change in plans.
6. The scientist will __(investigate)__ the cause of the disease.

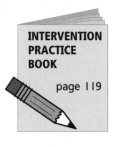

FLUENCY BUILDER Tell students to follow along as you read the words at the top of *Intervention Practice Book* page 119. Then focus on one column at a time. Read each word in the first column aloud and have students repeat after you. Follow the same procedure with each of the remaining columns. Then let students practice reading the words aloud in pairs.

INTERVENTION PRACTICE BOOK

page 119

BEFORE

Before Reading
"The Down and
Up Fall"
pages 716–728

USE SKILL CARD 30A

★ Focus Skill Author's Purpose

PRETEACH **the skill.** Point out that authors write to entertain, to persuade, or to inform. Authors also share their opinion about a subject.

Have students look at **side A of Skill Card 30: Author's Purpose**. Read the definition and the paragraph aloud. Next have students look at the chart. Point out the *Details* and *Language* boxes. Explain that an author chooses details and language to express his or her feelings about a subject. Ask:

- **What do the details in the chart describe?** (*a new school*)

- **Does the author use positive or negative words to describe the new school?** (*positive*)

- **How do you think the author feels about the new school proposal?** (Possible response: *The author feels enthusiastic.*)

Prepare to Read: "The Down and Up Fall"

Preview. Tell students that they are going to read "The Down and Up Fall." Remind students to think about the author's purpose as they read. Reinforce the idea that sometimes an author can have more than one purpose in mind. Then preview the selection.

LEAD THE WAY
pages 716–728

- **Pages 716–717:** I see the title, the author's name, and the illustrator's name. I also see a picture of a girl and a colorful parrot. The story is called "The Down and Up Fall." That's an interesting title! I wonder what it means.

- **Pages 718–719:** These pages have a border that reminds me of the jungle. I notice the word *parrot* repeated throughout. This gives me another clue that the story must be about a parrot.

- **Pages 720–721:** I see an illustration of a monkey and the girl from the opening pages. She must be important to the story, too.

- **Pages 722–727:** The illustrations have plants, flowers, and jungle vines. I see the girl, the parrot, and a boy. On page 727, the girl and boy are talking. I wonder what they're talking about.

Set purpose. Model setting a purpose for reading the story.

MODEL From my preview, I know that the story has to do with a parrot and a "rain forest" classroom. I will read to find out what the parrot does and if the story is funny.

Reread and Summarize

Have students reread and summarize "The Down and Up Fall" in sections, as described in the chart below.

Pages 718–719

Let's reread pages 718–719 to recall what we learned about Bolivia.

Summary: The science teacher invites Bolivia to bring Lucette, her pet parrot, for a visit to school. Bolivia thinks Lucette will be scared. But she is happy to be able to show Lucette a "real" rain forest.

Pages 720–721

Now let's read page 720 to recall what happens when Lucette arrives at school.

Summary: The kids are really excited to see Lucette and they crowd around her. Bolivia is amazed by the rain forest.

Pages 722–723

Let's reread to find out about what happens in the rain forest.

Summary: Bolivia and Lucette make themselves at home in the rain forest. The sights and sounds fascinate them.

Pages 724–725

Now let's reread page 724 to learn about the problem with the snakes.

Summary: The assistant principal visits the rain forest and is scared of the snakes. Suddenly, the sprinklers come on. Everyone gets wet.

Pages 726–728

Let's read to find out how things turn out for the characters.

Summary: The custodian turns off the sprinkler system and everyone agrees that Mr. Peters has created a very realistic rain forest. He says that his next project will be to create a moonscape.

FLUENCY BUILDER Redirect students to *Intervention Practice Book* page 119. Point out the sentences at the bottom of the page. Read the sentences aloud, modeling how to use expression, pacing, and tone. Let students know that their goal is to read naturally, as if they were speaking in a "regular" conversation. After each sentence, students can repeat after you. As you circulate while students read, monitor for problems with pronunciation and provide instant correction.

> INTERVENTION
> PRACTICE
> BOOK
>
> page 119

Directed Reading: "Air Force Kids," pp. 238–245

Pages 238–239

Read aloud the title and help students understand that "Air Force kids" are the children of men and women who are in the U.S. Air Force. Read aloud page 239. Ask: **How do you think Ricardo feels about meeting Paul? How can you tell?** (Possible response: *He feels excited. I can tell because Ricardo invites Paul to go exploring and he signs his letter "Your new friend."*) **INTERPRET STORY EVENTS**

Pages 240–241

Have students read page 240 to find out all the places where Ricardo has lived. Ask: **Why does Ricardo call himself "an American who never lived in America"?** (Possible response: *His parents are American, but he has always lived overseas.*) **MAKE OBSERVATIONS**

After students read page 241, ask: **How can you tell that Ricardo likes soccer?** (Possible response: *He gives details about the game and calls himself "Your soccer pal."*) **DETERMINE CHARACTER'S EMOTIONS**

Page 242

Ask: **What is Ricardo's news, and why is it both good and bad?** (Possible response: *Ricardo may move to California, which he is happy about. The bad news is that he would miss meeting Paul.*) **INTERPRET STORY EVENTS**

Ask a volunteer to reread aloud the second paragraph on page 242 while students listen to find out what Ricardo hopes. Model using the self-question strategy:

> **MODEL** When I listened to this paragraph, I couldn't tell what Ricardo hoped for because I got stuck on the word *compromise*. I asked myself what the word might mean. Ricardo said that maybe his mom could "compromise" with her boss. I think that must mean "strike a bargain." I'll keep reading to see if my definition is correct. (Focus Skill) **SELF-QUESTION**

Pages 243–244

Then have students read page 243 to find out more news. Ask: **Why is Ricardo feeling so enthusiastic?** (Possible response: *He finds out the trip to California is put off for a year; he'll get to meet Paul and see Spain's World Cup soccer team play.*) **DETERMINE CHARACTER'S EMOTIONS**

Have students read page 244 to find out how the story ends. Ask: **Do you think you would like to be an Air Force Kid? Why or why not?** (*Responses will vary.*) **INTERPRET THEME/EXPRESS PERSONAL OPINIONS**

Ask: **What do you think is Sal Ortega's purpose for writing this story?** (Possible response: *to entertain*) (Focus Skill) **AUTHOR'S PURPOSE**

**INTERVENTION
PRACTICE
BOOK**

page 121

Summarize the selection. Ask students to think about what life is like for children who live on U.S. Air Force bases around the world. Then have students complete *Intervention Practice Book* page 121 to write a sentence that summarizes the events of the story.

Answers to *Think About It* Questions

1. Ricardo and Paul have become friends by writing letters. Ricardo wants a chance to become friends with Paul in person. **SUMMARIZE**

2. Possible response: He will probably feel comfortable about the new school because he has learned about it and already has a friend. **INTERPRETATION**

3. Letters should follow the friendly-letter format and should describe activities and events at the school on the base in Spain. **WRITE A LETTER**

AFTER

Skill Review
pages 736–737

USE SKILL CARD 30B

(Focus Skill) Author's Purpose

RETEACH the skill. Have students look at **side B of Skill Card 30: Author's Purpose**. Read the skill reminder aloud and invite students to read along. Ask a volunteer to tell the three most common purposes for writing. (*to entertain, to persuade, to inform*)

Have a student read aloud the letter. Then direct them to create a chart similar to the chart shown on the skill card. Explain that the notes they make in the *Details* and *Language* boxes will help them think about the author's purpose and perspective. After students have finished, ask them to share what they wrote with the group. Discuss any differences among students' charts.

FLUENCY BUILDER Be sure students have copies of *Intervention Practice Book* page 119. Tell students that you'd like them to work with partners. Have one student read each sentence aloud three times. Have the student self-evaluate. (*How well did I read?*) after each sentence. After the third reading, the listener should tell how the reader improved. (*He or she read more smoothly, knew more words, read with more expression, and so on*) Then have partners switch roles.

INTERVENTION PRACTICE BOOK

page 119

Expressive Writing: Story Introduction

Build on prior knowledge. Tell students that they are going to work together to write an introduction to a story about Ricardo and Paul. Display the following information.

Prewriting Questions	Responses
I. Who is my audience?	I. fourth-grade students
2. What is my purpose for writing?	2. to entertain
3. Who are my characters?	3. Ricardo and Paul
4. What will the characters do?	4. Ricardo and Paul go to the World Cup soccer match.

Construct the text. "Share the pen" with students in a collaborative group writing effort. Discuss ideas for a story plot, reminding students that most plots focus on a problem and a solution. Then guide students in writing the introduction.

- Write one sentence that introduces the setting of the story.

- Add two sentences that introduce the characters.

- Conclude the introduction by writing one sentence that summarizes the plot, or the problem that the characters in the story will face.

Revisit the text. Ask volunteers to read aloud their introductions. Have students comment on the writing. Ask: **Would more details make the writing more interesting or enjoyable?** Encourage students to add specific nouns and active verbs to the introduction. Then have the students proofread their introductions. Tell them to check for proper grammar and spelling.

> **On Your Own**
>
> Assign the following topic to students: *Write a story starter for a trip you took with a friend. Tell who went on the trip, where you went, and something that happened on the trip.*

Correct Spelling and Phonics

RETEACH **syllable patterns.** Tell students that you are going to say words that have different numbers of syllables. Remind students that each syllable contains one vowel sound. Dictate the following words, and have students write them. After they write each one, display the correct spelling so students can proofread their work.

1. arctic*	2. corridor*	3. animals*	4. teacher*
5. giggle	6. volunteered*	7. alphabet	8. together*

*Word appears in "Air Force Kids."

Dictate the following sentence for students to write: *I volunteered to copy the alphabet for my little sister and her classmates.*

Build and Read Longer Words

**INTERVENTION
ASSESSMENT
BOOK**

Write the word *previewing* on the board. Remind students that they have learned how to read words according to syllable patterns. Cover the prefix *pre-* and ask what root word students see. (*view*) Then cover *view* and have a volunteer read the suffix *-ing*. Tell students to separate the word as follows: *pre-view-ing*. Write these words on the board: *boastful*, *piloting*, *commonplace*. Guide students in explaining the syllable pattern(s) that enable them to figure out each of these words.

FLUENCY BUILDER Have students select a page from "Air Force Kids" to read aloud to a partner. Encourage students to choose passages that they found particularly interesting, or have them choose from one of the following options:

- Read the first letter from Paul to Ricardo on page 238. (Total: 90 words)

- Read Ricardo's letter to Paul on page 241. (Total: 89 words)

Students should read the selected passage aloud to their partner three times. Then have the student rate each of his or her readings on a scale of 1 to 4. The listener can point out the progress that his or her partner made before switching roles.

Review Vocabulary

Review the Vocabulary Words before the weekly assessment. Divide the class into groups of six. Assign a Vocabulary Word to each student in the group. Ask students to pronounce, spell, and then define their assigned word so that the whole group can hear it. Have students exchange words if they need additional practice. Then suggest that students write a sentence for each word.

INTERVENTION
PRACTICE
BOOK

page 122

 Author's Purpose

Distribute *Intervention Practice Book* page 122 to review Author's Purpose before the weekly assessment. Select a volunteer to read the paragraph aloud. Tell students to think about the author's purpose as they listen. Guide students to complete the diagram.

Review Test Prep

Invite students to turn to page 737 of the *Pupil Edition*. Call attention to the tips for answering the test questions. Tell students that paying close attention to the author's purpose and viewpoint can help them answer not only the test questions on this page but also other test questions like these. Remind students to consider eliminating incorrect answers first to narrow their choices as they determine the correct response.

LEAD
THE WAY

page 737

Read aloud the test questions and the tips. Encourage students to think about the content of the passage and to ask themselves why they think the author wrote it.

INTERVENTION
ASSESSMENT
BOOK

Self-Selected Reading

Have students select their own books to read independently. They might choose books from the classroom library shelf, or you may wish to offer a group of appropriate books from which students can choose.

- *The Amazing One-of-a-Kind Parrot.* (See page 737K of the *Teacher's Edition* for a lesson plan.)

- *Class President* by Johanna Hurwitz. William Morrow, 1990

- *Chameleons are Cool* by Martin Jenkins. Candlewick, 1997

After students have chosen their books, give each student a copy of My Reading Log, which can be found on page R38 in the back of the *Teacher's Edition*. Have students fill in the information at the top of the form. Then have them use the log to keep track of their reading and to record their responses to the literature.

Conduct student-teacher conferences. Budget time to confer with each student about his or her self-selected reading. Encourage students to share what they've written in their Reading Logs and explain their responses to the literature. Ask questions about the plot of their favorite book. Then have them comment on the author's purpose and perspective.

FLUENCY PERFORMANCE Invite students to read aloud to you the passage they practiced from "Air Force Kids." Keep track of the number of words each student reads correctly and incorrectly. Ask each student to rate his or her own performance on the I to 4 scale. Offer students the opportunity to reread the passage until they are happy with their oral reading.

See *Oral Reading Fluency Assessment* for monitoring progress.